WITHDRAWN

DR. DONALD F. SABO, JR.
is a lecturer in the Department of
Sociology, State University of New
York, Buffalo. He is coauthor of
Humanism in Sociology and is a
former college defensive football
captain.

DR. ROSS RUNFOLA,
a professor of Social Science at
Medaille College, is the author of
numerous articles published in the
area of sports sociology.

SPORTS & MALE IDENTITY

Donald F. Sabo, Jr.

Ross Runfola

PRENTICE-HALL, INC.   A SPECTRUM BOOK Englewood Cliffs, N.J. 07632

Library of Congress Cataloging in Publication Data

Sabo, Donald F
    Jock: sports and male identity.

    (A Spectrum Book)
    Includes index.
    1. Sports—Psychological, aspects—Addresses,
essays, lectures.   2.   Masculinity (Psychology)—
Addresses, essays, lectures.   3.   Identity (Psycho-
logy)—Addresses, essays, lectures.   I. Runfola,
Ross, joint author.   II.   Title.
GV706.4.S22   796'.01   80-11147
ISBN 0-13-510149-2
ISBN 0-13-510131-*X* (pbk.)

Design and production by York Graphic Services, Inc.
York, Pennsylvania 17404

© 1980 by Prentice-Hall, Inc.,
Englewood Cliffs, New Jersey 07632

A SPECTRUM BOOK

10   9   8   7   6   5   4   3   2   1

Printed in the United States of America

PRENTICE-HALL INTERNATIONAL, INC., *London*
PRENTICE-HALL OF AUSTRALIA PTY. LIMITED, *Sydney*
PRENTICE-HALL OF CANADA, LTD., *Toronto*
PRENTICE-HALL OF INDIA PRIVATE LIMITED, *New Delhi*
PRENTICE-HALL OF JAPAN, INC., *Tokyo*
PRENTICE-HALL OF SOUTHEAST ASIA PTE. LTD., *Singapore*
WHITEHALL BOOKS LIMITED, *Wellington, New Zealand*

CONTENTS

PART THREE
VIOLENCE, SPORT, AND MASCULINITY

Introduction
The Editors
The Super-Bowl Culture of Male Violence
Eugene C. Bianchi
Violence and the Masculine Mystique
Lucy Komisar
The Culture of Young Hockey Players:
Some Initial Observations
Edmund W. Vaz

PART FOUR
HIGH FROM THE GAME:
SPECTATORS AND THE SPECTACLE

Introduction
The Editors
The American Seasonal Masculinity Rites
Arnold Beisser
Autumn Begins in Martins Ferry, Ohio
James Wright
The Changing Role of Homoerotic Fantasy
in Spectator Sports
Edgar Z. Friedenberg
Two Views: Men Attend, Women Comprehend
Larry Merchant

PART FIVE
WOMEN, SEX-ROLE STEREOTYPING
AND SPORTS

Introduction
The Editors
Sport: Women Sit in the Back of the Bus
M. Marie Hart

PREFACE

Sports and masculinity are virtually synonomous in American culture. Sportswriter Roger Kahn said it well more than a decade ago: "The number of boys who would like to be Mickey Mantle is beyond calculation. Compare it to the number who would like to be Robert Frost."[1] Today O. J. Simpson has replaced the famed Yankee slugger as the quintessence of American manhood, but the rest of the male cultural script remains unchanged. For many, sports is a major rite of passage from boyhood to adulthood. Given the choice, how many American boys would trade their jockstraps for a poet's pen?

But does a boy really have a choice in a society that places a premium on performance and conformity in an endless quest to prove oneself a man? In America, sports continue to be the strongest reference point for promulgating the most sacred values of a male-dominated, success-oriented, status-seeking society. From presidential addresses to pee-wee hockey leagues, sports weave their way into our lives. Nixon characterized himself as the nation's "number-one football fan." The Watergate tapes abound in locker-room linguistics. President Ford's prescription for a recessionary economy and a growing lack of faith in government consisted of periodic pep talks and the brandishing of WIN buttons. Sports is big business, and sports-related expenditures in the United States approach $25 billion annually. Sports shops, tracks, fields, and multi-million-dollar stadiums pockmark the American cultural landscape. Jock celebrities endorse everything from political candidates to pantyhose and coffee makers. In many newspapers, more typespace is devoted to sports than to national news. Modern communications technology has

---

[1] "Money, Muscles and Myths," in Eric Larrabee and Rolf Meyersohn, ed., *Mass Leisure* (New York: Macmillan, 1958), p. 267.

ushered in an era of mass spectator sports, and millions of fans display their ardor through bumper stickers, pennants, shoes, hats, jerseys, and jackets.

Sexist culture revolves around the ideology of male supremacy. Alfred L. Kroeber and Clyde Kluckhohn find that the essence of a culture consists of traditional ideas *and the values attached to them.*[2] A primary function of sports is the dissemination and reinforcement of such traditional American values as male superiority, competition, work, and success. Sports are among the most crucial socializing forces in the development of the superman syndrome in American society. Through sports boys are trained to be men, to reflect all the societal expectations and attitudes surrounding such a rigid role definition. Sports act as a mirror of the dominant culture and a link between sexist institutions.

Given these assumptions, the analysis of sports offered by the readings in this book can help us understand the ethos and organization of our entire society. More particularly, the articles that follow provide an avenue for furthering our understanding of the male role in a sexist society.

What is the relationship between sports and masculinity? A lack of playful spontaneity and identification with work are hallmarks of the male role. Over three centuries ago, John Locke recognized the true worth of children's games: "Children have as much a mind to show that they are free, that their own good actions come from themselves, that they are absolute and independent, as any of the proudest of your grown men."[3] Unfortunately, much of

---

[2] Alfred L. Kroeber and Clyde Kluckhohn, "Culture: A Critical Review of Concepts and Definitions," *Papers of the Peabody Museum of American Archaeology and Ethnology,* Harvard University, vol. 48, no. 1, 1952.

[3] Quoted in Gregory P. Stone, "The Decay of Little Children," *Quest* 4 (April 1965): 74.

the freedom of which Locke speaks ends with the coming of organization. Given the competitive ethic in American culture, it was inevitable that when adults brought organization, they also brought the outside world. Philosopher Kenneth Schmitz believes adults "kill the spirit of play within sport and reduce sport to something less than its fullest human possibilities."[4] As Schmitz views it, little leagues and other adult-inspired organizations conflict with the true spirit of play by exaggerating the importance of technique, efficiency, and winning. Just as boys work at becoming sports stars, men work at acting out the everyday expectations of the male role.

Part of the definition of being a man is to be a competitor. One of the most famous sports maxims of all time was Vince Lombardi's remark, "Winning isn't everything; it's the only thing." Within American sports, excessive concern with winning has led to an authoritarian coaching system, recruitment violations in college sports, exorbitant violence, and drugtaking. If this blind commitment to victory was found only at the college and professional levels, it would be cause enough for concern. Unfortunately, small boys are programmed for excessive competition and victory as early as their Pop Warner and little league days.

To be "a man" in our society means to maintain a stoical degree of emotional control, and one of the few socially acceptable settings in which a boy or man can cry is upon losing an athletic event. But with Spartanlike fervor, coaches teach boys to suppress their emotions. Loss of emotional control is at once perceived as unmanly and unproductive because it impairs individual and team performance. The fact that the ability to shut off feelings, though it may be an asset to a young athlete, can create problems in

---

[4]"Sport and Play: Suspension of the Ordinary," paper delivered at the 13th annual meeting of the American Association for the Advancement of Science, Dallas, Texas (December 1968).

later years by limiting an individual's ability to build worthwhile human relationships, is ignored.[5]

Aggressiveness is another primary ingredient of the male role. There is a profound feeling within the sports establishment that there is a strong causal connection between the development of controlled violence and winning. In American sports, the opponent is often dehumanized as an enemy who stands in the way of victory. Vince Lombardi often reminded his players that "you have to have that fire inside you to play this game [football], and there's nothing that stokes the fire like hate." As unconscious co-conspirators in the weaving of the masculine mystique, parents and coaches teach young boys the value of controlled violence in destroying opponents. The same kind of aggressiveness is useful later in the adult drive to the masculine Superbowl, where success in business, politics, and other pursuits is measured by the accumulation of possessions, power, and prestige. Moreover, the links between violence and the masculine mystique have grown more obvious in recent times. The "demonstration of masculinity and toughness" is the central tenet of the "subculture of violence."[6] For many males, violence and physical aggression are a way of life. The associations between violence and masculinity, in part created by sports, appear to reinforce misogynistic elements of male sexuality and may be related to the prevalence of rape and wife-beating, the rising tide of sado-masochistic sexual imagery in men's magazines, and the eroticized violence against women in television and cinema productions.

Just as American boys are prepared on the playing field to be future custodians of the Republic, girls learn to

---

[5]Jack O. Balswick and Charles W. Peek, "The Inexpressive Male: A Tragedy of American Society," *The Family Coordinator* (1971), pp. 363–68.
[6]Marvin Wolfgang and Franco Ferracuti, *The Subculture of Violence: Toward an Integrated Theory in Criminology* (London: Tavistock, 1967).

support their men on the sidelines as cheerleaders or to fit the housewife-mother stereotype by preparing dinner after the big game in their "Easy Bake Ovens." Many women play a lifelong game, deliberately underachieving to win the biggest prize of all—the love of a man. The masculine value placed on sports thus thwarts the developmental potential of both women and men. Marie Hart, a prominent sports sociologist, encapsulized the sex role dilemma fostered by sports when she said "American society cuts the penis off the male who enters dance and places it on the woman who participates in competitive athletics."[7]

The constellation of expectations, beliefs and values that have been traditionally regarded as masculine do much to structure the sexual attitudes and behavior of men.[8] For many males, the onset of puberty and the awakening of sexual interest occur in an athletic setting. Symbolically and linguistically, the worlds of sport, dating, and sex become fused. Male-female relationships are defined as a "game" in which there are "winners" and "losers" and participants vie for dominance. Sexual relations become a matter of conquest and an extension of male competitiveness. "Did you score last night, Steve?" Females are often perceived as opponents, and various strategies or game plans are developed to get them to submit. Athletic and sexual prowess are naively equated, and the technical competence of a man's performance is rated more important than sensitivity to a partner's psychological and sexual needs. The absence of sensitivity is also reflected in the satisfaction men get from retailing their "moments of glory"

---

[7] Quoted in Jack Scott, "Women in Sport: She Dives Like a Man," undated essay, Institute for the Study of Sport and Society, Oberlin College.
[8] See John Gagnon and William Simon, *Sexual Conduct* (Chicago: Aldine, 1973); Judith Laws and Pepper Schwartz, *Sexual Scripts* (Hinsdale, Ill.: Dryden Press, 1977); and David A. Schultz, *Human Sexuality* (Englewood Cliffs, N. J.: Prentice-Hall, 1979), chap. 7.

(real or fabricated) to one another over a lunch table or a beer as a way of gaining status.

The widespread cultural influence of athletics is perhaps most visible in the national preoccupation with sports, which verges on a mania. The tremendous escalation of interest in mass spectator sports in the sixties and seventies—especially the more violent variety—is often seen as a way of discharging individual and social frustrations, with athletes as professional surrogates. Perhaps more significant, however, is the way in which spectator sports maintain traditional masculine ideals and values in a period in which they are being challenged. The American woman is growing more assertive on many fronts. Her increasing involvement in the economic sector and her raised consciousness no longer permit simple acquiessence to traditional social and sexual passivity. The modern women's movement is both an expression of woman's changing social role and a driving force behind it. Its ideology has helped many women adjust psychologically to institutional and personal change.[9] For men who feel threatened or confused by women's emerging social and sexual equality, sports spectacles may be a link with a more patriarchal past. In this sense, sports constitute a major cultural element that ritualistically maintains traditional male supremacy in the face of egalitarian trends. The impulse that drives many men to become superconsumers of both sports and sports-related products may be an attempt to confirm their masculine identity in a society that provides fewer opportunities to prove one's "manhood."

On the other hand, if women have acted in recent times, men have reacted. Independently or through the incipient ethos of men's liberation, they have begun to ex-

---

[9] Constantina Safilios-Rothschild, *Love, Sex, and Sex Roles* (Englewood Cliffs, N. J.: Prentice-Hall, 1977).

amine the social origins of masculinity, to probe the positive and debilitative aspects of the male role, and to recognize that institutionalized and attitudinal sexism harms them as well as women. This anthology provides a touchstone for men who want to free themselves from the rigid constraints of traditional masculinity. It shows that, contrary to popular sentiment, men have much to gain from sexual equality.

All the selections in this book share the critical assumption that sports shape many undesirable elements of the male role and perpetuate sexist institutions and values. The book is intended primarily for men, to raise their consciousness and stir their self-awareness. We must understand ourselves if we are to reshape the society that molds us. New consciousness is built upon an understanding of the old. This anthology is intended as part of a liberating process, a process which is personal, political, and scientific in the sense that it furthers our knowledge of the society we live in and suggests new routes for personal and institutional change.

The book has six sections. Part One analyzes the interrelationships between sports and larger social institutions. Sexism is not merely the product of male chauvinistic attitudes; it is also rooted in underlying institutional processes. Part Two examines sport as a socializing agency that shapes male identity and behavior. The links between sports, violence, and masculinity are identified in Part Three, while Part Four presents a profile of the American sports fan. Under the conceptual umbrella of sex role stereotyping, Part Five explores women's changing role in sports and its implications for men. The selections in Part Six present several alternatives to the image of masculinity inherent in sport as well as recommendations for changing the structure of athletics in American society. Finally, the editors' concluding remarks are followed by a bibliography of pertinent materials.

The ideas and energies behind this book are many. We are especially indebted to our contributors. For their insights and support, we also want to thank Donald Bain; Jessie Bernard; Roger Bonnefant; Marie Coleman; Naomi Cooper; Charles Dick; Harry Edwards; Michael Farrell; William Fisher; Frances Gabriel; Aleksander Gella; Llewellyn Gross; Charles Haynie; Marge Holton; Barbara Howe; Paul Jayes; Stacy Johnson; Robert Krollman; Sheila Kuch; Lionel Lewis; Lynne Lumsden; Diane Marlinski; the Medaille College Library; Dave Meggyesy; Frank Moorman; the National Women's Sport Foundation; Steven Novick; Ray O'Connell; Michael Outram; Robert Paskoff; Jimmy Piersall; Milton Plesur; the Popular Culture Association; Elwin Powell; Frank Ralabate; Kevin Ransom; Isabelle Runfola; Jennifer Runfola; John Runfola; Joseph Runfola, Sr.; Joseph Runfola, Jr.; Ross Runfola, Jr.; Donald F. Sabo, Sr.; Jeffrey Sabo; Linda Weisbeck Sabo; Mary Kay Sabo; Jack Scott; Micki Scott; John Sirjamaki; Barry Snyder; Melvin Tucker; Douglas Turner; Antoinette Weisbeck; Ralph Weisbeck; Sidney Willhelm; and Ray Van Dette.

INTRODUCTION

Knute Rockne, the legendary Notre Dame football coach, was a powerful orator who exercised a spellbinding influence over the young men under his tutelage. His fiery pep talks invariably transformed "his boys" into the Fighting Irish, an invincible juggernaut.

In one well-chronicled game Notre Dame was behind at half time by three touchdowns against a team they had been touted to walk over—even if most of the players had skipped out on the traditional morning mass before the game. Lethargic Notre Dame filed into the locker room and sat down to solemnly wait for Rockne to enter and give one of his blistering wintergreen-in-the-jockstrap pep talks. But the minutes clicked by and Rockne did not appear. The players, assistant coaches, trainers, and team priests sat in silence with bowed heads, the tension growing. A referee stuck his head in and shouted, "Two minutes left in the half time." Still no coach.

Finally, Rochne stepped inside the locker room door moments before the team would have had to return to the battlefield—they were going out to do battle, most certainly not play. All heads turned toward the Coach, and he dramatically waited until the room was still.

"Oh, excuse me, ladies," he began. "I was looking for the Notre Dame football team." I'm sure you don't need me to tell you which team won the game.

An even sadder story was told by Nathan Hare in an article in *Black Scholar* magazine. He was writing about the extreme emphasis on masculinity in sports and mentioned a boxing match many people remember, the one involving Benny "Kid" Paret and Emile Griffith, in which Paret was killed. At the weigh-in ceremony before the bout, Paret called Griffith "a woman" and "a fruit." Apparently he used those terms because Griffith had once been a choir boy and had become a designer of women's hats. Paret's widow, Lucy, blamed this incident for the bad blood between the fighters and the savage fury of Griffith's punches, which killed Paret.

Fortunately, organized competitive sports in the United States rarely kill. However, as this sensitively edited collection of articles vividly shows, they all too often maim the body, and even more insidiously twist and impoverish the soul. Macho values in athletics also make it next to impossible for anyone male or female, to fully enjoy their participation in sports.

If my remarks elicit skepticism, or even if you feel anger—"this guy must be some commie, fag, or intellectual," of which I am only one—waste no more time on my contribution and get right into reading the articles. I guarantee a full refund to anyone who still disagrees with me after they have read the book. Just send me one dollar and ten jacket covers of this book, and your refund will be promptly mailed to you.

Some readers may be tempted to close the cover of this book, grumbling that it is simply another anti-sport diatribe. However, to accuse the editors of this collection of anti-sport bias would be like calling someone anti-eating simply because they point out that much of our food is polluted with carcinogenic sprays, dyes, steroids, and preservatives. It's not pleasant to hear that such mainstays of American life as hot dogs and Pop Warner football can be dangerous. But we ignore such warnings at our own peril.

It is important to note that this book does not just expose and condemn the structure of contemporary American sport. It also provides the reader with an excellent vision of how sports might function in a humane, liberating manner.

My one bone to pick with the editors is their belief that the book is primarily for men. At a time when opportunities for girls and women in competitive sports are growing by leaps and bounds (though admittedly not fast enough), it is imperative that women have a thorough understanding of the present athletic system. Those who do not understand history are doomed to repeat it, and there has already been a major recruiting scandal in women's intercollegiate athletics. Surely it was wrong to blame Eve for all the problems in the Garden of Eden, but it would be equally wrong to think that women cannot be corrupted and desensitized as well as men. While this book focuses on the role of sports in shaping the masculine character, its conclusions clearly imply a better quality of life for *both* men and women.

Many political activists blindly sneer at all efforts at personal growth as bourgeois and countercultural, if not downright hippie dippie. On the other hand, too many folks who are into personal liberation dismiss political activism as a bummer to staying mellow and centered. The editors wisely urge a synthesis of these extremes. "If we wish to humanize our identities," write Sabo and Runfola, "we must also transform the society that shapes our lives."

One often hears the derisive comment, "Oh, that's academic," in talking about something meaningless or insignificant. Not without justification, most of the populace view things academic as likely to be irrelevant. This book will be praised and damned, but it will not be called academic. It is scholarship at its finest, rigorous but passionate: social science in the service of human liberation instead of the Rockefeller Foundation.

In this age of increasing ecological awareness, I give all the books I read what I call "the tree test." "Was this book worth the trees sacrificed for its creation?" I ask myself. Most books fail miserably and should be deposited at the nearest recycling center. *Jock? Sports and Male Identity* passes the tree test with flying colors. I hope you enjoy it and learn as much from it as I have.

Jack Scott
Trout Lake, Washington
Summer 1979

SPORTS
AND SEXISM

INTRODUCTION

Traditional notions of male dominance and female submissiveness, the norms safeguarding men's privileged position in family and society, and the discriminatory attitudes women face daily in political and economic life are rooted in a complex system of institutions. The institution of sport functions in part to preserve the unequal distribution of wealth, power, opportunity, and authority between men and women found in the major social, political, and economic institutions of American society.

In addition to socializing boys into traditional male sex roles, sports are intricately interrelated to broader institutional processes. As A. S. Daniels observes, "In the complex fabric of total society, sports have influences upon, and in turn are influenced by, politics, social structures, economics, religion, the military, education, technology, music, art, science and literature."[1] Perhaps the most important function of sports in American society is to integrate varied institutional complexes within a value system that promotes and maintains sexual stereotypes, male dominance, the competitive ethic, and the belief that aggression is a positive and necessary ingredient of social life. Lewis Mumford finds that, in modern civilization, mass sports both facilitate social integration and serve to stabilize the existing state.[2] Corporate executives and steelworkers coming from otherwise divergent social and economic backgrounds can sit down together, sip a beer, and discuss the latest football scores. Like male privilege, male communication networks reach across many social barriers such as class or religious affiliations.

The first set of readings view sport as a primary institutional element in American society. As a central rite of passage for boys and pastime for men, sports are the source of a widespread consensus on values and feeling of solidarity among men. Paul Hoch finds that the most obvious way males are prepared for leadership roles in society is through participation in exclusionist sports that foster the ideology of male supremacy. He argues that an unfortunate residue of sexual apartheid in sports is sexual repression, which in turn leads to the alienation of workers, who look to sports as an opiate for their frustrations.

The Superbowl, of course, is the most graphic example of a sports spectacle as an opiate for the masses of male sports fans. On that day, the American male suspends all significant family activity and is lulled into a state of deadened passivity by the artificial sights and sounds of behemoths competing in a pseudomilitaristic struggle for possession of the keys to the football kingdom. On the sidelines, far from the action, buxom cheerleaders in skimpy outfits cheer their heroes on to victory, while wives throughout the nation serve their husbands dinner by the television set. Like many sports events, the Superbowl is a male-centered ritual with female participants occupying subservient and auxiliary roles. There is little or no unity or commonality of experience between the sexes. The social scenerio is designed to differentiate and separate men from women. To put it simply, men are "on the team" and women are not.

Warren Farrell sees the Superbowl as a repository of masculine imagery in society at large, an event that stresses sexism, masculinity, patriotism, and power. He observes the adeptness with which corporate advertisers channel the machismo strivings of an essentially passive audience toward consumptive behavior. As Farrell shows, media sports events provide a lucrative marketplace for corporate goods with a demonstratively masculine appeal, reminding us of Alvin Gouldner's words, penned in another context: ". . . the ultimate alienation is not that we fail in what we seek, but what we seek is not ours."[3] Unlike those who regard masculine traits as the products of innate physiological factors, he argues that male aggressiveness is primarily an outgrowth of social and cultural conditioning.

Mark Naison attempts to examine why the male fascination with sports borders on hysteria. He argues that this mania can be understood in part in relation to the women's struggle. During and after World War II, women's economic roles underwent a dramatic change, triggering concomitant transformations in domestic life. Women's growing participation in the economic and educational sectors and the subsequent effects on marital, familial, and sexual life were paralleled by the development of mass spectator sports. While millions of women made their way from home and hearth to the workplace, millions of their men grew enthusiastically involved with sports. Naison sees a relationship between these two processes and suggests that many males view sports as the last bastion against a growing feminist onslaught.

FOOTNOTES

1. A. S. Daniels, "The Study of Sport as an Element of the Culture," *International Review of Sport Sociology* 1 (1966): 156.
2. Lewis Mumford, *Technics and Civilization* (New York: Harcourt, Brace Jovanovich, 1934), pp. 303–07.
3. Alvin Gouldner, *The Coming Crisis of Western Sociology* (New York: Avon Books, 1971), p. 193.

SCHOOL FOR SEXISM

PAUL HOCH

Sexual apartheid in sports originates from more or less the same roots as the racial apartheid in the sports of South

---

Africa. Both were established on the sports fields of England's all-white, all-boys public schools which originated our kinds of team sports in the nineteenth century/ No, despite what you might read in the British press, sports apartheid in South Africa was not an Afrikaner invention. It derives from the English-speaking private schools, universities, and such clubs as the Wanderers in Johannesburg, many of which have played their part to this day in keeping that country's international teams lily white. The most obvious reason blacks and women were excluded from English public school sports is that they were not admitted to these schools in the first place. The function of these places was properly to train and socialize an all-white, all-male imperial ruling class. Team sports were one way the elite was more solidly welded together. And since it was a male elite that was going to be toughened up for their role as world imperialists, perhaps the most popular of the early team sports turned out to be the ultra-macho game of rugby. Now in rugby, perhaps even more than its American successor football, the broken bones come so fast and furious that this "game" might better be called a kind of carnage. Even after it spread beyond the public schools, or got watered down into American football, it was obviously not a game for women. The public school team sports were part of the socialization process whereby the male Anglo-Saxon elite learned to recognize one another, and use their elite exclusionist sports as a preparation for their more general notions of elitist rule.

Sports like cricket and rugby were, thus, part of the ideological-social cement that welded the male ruling class together. Other exclusively male bonds were the exclusionist men's clubs, men's activities like gambling, men's prerogatives to "serious" conversation (and monopolization of "unladylike" subjects like politics), and the widespread belief that sex was simply a woman's "marital duty" (which *only her husband was supposed to enjoy). The new all-male sporting traditions formed part of this ideological base behind which men —and especially the male ruling class which originated these activities —got themselves solidified and gradually extended their exclusionist monopoly over more and more areas of meaningful life. The frivolous and household pursuits could then be safely left to the "ladies."*

Even today sports remain one of the prime ways young men are brought together (even though they might be competing against one another), while comparable girls' pursuits, like playing with dolls, learning to be housekeepers, shopping, or whatever, are for the most part carried out in the comparative social isolation of separate households. The boys gather the contacts that will enable them to dominate society, while the girls slowly acquire the habit of living through their menfolk. Over and above these rationales for the exclusion of women was the general male supremacist and anti-sexual atmosphere of the Victorian era in which the team sports developed. (Particularly ironic because a woman male supremacist sat on the throne.) There, of course, remained the strong suspicion in those times that any unnecessary contact between the sexes was bound to lead to damnation. To have them playing sports together might well bring down the Empire.

And to this day the world of jockery still maintains a vividly anti-female aura. In their book Modern Sportswriting, *Gelfand and Heath casually remind their readers that, "Some news pictures of female tennis players are chosen by deskmen primarily because they have more sex appeal than other pictures available." . . . . In short, such female participation in sport as there is is treated as just another girlie show.*

In the sexually repressed atmosphere that makes such

attitudes possible, the male athletes don't fare that well either.

In his book Ball Four *(pp. 36–38), Jim Bouton gives the almost unbelievably sick details of one of major league baseball's most popular pastimes—"beaver shooting." This involves such things as sneaking under the seating of stadiums, "so that to the tune 'The Star-Spangled Banner' an entire baseball club of clean-cut American boys would be looking up the skirt of some female." Other common Peeping Tom techniques used by ballplayers include "peering over the top of the dugout to look up dresses," hanging from fire escapes to look into windows, drilling holes in walls, or holding a mirror under the crack of a hotel-room door. Bouton admits that some people might look down on this sort of thing. "But in baseball if you shoot a particularly good beaver, you are a highly respected person, one might even say a folk hero of sorts." He tells about one hotel that had various L-shaped wings which made it particularly vulnerable to beaver shooting from the roof. "The Yankees would go up there in squads of fifteen or so, often led by Mickey Mantle himself." If anybody spotted something, "there'd be a mad scramble of guys climbing over the skylights, tripping over each other and trying not to fall off the roof." Just after Bouton joined the Yankees, and found himself up on the roof with the team at 2:30 in the morning, he recalls saying to himself, "So this is the big leagues." It resembles much more the sexual deprivation of early adolescence. Imagine; our great American sports heroes have so little opportunity to make love to American womanhood that they have to play peekaboo on rooftops and fire escapes just to catch a glimpse of a female body.*

In fact, the sort of drooling, Peeping Tom atmosphere seems to have penetrated almost every aspect of competitive sports. In 1971 the cameramen at the ABC-NCAA telecasts of college football would every once in a while bea-

ver shoot a particularly fetching lady at the game, and captions like "Not that bad," or "Strong!" would flash across the TV screen underneath her picture. The Enden Shampoo commercials for the professional games were more of the same. The general idea was that football heroes who use Enden will always reel in the beautiful girls. Like big Ben Davidson who reels in three of them in one commercial. Or Alex Karras who warns you solemnly against the perils of being a loser, and then points to his beautiful girl, saying, "She's no loser! She's got me!"

But even when the players manage to get into bed with one of their "baseball Annies" or other "easy lays," they are not much better off:

> The artificial light falling on false eyelashes, oily cosmetics and the smell of cigarette smoke inclined me toward sexual depression. The attention we got from those women (and men too) was sad. The frustration of a stagnant society drained them. There was nothing left but to suck energy from each other and from us. No matter how they tried to disguise it, it always looked shabby and sordid to me. (Chip Oliver, HIGH for the GAME p. 117.)

The sexual repression (including the sexual repression of compulsive cosmetics sexuality) is beaten right into the players along with the sports. They are supposed to be clean livers: not too many women; bedcheck at 11:00 P.M.; and, of course, no sex within at least forty-eight hours of the game. The superstition is that sex weakens you. Physiologically, this is sheer nonsense. If anything, a little healthy lovemaking gets rid of tensions, clears the mind, and may even reinvigorate the body. But what it does "weaken" is those sado-masochistic tensions which come from sexual repression, which might make one hard-hitting killer on a football field. And, more generally, if athletes were less sexually deprived, they would certainly be far less willing to take orders from despotic coaches and managers. The atmosphere of a pro training camp, suggests a kind of "jock convent." Whether they know it or not, "male" sports are one of the things that have made the jocks accomplices in their own sexual (and, hence, political) repression. . . .

American society's general prohibitions against men touching men, or women touching women—or either sex touching the other in any way that doesn't lead straight into bed ("a pass")—works to channel sexuality into the narrow bounds of genital-to-genital intercourse. Men are further prohibited from showing any real emotion, so that even intercourse becomes for many a part of the act of "staying cool." More than that, it becomes the main arena of the constant battle to "prove" what is defined (especially by such writers as Norman Mailer) as one's "masculinity." The battle is fought on the playing fields, too, especially in the ultra-macho game of football. Here, as we've said, it's a particularly narrow kind of "masculinity," the kind measured in brawn not brain, in scoring those touchdowns. The next time you watch a pro football game try to count the number of times the announcer calls out the weights of the players, particularly the big burly interior linemen. "And there's big Ben Davidson tipping the scales at two hundred and eighty pounds. . . . And there's Bob Lilly, a solid two-sixty pounds of beef. . . ." You might think they were calling out the weights of prize calfs at a cattle show. Men reduced to slabs of beef. Depicted as heavyweight objects. It's the male equivalent of the way they describe bathing "beauties" and cheerleaders.

An unusually perceptive article in the Toronto Telegram's Weekend Magazine noted, "football represents the deep-seated desire of every red-blooded American male to be a Superman, all-powerful and immortal . . . the average man's ultimate trip, the fulfillment of the American dream." On the other hand:

> Cheerleaders and baton twirlers, for their part, typify pure American womanhood. There's a hint of good, clean sex in their short skirts and well-rounded sweaters, mind you—but the image is strictly virginal. The message is: Look, don't touch.
>
> In fact, the male's attempt to prove his superiority is very much in evidence. Cheerleaders are relegated to a position of worshipping at the altar of a ritual they can never really be part of.

Football is America's No. 1 fake-masculinity ritual, and the worshiping females are used to give the mock ritual its validity. More than that, the cheerleaders' tiny skirts and rounded sweaters also help inject the proper tension into the atmosphere. They are the modern day equivalent of the Vestal Virgins that the Romans maintained to bless their mass gladiatorial spectacles.

As a symbol of just how much sexuality has been subordinated to the demands of the production ethic, the only time one player is allowed to touch another in a friendly way is when he has just scored a touchdown. Nor does the brutalization of sexuality end with the game. It is even visable in the attitude of the athletes toward their wives. "I'm really gonna punish my ole lady tonite," declared one pro footballer. "Put the wood to her. Make 'er suffer." It is as if the jocks were so brutalized on their jobs that one of the few consolations left to them was having the upper hand with their wives. They certainly do not have it with their coaches. So sexism becomes an opiate for political repression.

It is no secret that around such sexually repressed all-

male terrains as locker rooms, boys prep schools, or prisons, women are just "cunts," "gash," "pieces of ass." (It's as if sex had to be dirty to be any fun.) Even the verbiage of a football game goes hand in hand with that of a brutalized sexuality: "Ramming into the middle . . . sliding into the pocket . . . smashing in . . . beating . . . thrashing. . . ." The words for brutalized sex seem to be the same as those for brutalized sports, and are used by the athletes for both. Similarly, the movements of the cheerleaders are plugged into what amounts to a set of stereotyped military drill routines. Watching the drum majorettes and girls' drill teams prancing about in their mini-skirted mock uniforms, in precision goose steps, it is hard to miss the symbolism of sexuality subordinated to militarism, sexuality used as an advertisement for militarism, and frustrated sexuality used as a spur to militarism and machismo generally.

It is obvious that college and professional footballers would not go through endless hours of agonizing calisthenics and brutalizing scrimmages under the yoke of fascist coaches for money alone. Nor do pro hockey players crack each other's bones with their sticks for "love of the game." Nor do boys run themselves ragged to play on varsity teams because they like "clean living." None of this could happen without the spur of intra-male competition—the endless dog-eat-dog struggle to be the biggest jock (cock?) on the block. Sports is one of the central arenas in which this struggle—with all its physical and, especially, mental brutality—is carried out. (Never mind that the wealth and power that make a player subservient to an owner are not even at stake.) This is the competition behind the competition. "This," we are told, "is where they separate the Men from the boys."

In his article on "Masculine Inadequacy and Compensatory Development of Physique," Robert G. Harlow noted that various observations on the characteristic behavior of *weight lifters suggested an "abnormal accentuation" of certain signs of masculinity. In particular, the secondary masculine characteristics—such as brawn—became for these men the very criteria of their manhood, and:*

> *. . . in general, the weight lifter is characterized by excessive anxiety concerning his masculine adequacy; that his weight lifting and subsequent strength and physique development are attempts to demonstrate both to himself and to others his male potency. (*Contemporary Readings in Sport Psychology, *William P. Morgan, ed., 1970.)*

He notes that, whereas thirty years ago the number of American men interested in weight training could be counted in hundreds, there are at least a million men interested in it now. . . .

Of course the intra-male competition is bigger than all the sports fields. It goes on in all its brutality in bars, swingles clubs, factories, offices, prisons—anywhere and everywhere that men who have been denied control over their jobs and lives gather. Instead of struggling against those forces that keep us all—black and white, men and women, young and old, long hair and short—in subservience to the power of capital, the frustrations and aggressions get turned inward into a misdirected competition of each oppressed male against every other in a never-ending rat race for the prize of "masculinity." In his aptly titled book The Prisoner of Sex, *Mailer admits that this race never ends. No matter how many times the prisoners debase themselves and their women to "prove their masculinity," it isn't enough. Each day the contest begins anew—it's very much like sports—and the prisoners have to prove themselves yet again. One wonders why the Mailers of this world continue to run. . . .*

Women are the prizes of this game. Without sexual repression, no game. No intra-male competition, a stronger and more united proletariat. Hence, no capitalism. To keep the system going, you have to—in so far as possible—keep the women out of the game. Play up the "differences" between men and women. Keep the women off to the side. Outside production. Off the field. And, besides, if you had men and women tackling each other on the playing field of this sexually repressed society, they might like it so much that they'd just adjourn to the bedrooms. You couldn't get anyone to play the game. You couldn't get anyone to work. You couldn't get anyone to take orders. End of game.

The argument is often made that, because of biological differences (admittedly exaggerated by socialization) women are simply not able to stand the faster, more bruising, pace of many of today's male sports. This may well be true. But what if we should decide that this fast, bruising hypercompetitive pace of many male sports is simply too sick, brutalizing, and oppressive to the jocks themselves? Couldn't we have less brutal sports that both men and women could play together? (Mixed doubles in tennis might be one example.) And, if the women didn't play 100 per cent as "well" as the men, why should anybody even care! In fact, why bother with scoring or winning the game at all? Wouldn't it be enough just to enjoy it? . . .

Of course, it is important to see that the fight against sexism in sports, or in society generally, is not won by fitting a few females into the slots of the same repressive system (in this case, the same macho sports). It is hard to see what great benefits black people derived from being "allowed" to make it into professional sports. In fact, at a recent symposium at Queens College in New York, one of the leaders of the black movement in sports, Harry Edwards, said that in his opinion blacks had been deceived into an overemphasis on sports. The irony is, then, that black liber-ationists seem to be withdrawing from sports at the same moment as women's liberationists are clamoring to get in. The apparent incongruity will be resolved only if the mass participation of women in sports is geared to changing the distorted, ultra-macho character of the sports themselves. What we don't need is a new generation of female *gladiators.*

THE SUPER-BOWL PHENOMENON: MACHISMO AS RITUAL

WARREN FARRELL

There is nothing wrong with watching a football game. There is something suspect when a man gives lip service to "I wish I could spend more time with my wife and children" and then watches three football games in a weekend. There might be something suspect in football being held in such priority that sixty-five million people can arrange their day to allow a three-hour bloc of time for one event—the annual Super Bowl.[1] Sixty-five million persons is between one third and one quarter of the American population, the very great majority of whom are men[2]—doubtless more than half the men and boys who are old enough to watch TV in the United States.

Sixty-five million (as opposed to, say, one million) American (as opposed to non-American) males[3] (as opposed to females) have chosen one activity above thousands of alternatives. This alone makes the phenomenon worthy of analysis. What are all these millions attracted to?

Excerpts from "Super-Bowl: Sexism, Patriotism, Religion, Gangs and Warfare" from *The Liberated Man: Freeing Men and Their Relationships with Women*, 1974. Reprinted by permission of Random House, Inc.

When one adds to this the fact that this may involve persuading their attachés or live-in friends to rearrange schedules to allow the men to do this and then serve them beer and chips during the game, some attention might profitably be paid to the needs served and both the conscious and unconscious ways in which football makes its appeal to American men. A systematic analysis of every part of the Super Bowl (the pregame and half-time activities, the game, and the commercials) provides some fascinating answers.

The Super Bowl's first appeal to the viewers is patriotism and power. If we follow almost any Super Bowl from beginning to end we can see it first in the pregame activities. In the 1972 Super Bowl alone, for example, patriotism is represented in the pregame activities by the U.S. Air Force, which uniformly and with precise discipline marches onto the field. They are immediately followed by four flights of Phantom jets—the Tactical Fighter Wing of the U.S. Air Force—which thunder overhead, again with precision and discipline. Power and patriotism are linked. Speed and displays of force are inseparable from patriotism. The Phantom jets are just leaving the viewer's field of vision when the male announcer invokes in a deep voice (with background noise fading to silence) a plea to "remember our veterans in your prayers." Religion is now linked to power—but American power. There is no question that a God exists and that this God approves of power only as displayed by brave Americans.

The announcer's invocation needs a visual focus now that the jets are gone. The camera zooms in on the American flag. Patriotism is reinforced by music. The U.S. Air Force band plays "The Star-Spangled Banner." Feeling is running high—our jets, our Air Force, our flag, our anthem, and finally, our boys. The unquestioned power of our country is associated with the discipline and uniformity of every *Air Force jet* and *Air Force marching-band* member. No deviance is tolerated in this display. Freedom of choice seems to be every man choosing short hair since there was no man in the pregame activities without it. The power of "The Star-Spangled Banner" reached enormous heights, but it is followed by a final call to patriotism—the U.S. Marine Corps' silent drill team marching in quiet but precise step. This is the silence following the climax. Now the American male may watch the game. . . .

On the field a series of rituals are taking place which are designed to reinforce and provoke the utmost aggressiveness of which each man is capable. The pep talk is one ritual. The boy is manipulated by a number of reinforcing loyalties—the loyalty to his school, the coach, his team and team pride, and his own personal pride. In the game itself the loyalty to family and neighbors is added. Prior to the game the team captain yells, "Okay, let's go get them!" and the team screams, "Yeah!" repeatedly. A third ritual, described by Dave Meggyesy, formerly of the St. Louis Cardinals, as part of his high school team's preparation, is a special church sevice by a minister (a former college athlete), who gives an inspirational talk.[4] Almost every type of tactic is permitted when the boys go all out for victory. The side with which one identifies is seen as all good and the other as all bad.

If the effect of professional football is not clear by the end of the first half of the game, it becomes clear at half time. The first event is the introduction of young male children who will competitively vie with each other for honors such as the best passer. Seven-year-old boys test their strength before sixty-five million people, and the young boy at home sees already that he is not quite the man some of his peers are. Furthermore, the other person with whom he identifies is sitting an arm's length away, glued to the TV set. Both the football game and the presence of his father increase the boy's sense of identity with both, but somehow he often feels he is not yet worthy of being a part of what is on the field or deserving of the full attention of his father. If the father is a rabid football fan and the boy a fair-to-middling athlete, the father's presence reinforces the son's need to identify without enabling him to get the feedback to fulfill that need. There is no consistent transmittal of that warm feeling which tells the son he is accepted. Such a boy will either try to prove himself on various playing fields or will live vicariously through men who can.

No sooner do the boys clear off the field than women (called "girls") come onto the field. They are scantily clad, swinging their hips in unison, with outfits cut to reveal their buttocks and bosoms. As the cameras zero in on the former their legs slowly withdraw in a coy but obvious "see if you can get me."

The "girls" are not only selling the importance of slim, sexually coy bodies. They are selling the importance of white bodies (not a brown or black face was among the hundreds onto which the camera focused). But the sexism of selling bodies and the racism of uniform whiteness was not enough. These women were used to sell American patriotism. The scanty outfits were red, white, and blue "Aunt Sam" outfits, and in case the point was missed, each girl had a plastic American flag molded into an umbrella. As the distorted flag umbrellas were opened and closed the announcer explained the theme—"remembering the birth of America."

The next group of ladies appears in frilly red tights cut similarly to those of the last group. These women sing "Hello, Dolly" and literally lay around in a circle on the field and spread their legs, lift them up and spread them again. Carol Channing also sings "Hello, Dolly" but in front of a fifteen-foot football. The U.S. Air Force Academy Choir replies to Ms. Channing by singing "Hello, Dolly." Suddenly dozens of dollies appear—it's the women in the red tights who now promenade off the field by passing the men. The camera zooms in to pick up the eye contact between the men and the women, the essence of the half-time game. The proper distance is always maintained. The men have made their eyes while maintaining their stiff all-male ensemble, and the women have made their appeal without physically being "had." The half time ends. The women who are on the field because of their bodies leave the field to make way for the men who will come on the field because of their bodies.

The viewer has now come through half a game and the half time. On the conscious level the man's power has been supported by his identification with the football players and his fantasizing an "I'd like to get her" relationship with one of "the girls" the camera brought into his living room. In fact, during the Cornell at Dartmouth game the ABC cameras picked out individual women in the stands and rated them. The evaluations (by males) were literally placed on the TV screen as "not too bad," "terrific," and other more condescending phrases. An ABC-TV spokesman indicated in a telephone interview that this was used on four broadcasts.[5] It was not an isolated incident and the pressure brought to bear on the network was obviously not great enough to make them discontinue its use (the spokesman said he "did not remember any reactions to this").

The armchair viewers of the Super Bowl meanwhile have been treated to a spectacle which the crowd at the stadium has missed—the commercials. The theme of all but two of the commercials was muscle, strength, power and speed (no different from the football game). . . .

A beer advertisement first prepares us for the introduction of the beer. We see a rowing team of all men. The camera focuses on their muscles—the strength and power of the men become clear, but they all take directions per-

fectly from their leader. The importance of strict obedience is coupled with victory, and victory coupled with being a man. The beer is introduced as the well-earned reward, with the concluding comment, "It's sort of good to be with men who won't settle for second best.". . .

The razor-blade ad follows a similar pattern. The blades are tungsten, but they are not introduced until they are associated with a powerful steelworker drilling through tough tungsten steel. His shirt sleeve is cut short (and ragged) to reveal his muscles. Sparks bounce off his helmet. He balances himself above the city drilling the steel that makes the city (a far cry from "softer hands with Dove"). Now the tungsten blades can be introduced. They are blades "as tough as steel, for men with tough beards."

The marketing researchers know where it's at. Most of the ads were car ads—cars with "wide-grip tires" (not "pretty white walls"), with tremendous speed, and generally from the sports-car lines of whatever company is advertising. Men want adventure, freedom, a feeling of power, strength and status. They think that they are untouchable and unemotional, and are unaware that they are totally psychologically dependent on an authority figure. But marketing researchers are reinforcing this dilemma even more adeptly in the 1973–1974 football season. The new theme is selling products through the fear of becoming effeminate (as opposed to the aspiration of becoming masculine). . . .

The game draws to a close. The winning coach is Tom Landry, "the man they say is unemotional." The winning team is the Dallas Cowboys, "the team they say is unemotional." But the victory is tremendous, a clear-cut triumph: 24 to 3. The cameras pick the victorious coach out of the crowd. He barely cracks a smile. The time for emotions is certainly here, and a few of the football players do express happiness, but the game ends on a note of patriotism, not emotionalism. The National Football League champions are repeatedly referred to as the world champions. There are no boundaries to male power and no limits on male fantasies—except emotional limits.

Super-Sports

If this relationship between masculinity, sexism, patriotism and violence stopped with professional football, there would be enough need for concern. However, the relationship can be seen in almost every sport. With some exceptions the more violent the game or match, the larger the crowd it draws. The emphasis on violence is not unrelated to what is making ice hockey grow. The television advertisements for ice hockey stress quite clearly the blocking, hard-hitting and violent aspects of the sport. Soccer is the most popular sport in the world but has barely caught on in the United States. Persons who have lived in the United States and other countries observe that even when soccer is played here, the emphasis on body contact is great—a phenomenon peculiar to this country.

On almost all the levels on which sports are played, sexism is a fundamental part. What high school basketball game is without cheerleaders to support the men's efforts? In many schools cheerleaders even support grammar school teams, and for a girl, "making it" as a cheerleader is as important a step in her view of herself as feminine as making the team is in the man's view of himself a masculine. Cheerleaders are still essential in college football, high school football and college basketball. . . .

On Aggression

The lay person will occasionally remark, "Men just have an aggressive instinct," or "Boys will be boys," thus de facto assuming the inevitability of male aggressiveness while biologists and psychologists are still debating about its innateness. Assuming aggression to be natural, the "constructive theorists" talk about how natural aggression can be most constructively channeled.

The examples often given possess a subtle fallacy. They do not suggest that the encouragement of aggression be minimized, but only that aggression be channeled once it has already been encouraged. For example:

> If we block normal outlets of aggression, we may turn it inward. When we pacified the bopping gang of a decade ago, its members turned to narcotics and self-mutilation. And middle-class hippies (also without aggressive outlets) followed in the same path, adding their own variations.[6]

These examples, though, are specious. Pacified gang members and hippies grew up in an environment which encouraged many of the aggressive activities considered natural for a boy. Aggression is stimulated in boys through almost every avenue of socialization.

Most biologists today agree that men do not have natural aggressive instincts, but that aggressiveness is a product of two factors—a tendency and one's environment—and that the two interact to produce aggressiveness or passivity.[7] The implication is that environment is a variable and that by its very nature, aggressiveness is open to environmental influence.

The question should be whether the environment should reinforce that aggressiveness or discourage it. Should we encourage aggressiveness as if it were good of and by itself, or should we channel what aggressiveness there is and do no more to encourage it than is considered humanly functional? Conversely, should a woman's al-

leged tendency toward passivity be encouraged to th
of dependency, or should her family and school m
effort to encourage at least enough aggressiveness .u enable her to assert herself and function independently? Our
logic about aggressiveness compares to the logic of a doctor who says, "Boys naturally have more iron than girls;
therefore, boys should take even more iron tablets."

In fact, we do give more of these kinds of "iron tablets"
to boys than we do to girls. This socialization process starts
with dollhouses, football and children's literature, and continues through the double standard of the courting and sex
life of most people.

According to Sears, Maccoby and Levin (1957), a significantly larger proportion of boys were permitted to express aggression toward their parents; boys were allowed
to show more aggression toward other children, and were
more frequently encouraged to fight back if another child
started a fight. Girls got somewhat more praise for "good"
behavior, and were somewhat more often subjected to
withdrawal of love for "bad" behavior. Physical or antisocial aggression is less sanctioned for girls than boys in our
culture, and physical aggression is expected and rewarded
for boys more than it is for girls. Bandura (1965)[8] showed
that preschool children's imitation of aggressive models
was easily encouraged by positive reward.

Boys were also more subject to hostility and aggression from their parents than were girls. Girls more often
than boys reported that both parents were affectionate and
less often than boys reported that parents were rejecting,
hostile and ignoring. Both sexes said that their mother gave
more affection than their father.

Aggressive behavior to a certain degree is certainly
positive, but our association of aggression with virility
masks its dysfunctional qualities in the everyday life of the
average male. We know that the masculine personality

type is patriotic and conservative, wanting to do what is best for his society.[9] *However, Leventhal and Shemberg find that men scoring high in masculine interests do not inhibit aggression even when the approval of society is in question concerning the aggression's suitability.*[10] *(This finding was contrary to their hypothesis.) However, women expressing feminine interests were able to be both aggressive in societally approved situations and inhibit aggressions in societally disapproved situations. This was also true of men who did not score high in masculine interests.*

Since aggression may in some cases be protection against the blows of others some may fear that a breakdown in sex roles would lead to "passive men who cannot even defend themselves." Meanwhile Jerome Kagan, a leading authority in child development, finds that it is the boy with a weak identification with his father and a moderately strong one with his mother who is likely to be passive, feel inadequate in comparisons with his peers, be reluctant to defend himself against attack, and have difficulty suppressing anxiety.[11] *When sex roles are broken down, however, the father will have a much greater opportunity to provide a stronger identification for the boy, since he will be free to be with the boy more often once he stops his striving and shares responsibility for childcare.*

The insecure man is one who often gets trapped into proving himself a man. It is through this need that society can manipulate him. He is especially subject to being manipulated into committing violent acts by the approval of the football coach or the Army general, the gang leader, other peers, their parents, the public or fans. The one thing he cannot do is defend what he believes in against the clamor of the crowd. It also may be doubted that he really knows what he believes in.

Passivity is termed a woman's value. Part of what al-

lows us to be so comfortable with aggressiveness is merely the fact that it is men who are aggressive and men's value systems predominate. Even if there is an innate tendency toward violence and aggression in people, it is our obligation to curb rather than reinforce this tendency. Instead, we have been either unduly reinforcing it or actively creating it.

FOOTNOTES

1. The *New York Times*, January 15, 1972, estimated this number of Americans as the number watching the Super Bowl on January 15, 1972.
2. Ibid.
3. Most of whom are males.
4. Dave Meggyesy, *Out of Their League* (Berkeley, Calif.: Ramparts Press, 1970), p. 24.
5. The telephone inquiry was made of an ABC-TV general producer on February 9. 1971.
6. Patricia Cayo Sexton, *The Feminized Male* (N.Y.: Random House, 1969), p. 130.
7. See Peter Corning, "An Evolutionary-Adaptive Theory of Aggression," American Political Science Association meeting, Chicago, September 1971, for a review of the literature. Corning was at Stanford University, as of 1974.
8. A. Bandura, "Relationship of Family Patterns to Child Behavior Disorders," Progress Report, 1960, U.S.P.H. Research Grant M1734, Stanford University.
9. Theodore N. Ferdinand, "Psychological Femininity and Political Liberalism," *Sociometry*, Vol. 27, No. 1, March 1964, p. 75.
10. D. B. Leventhal and K. M. Shemberg, "Sex Role Adjustment and Nonsanctioned Agression," *Journal of Experimental Research in Personality*, Vol. 3, 1969, pp. 283–286.

11. Jerome Kagan, "Acquisition and Significance of Sex Typing and Sex Role Identity," in Martin L. Hoffman and Lois Wladis Hoffman, *Review of Child Development Research* (Russell Sage Foundation, 1964).

SPORTS, WOMEN, AND THE IDEOLOGY OF DOMINATION

MARK NAISON

Since the Second World War, sports have become a more visible and important part of American mass culture than ever before in our history. Through television coverage and heavy journalistic promotion, mass spectator sports have been made one of the major psychological reference points for American men, perhaps the single most important focus of emotion and energy in their leisure time. The corporations that finance this activity are capitalized at billions of dollars and are granted political privileges—gifts of land, stadiums constructed at public expense, immunity from anti-trust legislation—that are normally extended only to "public utilities." This special status is reinforced by the American educational system, which sponsors an intensive program of spectator sports from grade school up and explicitly seeks to "train" athletes for professional ranks in its higher levels.

The support that organized sports has been given by government, business, and education is not coincidental. The sports industy has been self-consciously used as a safety valve for social discontent and a vehicle for the political and cultural unification of the American population.

"Sports, Women, and the Ideology of Domination" from "Sports and the American Empire," *Radical America* (July/August 1972), 95–96, 107–110. Reprinted by permission of Mark Naison and *Radical America*.

Since the Second World War, sports has been one of the major areas for the assimilation of new racial groups (Blacks and Latins) into the mainstream of American life and the incorporation of backward and developing sections (the South and Southwest) into the orbit of modern capitalist relations. Black players began to enter major-league sports in large numbers at the exact time (1947–1950) that a series of executive orders "integrated" the US Armed Forces, and the expansion of professional (major-league) football, basketball, and baseball to the South directly followed the passage of Federal Civil Rights legislation.

In addition, athletic events have increasingly reflected the dynamics of an emergent American imperialism. As the American political economy "internationalized" in the post-war period, many of its most distinctive cultural values and patterns, from consumerism to military preparedness, have become an integral part of organized sports. Professional sports events have become "spectacles" whose political and cultural impact lies as much in the marching bands, the cheerleaders, the commercial endorsements and the introduction of politicians and visiting servicemen as in the competition on the field. The spectator is dazzled by an image of American civilization that is so overwhelming that it seems incomprehensible and futile to try to change it or exist outside its framework.

In exposing the relationship between the "sports industries" and emerging women's struggle, I would like to draw attention to three coincident trends in the post-war political economy.

First, the growing importance of women in the labor market and the effect of this on male-female relationships in the family, the workplace, the educational system, and the bedroom. As Selma James points out, the entry of women into the labor market during the Second World War "created in women a new awareness of themselves . . . expanded their conception of their capacities, and cracked . . . open the economic basis of the subordination of women."[1] When the pattern persisted after the war (by 1966, one third of married women were working), it created a crisis of "roles" in both working-class and middle-class families. With the economic basis for male "authoritarianism" in the family (the single paycheck) weakening male-female relationships entered a period of struggle, sometimes hostile and politicized (among the middle class), sometimes veiled behind a mutual concern for survival (among the working-class and poor). As James described it: "Men, particularly young men who have been trained to exercise domination, but have had little opportunity to do so, find themselves lost in their relations with these new women."[2] Their diminishing power over their wives and children evokes feelings of frustration that must be exorcised through social activity or rendered insignificant by more satisfying experiences in other spheres of life.

Second, and equally significant for our purposes, has been the increasing bureaucratization and "Taylorization" of factory and office work and the bargaining away of worker control of the quality and pace of production by the labor movement. Between 1940 and 1956, the once-militant CIO unions, with the lure of "high wages," assumed the role of disciplining workers to managerial imperatives of "efficiency" and became what amounted to a middle layer of the managerial bureaucracy. Workers who once had unions and/or shop committees responsive to their needs found themselves faced with another hierarchy of relentless impersonality that did nothing to stop the speed-ups and changes in production methods that took away what little pride workers had in their job and product. In addition, the growing service sector of the economy brought with it an increasing "proletarianization" of white-collar work which was reflected in the rise of civil service unions, but not in a more satisfying work experience. For the majority of working Americans, craftsmanship, creativity, and feelings of community became experiences sought in their leisure hours rather than through their work.

A third significant phenomeonon is the emergence of the US as a full-blown imperial power, with a political and military "line of defense" on every continent. The entire society was mobilized behind the banner of anti-communism to higher levels of effort—as workers, as soldiers, as managers, as consumers. Never in American history had there been so co-ordinated an effort to discipline the American people to a common cause, in this instance the cause of world domination. Education, music, sports, in fact all aspects of culture became infused with the dynamics of the need to protect the empire.

The psychology of domination thus became an increasingly important theme in American life, but, as we have seen, at a time when the historic domination of men over women was diminishing and the control by workers over the productive process was shrinking. The result was that the American male, told constantly that he was a hero and a "world runner," was not confirmed in this sense of himself by his day-to-day experience. Whatever frustrations resulted from this contradiction had to be expressed outside the workplace, where a struggle for greater control of production might reduce "efficiency" or challenge some corporate priorities. One legitimate outlet became consumerism—which made the accumulation of property, appliances, and hobbies a focal point of energy and emotion, but through which more violent, aggressive feelings could not be fully released. The most socially destructive feelings, when they were not actually being lived (with wives, children, work companions, friends, racial and political opponents) found their outlet in two areas—commercialized sex *and commercialized sports, both of which reached new levels of development in the post-war period.*

The use of sports and sexuality as outlets for violent and guilt-provoking feelings is nothing new; they have served that function throughout the history of industrial society and probably much before. Violent games and rituals like rugby, hurling, boxing, wrestling, and cock-fighting have been part of the daily life of European and American working men for centuries, as have prostitution and pornography in their various forms.

What is new in post-war America is the scale on which they are organized, their expression in nationwide media (some of which, like television, are new inventions), and their penetration by corporate values and relations. In the last twenty years, for example, the imagery of sexual domination and exploitation has become a major theme in the culture, dominating the consumer market, the film industry, popular music, and the agencies defining values for courtship, marriage, and the family (such as popular magazines and medical books). Women, once seen as the repositories of morality and civilized culture, have been projected as sexual beings whose new freedom offers men unimagined possibilities for sexual consumption. The advertising industry and magazines like Playboy *offer a new and more hedonistic image of male domination to replace the declining authoritarianism in the family. With the help of filmmakers, psychiatrists, and progressive clergymen, they suggest that every woman should now provide what men once sought in prostitutes—a seductive, but fundamentally passive sexuality that would affirm men's feelings of competence. Female sexuality is projected as a legitimate "catch-all" for male anxieties, a narcotic that eases the pain of daily existence. In both reality and projective fantasy men are encouraged to find in sex and the experi-*

ence of control (over women, over themselves) what is lacking in their economic and social life.

The success of this "sexualization" of daily experience is questionable. Despite the incredible propaganda campaign, women have resisted sexual objectification, and most men find it difficult to get their wives and lovers to play the roles defined in Playboy. Nevertheless, what is unattainable in relationships is made available in fantasy. The growing culture of pornography in America—topless dancers, X-rated movies, sex novels and magazines—represent efforts to provide a vicarious experience that meets male needs for sexual dominance. In daily life, women have thus won a kind of quiet victory. By their own self-activity, they have forced the most repressive aspects of the "new sexuality" out of the household, out of sexual encounters, and into compensatory fantasies, art, and masturbation.

The growth of commercial athletics in the post-war period mirrors many of the same developments and the same struggles. The increasing coverage of sports in the national media, like the increasing use of sexual images and incentives, aims at the re-inforcement of ideals of male dominance that are being undercut in daily life. The major commercial sports—baseball, football, basketball, ice hockey, and auto racing—allow women to participate only as cheerleaders, spectators, and advertising images, a situation which hardly mirrors the increasing participation of women in the job market and their growing influence in the family. Moreover, these games are not so much played as they are observed. Unlike tennis, golf, volleyball, table tennis, and softball, games which a whole family can participate in and enjoy democratically, these five all-male sports have expanded nationwide, catalyzed the construction of new stadiums, and acquired enormous television, radio, and newspaper coverage without increasing significantly in the degree to which they are played. The American male spends a far greater portion of his time with sports than he did 40 years ago, but the greatest proportion of that time is spent in front of a television set observing games that he will hardly ever play.

FOOTNOTES

1. Selma James, "The American Family, Decay and Rebirth," *Radical America* (February 1971), p. 13.
2. Ibid., p. 15.

MALE IDENTITY AND ATHLETICS: RITES OF PASSAGE

INTRODUCTION

We have argued that the institution of sport promotes and preserves traditional sex differences in American society. Sex roles in marriage and society at large, however, have changed appreciably in the last century. Generally, increased social differentiation in modern industrial society has been accompanied by a trend toward social equality between women and men and a softening of traditional sex role differences. Partially because of underlying institutional changes and the spread of feminist thought, many women have come to regard the passive, dependent, housewife-mother image of femininity as personally unfulfilling and politically undesirable. Similarly, many men have begun to find that the contours of traditional masculinity do not fit their perceptions of themselves, of relationships, and of society at large. In short, the male role is not what it used to be, and for many men, the John Wayne image is but a parody of the past.

A multitude of social and historical forces have eroded the ediface of traditional masculinity. The Industrial Revolution ushered in momentous social and economic changes, and contemporary American society is passing through a transitional phase, in which the old definitions of manhood and womanhood are giving way to new ones. In the highly bureaucratized and mechanized setting of techno-industrial society, the functional significance of physical strength has been progressively displaced by a need for technical and informational expertise that can be provided by women and men alike.[1] Competition in the marketplace, formerly a center of predominantly male activity, has swept up increasing numbers of females in its flux. Male domination of farm, family and professions no longer goes without question. More egalitarian modes of courtship have evolved and more emphasis is placed on companionate marriages. No longer the sole definers and initiators of sexual encounters, modern males are more apt to meet with sexually experienced and vocal women. Virility has become a matter not of conquest but of cooperation.

These changes in female and male roles have been associated with the emergent ideological perspectives of women's and men's liberation. The influence of these developing ideologies is also evident in the social sciences. A number of new investigative areas have crystallized both intellectually and institutionally, including the sociology of women, the psychology of women, feminist studies, the sociology of sex roles, and, most recently, men's studies. Social scientific analyses are yielding fresh insights into the existing social order, as well as providing conceptual contexts for formulating innovative theory and policy recommendations for future social and political action. Our effort to understand sport as a central sexist institution is in part a reflection of this ongoing change in political and social scientific consciousness.

According to Marc Feigen Fasteau, men as well as women are victimized by the ideology of male supremacy fostered by sports. Instead of being taught to measure success in sports in terms of personal growth and pleasure, the ideal is often victory at any cost. This has unfortunate consequences for those who do not conform to the athletic ideal.[2] In addition, Fasteau believes that the preoccupation of youngsters with winning and the emphasis on competitiveness they encounter from childhood on structures their later behavior in political, economic, and military spheres, at the cost of more humanistic ideals.

Peter J. Stein and Steven Hoffman see the role of the athlete as a prototype of the traditional male role and find that athletes and nonathletes alike feel an inner conflict in trying to come to terms with its requirements. Stein and Hoffman's observations concerning male role strain are corroborated by co-editor Don Sabo's autobiographical account of his pursuit of the masculine ideal through sports.

The often fanatical and comprehensive involvement of men in sports is frequently met with derision or just plain puzzlement by women. For young men, however, the ego-satisfaction and social rewards of participating in sports may be the keystone of their identities. Even for middle-aged men who are former athletes or ardent fans, previous psychic affiliations with sports may remain an active personality dynamic. In "The Uniforms," poet Jeanne Foster Hill perceptively captures the centrality of the sports experience for men as well as the gnawing fear of failure it engenders.

A social scientist and former sportswriter, co-editor Ross Runfola finds that the dominant white culture makes a fetish of the supposed prowess of black athletes while simultaneously giving blacks few opportunities to realize their social, political, and economic aspirations. He contends that many black males see sport as a last avenue of escape from the ghetto. Successful breadwinning is a major dimension of male identity, and, more than any other social group, blacks have been systematically deprived of the social resources necessary for economic advancement and the achievement of status. Though racism permeates all sports, many ghetto males have overidentified with the handful of black sports heroes who seem to have achieved the American Dream. Making use of Eldridge Cleaver's concept of the black male as a "super-masculine menial," Runfola argues that white males are apt to recognize the physical achievements of black athletes while denying their intellectual abilities and social aspirations.

Since sports have always been a bastion of the traditional masculine ideal, it is little wonder that men deviating from its stereotypical contours are often labeled deviant or made to feel inadequate or abnormal. Nowhere in the sports subculture is the threat of stigmatization so apparent and the realities of social ostracism so complete as in the case of homosexual breeches of prevailing norms.

While homosexual behavior has always been a part of western patriarchal society, it has been largely a covert phenomenon. One function of the secrecy surrounding it has been to preserve the tenets of traditional masculinity and patriarchal ideology. Though, this ideology has come under attack from feminists, it has remained relatively unchallenged *by males themselves*. Gay activists, however, have left the historical closet and entered the open corridors of social and political life, where their increasingly visible presence has been met with growing intolerance. Opposition to the gay rights movement is perhaps better understood not primarily as an effort to preserve heterosexual sexual morality, but as an attempt to resist any further erosion of the distinctions between males and females and any further altering of their sexual status in the direction of equality. In short, the key significance of the gay rights controversy is mainly social and political rather than strictly sexual. Even more than recalcitrant feminists, gay or "nonmasculine" men represent a threat to the male-dominated social order. Whereas women have always been defined as "the enemy" in patriarchal folklore, nonconforming males are regarded as defectors from their own sex.

In everyday life, the powerful threat of being labeled a homosexual forces boys and men to behave in accordance with traditional masculine stereotypes. A young male who takes an interest in any nonsexual but culturally defined "feminine" activity, such as dance or nursing, is often considered "queer" and labeled a sissy or faggot. The threat of homosexual stigmatization, therefore, serves primarily to maintain sex role stereotypes and only secondarily as a vehicle for regulating sexual behavior.

Within the highly masculine social world of sport, the threat of homosexual stigmatization is ever present. An insufficiently aggressive wrestler or football player is called a pussy, while a poorly performing male swimmer is told to turn in his jock strap for a halter. It is no mere coincidence, therefore, that the cultural image of the jock is the polar opposite of that of the homosexual. Given the myth of rugged masculinity embodied in professional football in particular, it is not surprising that David Kopay, a star running back for ten years in the National Football League, created a sensation when he became the first gay jock to come out of the closet.

Kopay's story reveals how athletes and homosexuals alike are victimized by constrictive masculine stereotypes. Known for his uninhibited, aggressive play, Kopay used violence on the football field as an outlet for suppressed sexual drives and a way of proving he was no less a man because of his homosexuality. His quest for identity in the authoritarian and sexually uptight football subculture and his discovery of human freedom serve as a reminder to all men that understanding of self is a key to liberation from sex role stereotyping.

As Ross J. Pudaloff shows, the protagonists in great works of sports literature provide a vehicle for understanding the dilemmas of modern masculinity. For most men, a re-examination of their identity or a redefinition of the everyday male role is both difficult and emotionally threatening. Few social settings, especially those defined by predominantly masculine values and rituals, offer the individual either an impetus to change or a supportive interpersonal context that facilitates change. The world of sport is a constrictive social setting, but, as Pudaloff observes, the literature of sport furnishes a medium for exploring the full dimensions of masculinity. The reader's identification with literature's tragic sports heroes, his immersion in plot and fantasy, and his discovery of the myths that establish his reality allow for the budding of a fresh perspective of the masculine self and the male role.

FOOTNOTES

1. John Gagnon, "Physical Strength, Once of Significance," in Joseph H. Pleck and Jack Sawyer, *Men and Masculinity* (Englewood Cliffs, N. J.: Prentice-Hall, 1974), pp. 139–49.
2. For a contrary view, see Fred M. Apgar, "Emphasis Placed on Winning in Athletics by Male High School Students," *Research Quarterly* 48, no. 2 (1977): 253–59.

SPORTS: THE TRAINING GROUND
MARC FEIGEN FASTEAU

When learning a sport, men are nearly always impatient with themselves, feeling that they have to reach a certain level of skill right away, instead of enjoying the process of learning. In tennis, for example, men are impatient to play matches, frequently shortchanging themselves on the practice rallies needed to develop consistency and form. In skiing, male beginners and intermediates are often found on slopes much too hard for them, helplessly and sometimes dangerously out of control; learning nothing at all, and, except for the thrill of being afraid, not really enjoying themselves; proving that they can handle the tough slopes takes precedence over everything else.

The intimate association between masculinity and athletics becomes glaringly clear when women try to join the game. If women can play, then, by definition, participation

Excerpts from Marc Feigen Fasteau, *The Male Machine*, © 1974 McGraw-Hill Book Company, pp. 102, 104–114. Used with permission from McGraw-Hill.

does not prove anything about masculinity. Beating a woman proves nothing; losing to a woman is a major humiliation. As we have seen, this dynamic is at work in many all-male activities, but the resentment stirred up by women's attempts to break the sports barrier is more passionate than in most other areas. . . .

The feeling that success in athletics is a sine qua non of manhood is learned early. In a study of the attitudes of middle-income fathers toward their children, only one out of twenty fathers did not want his boys to be good athletes.[1] The father who pushes his son into sports with missionary zeal is so common as to be a part of our folklore. One man in his twenties, who described himself as having struck out more than any other nine-year-old on his Little League team, told me that his father literally carried him screaming and yelling to the games, where his relatives from a neighboring state across the river would sit in the stands to watch him play. And when he did poorly, his father wouldn't talk to him for several hours after the game. The fact that these extreme instances are funny, as well as sad, does not mean that the more usual climate is benign.

Pressure from parents, nearly always fathers, peers, and other male adults, results in a skewing of values which tend to make sports a compulsion for many boys, the mandated center of their lives. Some boys can live with this. Stuart, a twelve-year-old "three-letter man" described his life to a reporter:

> I've been in Little League since I was 8. But I've been throwing the ball since I was 4 or 5. I like soccer, basketball and baseball best. It's all I do, play sports.[2]

Stuart may be another Rafer Johnson in the making, but what if he isn't? There probably ought to be more in his life *than sports. Looking back on my junior high school days, I am sure that some of my afternoons could have been better spent on something other than playing whatever sport was in season.*

Boys who can't conform easily to the athletic ideal are made to feel inadequate. They either quit completely, developing a compensatory disdain for sports as a result and giving up its genuine pleasures for the rest of their lives; or they keep trying, setting standards for themselves that have nothing to do with their own talents or desires. Images of Richard Nixon and Robert Kennedy come to mind, the first uncoordinated and the other too small, both doggedly, probably desperately, hanging on as second-string college football players. . . .

The conventional wisdom about sports is that it is valuable beyond the experience itself, that it builds character, masculine character. The fathers in the study mentioned earlier were not concerned with athletics because they wanted their sons to grow up to be professional athletes but because "failure along these lines seems to symbolize for the father inability to be properly aggressive and competitive, now and in the future."[3] Men I interviewed thought sports were important for their sons because participation taught them how to compete in a rough world and how to get along with other people. But does sport actually build character? And, if it does, what kind of character?

Two psychologists who have studied the effects of athletic competition on personality for eight years and tested approximately fifteen thousand athletes from the high-school gym to the professional level, have tried to answer that question:

> We found no empirical support for the tradition that sport builds character. Indeed, there is evidence that athletic competition limits growth in

some areas. It seems that the personality of the ideal athlete is not the result of any molding process, but comes out of the ruthless selection process that occurs at all levels of sport. Athletic competition has no more beneficial effects than intense endeavor in any other field. Horatio Alger success—in sport or elswhere—comes only to those who already are mentally fit, resilient and strong.[4]

Men who survive the attrition of our culture's highly competitive, star-oriented sports system for the most part have personalities that conform to the traditional male stereotype: high in achievement need, respectful of authority, dominant among peers, self-controlled, and low in sensitivity to other people[5]. . . .

On the character-building front, there is also evidence that those who don't make it to the top suffer a great deal. . . . With the "winning is everything" approach, money, personnel, equipment, and emotional energy are spent on a few teams of the very best athletes, while other men either are discouraged from participating or take a psychological beating if they do. Substitutes on high-school, college, and professional teams—second-stringers who don't play much but are kept around for the good of the team—are often depressed and suffer substantial loss of self-esteem.[6] To some extent, of course, that's life, on or off the playing field. But people learn it soon enough. Why structure amateur sport—which, at least in theory, has as its purpose the pleasure and development of its participants—so that many of the participants and would-be participants lose rather than gain from the experience? People learn and gain confidence from facing challenges that, with effort, they can meet, not from struggling in a system geared to the interest and abilities of the very few. Amateur sport, if designed more for the broad range of ability and commitment of potential participants and made an opportunity rather than a compulsion, could build a lot more character than it does today. But that would require the coaches, and their various publics, to care more about this than about sending their football team to the Cotton Bowl. Contemplating the unlikelihood of that set of priorities, we are led directly to the question of why men watch sports and what they got out of it.

The great chunks of their lives that men spend as spectators of sports can be partly explained, of course, by intrinsic interest. Professional athletes are often incredibly skilled and graceful, and even college football has moments of drama. But game after game, sport after sport, season after season, it can't be that interesting. The same moves are made, passes thrown and caught, championships won and lost; among the pros, all the players are so good that excellence becomes routine. Visual, aesthetic interest alone is not enough to explain the emotional commitment of male sports fans. I like to watch fifteen minutes of a football or basketball game occasionally and, because tennis is the sport I play most myself, I watch tennis on television more often and I go to watch about one tournament a year. Even there, after a match and a half, I've had enough. The drama isn't personally involving enough to absorb me any longer.

But many men are caught up in emotionally meaningful ways. In most spectator sports, especially football, qualities thought to be particularly masculine are at a premium: strength, speed, coolness under pressure, teamwork, the risk of violence, and the drive to win: then there is the satisfaction of a clear-cut decision—one team is a winner, the other a loser. Men understand and identify with these values and codes even if they are not athletes themselves. By devoted spectating and rooting, they vicariously affirm their membership in the club of certified males. Nixon phones plays into the Washington Redskins locker room at half-time. Dave Meggyesy has described a particular brand of avid football fan known to the players as "jock-sniffers": "They were wealthy [men] who would contribute to the under-the-table fund [for the college team] for the privilege of rubbing shoulders with big-name football players."[7] The too-fat or too-skinny boys who take on the thankless job of team manager in high school or college are paying differently for the same associations. Ordered about ruthlessly, sometimes labled as "pussies" by playing members of the team, they hope that somehow, the aura of masculinity surrounding the players will rub off on them. Men watching sports are often doing the same thing at one remove. . . .

For men sports provide a kind of state religion, something they can care about and share in a way which reaffirms the most basic component of their identity; Philip Roth, writing about his love affair with baseball, spelled it out:

> To sing the National Anthem in school auditorium every week, even during the worst of the war years, generally left me cold; the enthusiastic lady teacher waved her arms in the air and we obliged with the words: "See! Light! Proof! Night! There!" Nothing stirred within, strident as we might be —in the end just another school exercise. But on Sundays out at Ruppert Stadium (a green wedge of pasture miraculously walled in among the factories, warehouses and truck depots of Newark's industrial "Ironbound" section), waiting for the Newark Bears to take on the enemy from across the marshes, the hated Jersey City Giants (within our church the schisms are profound), it

would have seemed to me an emotional thrill for-
saken, if we had not to rise first to our feet (my
father, my brother, and me—together with our
inimical countrymen, Newark's Irishmen, Ger-
mans, Italians, Poles, and out in the Africa of the
bleachers, Newark's Negroes) to celebrate the
America that had given to this disparate collection of men and boys a game so grand and
beautiful.[8]

This aspect of the male preoccupation with sport, although
pathetic, is more or less benign. But it has a darker side: the
use of athletic competition as a model for behavior and
problem-solving in other areas of life. Competition is the
central dynamic of organized athletics. Its other benefits
(and costs), unlike those of activities which produce a tangible product rather than abstract "victories," are personal
to the athlete and sometimes hard to measure. So it has
been easy to make athletic competition into a superficially
rational paradigm of total, unqualified pursuit of victory.
And because the subtler, personal rewards and pleasures
of sports are played down, in fact often destroyed by this
approach, the pursuit becomes a never ending one; one's
sense of achievement depends entirely on winning. Absolute team loyalty, unquestioning obedience to authority,
respectful fear and hatred of the opposition, disregard of
individual injury and suffering—all justified in the name of
victory—these are the axioms of the sports system. . . .

It is just this all-out competitiveness that makes fathers
view athletics as an important training ground for their
sons. For example, Joseph Kennedy, the patriarch of the
Kennedy family whose dedication to the precepts "win at
all costs" and "second place is losing" is well-documented,
made heavy use of athletic competition to inculcate these
values into his children. During summers at Hyannisport,

he organized arduous sailing, swimming, and tennis competitions for them. To make sure thay got the point,

> he trail[ed] his children's sailboats in his power
> launch to note their mistakes. Those who erred
> and lost races were sharply scolded and some-
> times sent in disgrace to eat dinner in the kitchen.[9]

Former President Nixon's belief that the qualities needed to
win in football are the same as those needed "to win" in life
is familiar to all of us.[10] Football terms and slogans appear
in his Administration's statements on almost every kind of
issue, but especially foreign policy. At a reception for the
quarterback of the Green Bay Packers, Nixon said,

> A word about your Secretary of Defense . . . [We]
> know that the defense is essential if you are going
> to be able to win the game. . . . The defense is
> important, as Mel Laird has said, not because the
> United States wants a war, but because with that
> kind of defense we can discourage anyone who
> might want to engage in an offense.[11]

. . . John S. D. Eisenhower, son of the former President and
once ambassador to Belgium, wrote a column for The New
York Times in 1973 that was a paradigm of this kind of thinking. Entitled "The Coach," it offered the trials of West Point
football coach Earl Blaik as a predictive parable about the
problems of Richard Nixon," our nation's Coach." Its bland
analogy between a football team caught cheating and a
national Administration in the throes of Watergate, between a football coach with one glorious obsession—"to
win"—and the President of the United States, and its easy
assumption that the only important objective for both is to
rebuild the team (Administration) so it can go on to "victory"

is at once incredible and disturbingly familiar in its "big game" approach to life. Here is an excerpt describing the "comeback" achieved through the Coach's personality and "fight:"

> *Gradually the Coach rebuilt. He took his defeats, using scrubs for a while, but he continued to rebuild with a determination that few men could muster. Gradually he and his new team came from the depths of defeat to eventual renewed success. When it finally came time for him to set aside his responsibilities as Coach, he had once more created a team that went undefeated for the season. The Coach, exonerated, retired, and the Institution was restored.* [12]

If the analogizing of national and international life to football went no farther than occasional and superficial use of sportspeak, no great harm would be done. Nixon, in all likelihood, would believe that winning is everything even if he had never heard of football. But sport—especially football—reflects society's dominant, traditional masculine ethos in a particularly clear and magnified form. For this reason, and because of its role as a key masculinity-affirming ritual, sports play an active part in the dialectic between the individual and the society which perpetuates these values. In particular, it supplies a language and rationale for men to use in nonsports situations, a language which is widely understood and which reduces the more complex real-life problems of choosing objectives and weighing human costs to the simplistic imperatives of a competitive game.

FOOTNOTES

1. David F. Aberle and Kasper D. Naegele, "Middle-Class Fathers' Occupational Role and Attitudes To-

ward Children," *American Journal of Orthopsychiatry*, Vol. 22 (1952), p. 366.

2. *The New York Times*, June 2, 1973, p. 33
3. Aberle and Naegele, *op. cit.*, p. 374.
4. Bruce C. Ogilvie and Thomas Tutko, "Sport: If You Want to Build Character, Try Something Else," *Psychology Today* (October, 1971), p. 61.
5. Ibid.
6. Telephone interview with Bruce C. Ogilvie, September 21, 1973.
7. Dave Meggyesy, *Out of Their League* (Ramparts Press: 1971)/(Paperback Library ed., 1971), p. 87.
8. Phillip Roth, "My Baseball Years," *The New York Times*, April 2, 1973, p. 35 (emphasis added).
9. Nancy Gager Clinch, The Kennedy Neurosis (Grosset & Dunlap, 1973), p. 31.
10. See, for example, Robert Lipsyte, "When You Lose, You Die a Little," *The New York Times Magazine* (September 16, 1973), p. 13.
11. Ibid.
12. Ibid.

SPORTS AND MALE ROLE STRAIN

PETER J. STEIN AND STEVEN HOFFMAN

Sport in American society is a prominent masculine rite. Every boy has to wrestle with the all-pervasiveness of athletics./The development of athletic ability is an essential element in becoming a "man"; sports is the training ground for "the traditional male role."/

In recent years there has been a growing interest in

Peter J. Stein and Steven Hoffman, "Sports and Male Role Strain," *Journal of Social Issues* 34, no. 1 (Winter 1978): 136–50.

the study of sports. Such writers as James Michener (1976), Robert Lipsyte (1975), and Michael Novak (1976) have provided a general analysis of sports in American culture. Disaffected athletes—Jim Bouton (1970), Dave Meggyesy (1971), and Gary Shaw (1972)—have provided first-hand accounts of the dehumanizing aspects of sports. Social scientists (Edwards, 1973; Talamini & Page, 1973; Ball & Loy, 1976) have contributed in a more systematic way to the study of sports. Similarly, writings on male roles, particularly from the perspective of the men's liberation literature, have emphasized how both athletes and nonathletes are harmed by the athletic element in the male role. Yet to date there has not been a systematic analysis of the processes by which this occurs. A growing number of recent publications (Fasteau, 1974; Farrell, 1974; Pleck & Sawyer, 1974; David & Brannon, 1976; Pleck, 1976a, 1976b) have suggested that "the male role contains many constraining and limiting features from which men need to free themselves" (Pleck, 1976a, p. 155).

Little work has been done in analyzing the problems for men which result from being or not being an athlete. In this paper we consider aspects of the experience of role strain for athletes and for nonathletes.

Methodology And Data Base

The concepts of role conformity, conflict, and role strain have a strong intellectual history in sociology (Goode, 1960, 1961; Turner, 1970; Parsons, 1951). Among the most recent works is Komarovsky's (1976) study of role stain among college men, in which she reports that over 80% of the college seniors interviewed experienced some form of role strain, ranging from mild to severe, in fulfilling role obligations. For Komarovsky, role strain involves manifest or latent difficulty in role performance or low rewards for role conformity. These seniors experienced role strain in their emotional, intellectual, and sexual relationships with women, relationships with parents, occupational plans, self-images, and experiences of intimacy and isolation. Their athletic experiences were not examined.

Komarovsky developed a typology of six modes of role strain: (1) ambiguity or anomie, (2) lack of congruity or "malfit" between personality and social role, (3) lack of resources for role fulfillment, (4) low rewards for role performance, (5) conflict, and (6) role overload.

This paper is primarily a theoretical analysis of role strain experienced by two groups of male college graduates—those who were members of high school and college teams (athletes) and those who did not participate in athletics beyond that required by the curriculum (nonathletes). The utility of Komarovsky's typology is examined and extended in light of the athletic experiences of our sample. Our data will be used for illustration; and extensive data analysis is reported in Hoffman (1978).

Interviews were conducted with 24 white men between the ages of 21 and 32—old enough to have had extensive sports experience, yet young enough for those experiences to be readily available to recall. Twelve men who participated in at least one full season of both high school and college level varsity football, basketball, or baseball constitute our athletes. The twelve men defined as nonathletes had not participated in any form of organized sports beyond compulsory high school and college requirements, had very little other sports experience, and considered themselves as nonathletes.

Although interest, participation, and success in sports can be represented along a continuum, for the purposes of this study we have dichotomized these dimensions. This definition also excludes from our study the large number of

American men who participate in some sports in some measure, but have not played on varsity teams in any of the particular three sports.

Basketball, baseball, and football are, in our estimation, most representative of competitive team sports in America. They are sports that have been developed in the United States and, unlike such other competitive team sports as ice hockey or soccer, are associated with American culture. Almost all males are exposed to these three sports as children and as adolescents. They are an integral part of most school physical education curriculums and most high schools and colleges field teams in these sports. As team sports the competitive environments they create are different from individual sports such as swimming and running, or two-person competitions such as tennis or boxing, in which elements of team play are less direct.

The Importance of The Athletic Role

Researchers have noted that boys tend to be socialized in childhood for the traditional male role, which includes an instrumental orientation toward the world and an emphasis on physical strength and athletic ability (Hartley, 1970; Gagnon, 1974). In the traditional male role, taught in part through sports, "interpersonal and emotional skills are relatively underdeveloped, and feelings of tenderness and vulnerability are especially prohibited" (Pleck, 1976a, p. 156). The ideal sportsman is tough, strong, and agressive.

Our interview data suggest that, as boys, all of the respondents were aware of these cultural scripts. Boys were expected to take part in sports and develop athletic skills. The importance of the athletic role was reinforced by the interpersonal and institutional contexts of childhood and adolescence. Both athletes and nonathletes had to cope with the social expectations of the athletic role.

The experiences of our respondents parallel findings of other studies. When asked about popularity, students in 10 high schools indicated that being an athletic star was the most important attribute in making a boy popular (Coleman, 1976). Another study of acceptability (Tannenbaum, 1960) found that all athletes had higher acceptability ratings than nonathletes; both brilliance and studiousness had much less effect on popularity than athletics.

Lipman-Blumen (1975) reports that athletes have more interaction and contact with peers, feel better about themselves, and have more group involvement and experience with others. She also points out, however, that although these experiences are valuable, at a certain point sports start to extract costs: pressure, time and energy, exclusion from other activities, and expected conformity to the traditional male role.

The role of the athlete was the most salient for the athletes we interviewed. For most of them, "sports was everything." Their participation in competitive sports, particularly in high school, influenced their conduct in most other roles. Their successes or failures in sports influenced the way they were treated in their roles as students, dates, friends, and brothers. However, their participation in sports also resulted in various experiences of role strain.

Modes Of Role Strain
Experienced By Athletes
AMBIGUITY AND ANOMIE

The failure of expected interaction in a role system leads to a situation of disorganization, ambiguity, and anomie. Komarovsky notes that ambiguity is experienced as confusion involving normative expectations of role partners or conflict between alternative possibilities (Mode 1).

For the male athletes interviewed, this mode of role strain involved ambiguity as to whether individual or team performance is more highly valued and a shift over time in the value of athletics in their lives. The male sex-role norms are very clear in valuing athletics, but in late adolescence and in adulthood there is more ambiguity in whether this is so valued and there is marked increase in negative stereotypes about athletes.

Many of the athletes experienced the role strain stemming from situations of ambiguity between individual achievement and team success. These situational strains occurred in a cultural context which stresses and rewards the performances of professional football, basketball, and baseball stars. This is reinforced by the prestige bestowed on stars by local high school and college newspapers.

Minimum levels of cooperation and reciprocity are incorporated in sports such as football, basketball, and baseball through a complex division of labor institutionalized in the different positions on a team. But the success of a team depends on a relatively high level of task and interpersonal cooperation and reciprocity. Each player on a team responds to his teammates athletically and emotionally, through his play. Through these actions an athlete establishes his standing and his value to other members of the team; these actions can facilitate cooperation or hinder it.

Turner (1970) suggests that in this mode it is the "failure of reciprocation" that leads to an ambiguous or anomic situation. Most of our athletes reported situational ambiguity involving diminishing reciprocity and increased individuality. For example, Respondent #5 reported that in his senior year the high school basketball team had more talented players than it did in the previous two years. Yet, despite such talent, the team posted a record of 7 wins and 15 losses. The major reason was the lack of cooperation among the players and the predominance of shooters or "gunners" over playmakers. "Everyone wanted to be a star and score in double figures, but no one would set up plays, set picks, and feed off. Almost everyone played as an individual, with very little team effort." From the perspective of the team, a situation of anomie prevailed. The closely coordinated division of labor, with its inherent normative structure, disintegrated; the players experienced confusion and a sense of ambiguity about their roles.

The second major source of ambiguity and anomie for athletes involved shifts in values over time. In childhood and earlier adolescence, athletics were stressed in their lives and reinforced by significant others. For most, a shift from high school to college yielded less and less satisfaction with competitive sports experiences and an increase in feelings of ambiguity about the personal value of sports (Mode 4). For some this ambiguity developed into role conflict involving growth of interest in other activities (Mode 5). This ambiguity was also fostered by the increase of negative stereotypes about athletes (dumb, lacking social skills, no other interests, no political awareness, macho, bully). Two of our respondents, both students at Ivy League schools, stressed their superior academic achievements whenever faced with such negative stereotypes. They sought to dissociate themselves from other team members whose behavior approximated these negative stereotypes.

PERSONALITY AND SOCIAL ROLE

A second source of role strain for the men in our sample involved lack of congruity between personality and the expected social role (Komarovsky's Mode 2). Turner refers to this mode as the inability to perform a role adequately. He notes that the intensity and frequency of strain is most *noticeable when the role is rigidly defined and the individual must fit into it regardless of his needs or preferences. This mode was experienced primarily by the nonathletes.*

For both the athletes and the nonathletes in our sample, football, basketball, and baseball were used to differentiate boys not only according to their athletic abilities, but their developing personality characteristics as well. Boys who possessed basic athletic skills of strength and coordination were also expected to exhibit competitiveness, assertiveness, leadership, and confidence. These behavior patterns were then reinforced and further developed through participation in sports. The combination of selectivity and socialization into the athletic role meant that athletes possessed the appropriate personality characteristics.

Insufficient Resources

A third major mode of role strain results from socially structured insufficiency of resources for role fulfillment (Komarovsky's Mode 3). This mode expands Merton's (1957) idea that a disjunction exists between widespread aspirations in a society and the access of individuals to legitimate means of realizing these goals. The competitive sports environment in America is dominated by the Vince Lombardi ethic: "Winning isn't everything. It's the only thing!" This ethic is at the base of the role strain experienced by athletes interviewed at all levels of competition from grade school through college.

The major task of football, basketball, and baseball teams is to win ball games. In the competitive, zero-sum structuring of these sports there is, by definition, only one team that can win. For athletes the combination of the value given to winning as opposed to meeting some minimum standard of performance, combined with evaluation systems that emphasize only who has won instead of who has played well, leads to role strain. If in order to fulfill his role the athlete (and his team) must win, the nature of the contest is such that some athletes must always fail.

This winning attitude was reinforced in a number of ways. For example, Respondent #11 reported:

> We learned that we had to win. I pitched well that year, but our team couldn't score runs. Our coach, who was used to winning, chewed out the entire team and, rather than praising those who played well and really tried, we were all responsible for not winning . . . At school winning was related to acceptance, popularity, and prestige.

The effects of the stress on winning were clearly expressed by Albert King, a high school superstar, following his first game for the University of Maryland basketball team:

> In college I get the feeling that you have to win, or they hate you. I don't want to be a star. If you're a star and the other team stops you, then what did you do? You lose, that's what, and nobody will like you. (The New York Times, 1977)

Few Rewards For Role Conformity

A fourth mode of role strain results from feelings that role fulfillment does not yield sufficient personal satisfaction, material benefits, or social esteem (Komarovsky's Mode 4). Turner refers to this mode as involving the failure of role performance to produce a sense of accomplishment.

Our interviews suggest the importance of distinguishing between internal and external rewards. The available rewards operate in the dominant context of a star system which is based on high rewards for a few at the expense of rewards for the many. Superstars receive publicity, pres-

tige, and glamour for performances, while teammates oftentimes feel devalued in their own performance. In all three sports, the average players reported that even though they performed well they felt overshadowed by the team's superstar. They sometimes felt comtempt and envy toward the better-recognized players. The players reported feeling good about their performance when values predominating the team were such that every member gained recognition for his contribution.

This failure to receive external rewards is related to the failure of reciprocation, stemming from unclear norms (Mode 1). As in that mode, the average team players felt that they played as well as they could but received neither the external rewards of social esteem nor the inner personal satisfaction from a task done well.

Other athletes reported that after a number of years of competitive sports participation, the cost of doing sports began to outweigh the benefits. The glory, the hoopla, the big game, the prestige stemming from their athletic achievements began to lose their importance. The long hours of work and practice were no longer paying off, and the role of athlete lost its value. Respondent #7 reported:

> *By the end of my freshman year I had had it. Even though I was the high scorer and we had the winningest freshman team in the history of the school, I couldn't see spending every afternoon from October through March practicing, especially with guys I didn't like. In my first year through playing I established who I was on campus. I was the hot-shot freshman guard.*

Athletes varied with respect to the importance they attached to internal as opposed to external rewards. In some cases both sets of rewards were present, in other cases the presence of one was not strong enough to outweigh the decreasing quantity, or absence, of the other. For example, Respondent #12, who had been the star scorer of a New York City high school basketball team, received a substantial athletic scholarship from a mid-western junior college. In exchange he was expected to play well, to help win ball games, and to practice seven days a week. He referred to his coach as "a man who lived and breathed basketball. We practiced about four hours after classes everyday and during the season he expected us to give our all to the game. We had a curfew, weren't supposed to get involved with women, but to rest a lot and conserve our energies for basketball. He even had a spot bed check a couple of times." As the season progressed, Respondent #12 decided that the material benefits did not overcome diminishing personal satisfaction. What had been fun and good times in high school changed to a situation that yielded little personal satisfaction, even though the material benefits were substantial.

Role Conflict

The athletes interviewed reported a number of examples of role conflict stemming from their participation in athletics. These involved conflict caused by problems of allocation of time, energy, and emotional commitment. In some cases the issue of allocation involved alternatives not intrinsically conflictful, while in other cases the alternatives involved mutually-exclusive choices (Komarovsky's Mode 5).

The components of the athletic role learned by our respondents involved an emphasis on toughness, independence, nonemotionality, insensitivity, blocking of pain, and a focus on concrete details and goals of winning. These characteristics proved to be satisfactory and desirable for athletes in high school, where these masculine characteristics were valued by other students and brought success in dating.

With a shift to college, more of the athletes experienced conflict due to their dates' expectations of different personality traits. Women they dated expressed a preference for greater openness, a sharing of feelings, more verbal communication, more sensitivity to feelings, moods, and nonverbal gestures.

The focus was on relating to each other and the men felt forced to reevaluate the characteristics stressed in their athletic role. They began to experience strain and conflict between these competing expectations. This role strain involved both interpersonal conflict with dates and some intrapsychic tension involving the surfacing of feelings about themselves and their athletic roles and heterosexual dating roles.

For some this role conflict was exacerbated by the strict definition coaches had of how energy, time, and emotional commitment should be allocated. The experiences of Respondent #12 illustrate the conflict generated by the coach's attempt to restrict dating and sexual activities since these might interfere with the commitment to sports. As far as the coach was concerned, there was plenty of time for dating after the season was over.

Unlike most high schools, college provides social contexts that provide alternate sources of status. While the traditional athletic role demands a substantial commitment to sports to the exclusion of developing other interests, in college, with the expansion of new experiences, our athletes began to feel the limitations and constraints of the athletic role.

Athlete #10, a football player, reported that in college he started attending concerts, political rallies, and religious meetings. "I was looked upon as a little suspect. . . . I'd gone to SDS meetings. . . . everything that I felt would enrich my life." He no longer fit the athletic role expected by his peers and was less and less accepted as a group member by both coaches and players. In their eyes, his new political interests were beyond the limits of the traditional role of athlete and reflected incompatible values. Political interests and activism, particularly radical politics, are incompatible with the politically conservative and traditional athletic role. The demands of these two roles, in terms of energy, commitment, life styles, and values, are incompatible (Scott, 1971; Hoch, 1972; Edwards, 1973).

Overload of Role Obligations

Strain stemming from an overload of role obligations refers to the situation where an actor cannot satisfy the demands for the same finite amount of time and energy from all role partners in his various statuses.

The athletic role as experienced by our respondents demanded substantial commitment of time, energy, and loyalty. The pressure and demands of tryouts, practice, and play encroached on the time needed for other obligations. Almost all of the athletes we spoke to played at least two varsity sports in high school. Football training began in August and the season stretched from September to the end of November; basketball started in November and ended in March, when it was time for baseball to begin. These athletes typically spent every afternoon and most of Saturdays practicing and playing ball. This overwhelming time demand resulted in time limitations to perform other roles, such as student and friend, with consequent role overload.

Interestingly, however, few athletes remember feeling the role overload during their high school years. In high school, athletic achievement provided rewards in terms of prestige and ingroup membership. The shift to college began to expand other opportunities for activities, as well as to diminish the overall importance of the athletic role. The growth of alternative areas of interest (academic, political, social), along with the more complex system of prestige rewards in college (Mode 4), made the athletes aware of the extensive demands of the athletic role. It is interesting to note that this mode of role strain seemed to gain in importance for athletes as they reflected on their competitive sports days. In retrospect, several wished that they had expanded their interests and activities beyond their concentration on sports. They felt grateful for having had the experiences of sports in childhood and early adolescence and having had the experiences of group membership, but the role of athlete seemed a limited one over the life-cycle.

Role-intrinsic Anxiety and Physical Damage

The high anxiety and actual physical damage experienced by out athletes represents a mode of role strain not identified in Komarovsky's typology. Quite apart from modes of role strain involving social norms, resources, competing demands, etc., the athletic role has certain negative consequences. This new mode of role strain involves role-intrinsic anxiety and physical damage.

The role of athlete demands high-level performance. This pressure to perform is learned early in the sports environment and is reinforced by coaches and other players throughout the athlete's sports career. This constant demand to perform is internalized by the athletes themselves and experienced as a strain.

Athletes with whom we spoke felt that every time they took the field they were expected to perform at least as well as their past best. This demand for excellent performance was reported by all the athletes. Their reactions to the demand varied, but they all worried about embarrassing themselves, failing, and not looking good. This pressure reduced the fun that was originally part of sports for them. Respondent #4 noted:

> Before any game ever, from Little League to college, nausea, butterflies, whatever you want to call it . . . I was afraid of losing, of failure, of performing poorly. . . . I was always far too self-conscious. I felt every eye was on me.

In some cases, the pressure to perform was so great that athletes continued to play with injuries. One respondent reported that he and his teammates continued to play on the college football team after a fellow teammate ran himself to death during an exhausting practice. Others continued to play with broken ankles; still others had operations so that they could continue playing, although this in one case led to permanent injury.

These seemingly extreme reactions to the demands for high-level role performance were quite common, actions made plausible by the set of attitudes fostered by the athletic environment. Our interviews revealed that playing with pain and discomfort was a normative expectation rather than an exception. From the point of view of those in this social system, not to play would constitute a conflict within the athletic role, i.e., athletes play with pain. This playing with pain necessitates denial of feeling, a dissociation which is part of the traditional nonemotive male role—men don't cry, they "bite the bullet."

Modes of Role Strain
Experienced by Nonathletes

While the athletes interviewed experienced various amounts of all the role strains identified by Komarovsky except lack of congruity between personality and social role, the nonathletes in contrast experienced primarily this second mode of role strain. Their major mode of role strain stemmed from the inability to perform in the athletic role. This results from a combination of lack of skills to participate in the sport and the incongruity between personality characteristics and the expected social role of athlete. The nonathletes reported intense negative feelings about this experience.

The role of nonathlete is rife with role strain. The child who is weaker and not well coordinated is chosen less and less often and begins to accept the definition of nonathlete. This development occurs throughout the early and middle grade-school years when his personality is being shaped. He experiences more and more role strain as his emerging personality does not fit the role of boy-athlete, terms which are closely linked in that age group. The men who did not play ball as children reported that the process of self definition as a nonathlete was gradual but definite. There was an initial casting of roles (athletes and nonathletes) which became more rigidly defined with each sports contest. Less skillful boys became labelled as nonathletes by the other children.

Once labelled, these boys found it difficult to break away from the role and the cycle of the self-fulfilling prophecy began. The nonathletes reported that they were typically late to games, did not bring their sneakers, and in many cases did not ask to be "chosen in." Respondent #18 reported that, in summer camp, part of his team actually started to beat him up in right field after he lost the game by not knowing where to throw the ball.

The nonathlete's definition of manhood is also focused on athletics. His inability to meet the role of athlete leads to his inability to be "one of the guys," or even "one of the boys in the family." Respondent #22 reported the following experience with its obvious negative psychological consequences:

> I was raised in the South and I certainly had some very strong impressions of what being a man was. My brother was three years ahead of me and he was really a tough athlete: first-string football, three-letter man, etc. So when I got into the ninth grade, I was expected to play football and I decided I wasn't going to do it. And . . . in my family all hell broke loose. My father would just launch in, in front of relatives, and imply that I was a sissy: finally it got so bad I gave in . . . I'll never forget being out on the practice field the first day and the coach saying: "If you're only here because your parents want you here, then you should just leave right now." And I wanted to leave so bad. And I just couldn't do it.

The nonathlete develops a negative set of attitudes towards the role of athlete. In his view, athletes are dumb, uninteresting, and callous bullies. In this way, he distances himself from others and provides a rationale for his lack of accomplishment. However, this attempt to redefine social reality lacks the support of others, and in its absence the nonathlete continues to feel role strain. Much of this conflict is turned inward and results in self-hatred. "The world of the boy who is always picked last in sports is very different from the world of the other boys. . . . It is a terrifying subterranean netherworld, full of hatred and violence which is expressed mostly against the self" (Pleck, 1976b, p. 262). Pleck articulates the feelings many of our nonathletes had difficulty expressing:

I didn't have sports as the major psychological reference point in my life, as nearly every other boy in grade school did, and I did not subscribe to the dominant system of values, images, and symbols it entailed. I saw the world differently from other boys. I identified sports as a major aspect of what I was supposed to be like as a male, which oppressed me because I could not do it, no matter how hard I tried. Sports expressed values about competition and aggression that I knew were awful. And I knew that these perceptions themselves, perhaps even more than my failure at sports itself, made me different from other people. (pp. 247–248)

Conclusions and Implications

The athletic role is a prototype of the male role. It separates the men from the boys. Our study discusses the types and forms of role strain experienced by men defined as athletes or nonathletes. It documents the strong link between the athletic role and the traditional male role in American society.

Both athletes and nonathletes experienced role strain. The athletes' preoccupation with and emphasis on high-level performance and winning were the underlying reasons for their experience of role strain. The nonathletes, on the other hand, were faced with their inability to make it in the pervasive child's world of sports. They experienced role strain and feelings of failure and nonmembership in the world of their male peers.

For the athletes—in this study, members of organized teams who played either football, basketball, or base-

ball—the demand for high-level performance was so pronounced that in some cases they played with great pain, risking permanent injury. In keeping with the traditional male role, it was unmanly to give expression to the pain and to acknowledge it. The star system with its differential rewards based on performance generated problems of cooperation and reciprocity among team members and materialized as another source of strain for athletes. Low rewards for cooperation and teamwork exacerbate the problem.

The inability of the nonathlete to perform at even the minimal level of competency severely limited his membership in male peer groups. This inability to perform in sports led to feelings of inadequacy and inferiority. Nonathletes experienced early casting into this role, and once so defined, the boy was not taught the proper skills and norms of the game and so continued to be nonathletic.

We do not mean to imply that positive experiences do not take place in sports. In fact athletes do learn, in varying degrees, to cooperate, compromise, and compete with peers. They learn strategic thinking, physical dexterity, and coordination. They learn competency and mastery of a skill. These functions can be very helpful to a person in leading a more productive adult life.

Our research leads us to ask the question of how sports can be organized so as to allow all participants to benefit from its crucial developmental functions, while minimizing the role strain for both athletes and nonathletes. We can speculate that the optimum condition for successful modern male-role performance is related to some group of athletic experiences of a less competitive and more cooperative nature. The introduction of these values into male-male relationships through sports may result in their eventual introduction in other areas of social interaction. Cooperation, *sharing, and compromising without suffering loss of self-esteem are hopeful aspects of change in the athletic role and in the male role.*

REFERENCES

Ball, D. W., & Loy, W. *Sport and social order: Contributions to the sociology of sport.* Reading, MA: Addison-Wesley, 1976.

Bouton, J. *Ball four.* New York: Dell, 1970.

Coleman, J. Athletics in high school. In D. S. David & R. Brannon (Eds.), *The forty-nine percent majority: The male sex role.* Reading, MA: Addison-Wesley, 1976.

David, D. S., & Brannon, R. (Eds.). *The forty-nine percent majority: The male sex role.* Reading, MA: Addison-Wesley, 1976.

Edwards, H. *Sociology of sports.* Homewood, IL: Dorsey Press, 1973.

Farrell, W. *The liberated man.* New York: Random House, 1974.

Fasteau, M. *The male machine.* New York: McGraw-Hill, 1974.

Gagnon, J. Physical strength: Once of significance. In J. Pleck & J. Sawyer (Eds.), *Men and masculinity.* Englewood Cliffs, NJ: Prentice-Hall, 1974.

Goode, W. A theory of role strain. *American Sociological Review,* 1960, 25, 246–258.

Goode, W. Norm commitment and conformity to role status obligations. *American Journal of Sociology,* 1961, 66, 246–258.

Hartley, R. American core culture: Continuity and change. In G. Seward & R. J. Williamson (Eds.), *Sex roles in changing society.* New York: Random House, 1970.

Hoch, P. *Rip off the big game.* New York: Anchor Books, 1972.

Hoffman, S. *The nature and influence of messages communicated through team sports as a medium of social interaction.* Unpublished doctoral dissertation, New York University, 1978.

Komarovsky, M. *Dilemmas of masculinity.* New York: W. W. Norton, 1976.

Lipman-Blumen, J. Toward a homosocial theory of sex roles. *Signs,* 1975, *2,* 15–31.

Lipsyte, R. *Sports World: An American dreamland.* New York: Quadrangle, 1975.

Loy, J. W., & Kenyan (Eds.), *Sport, culture and society.* New York: Macmillan, 1969.

Meggyesy, D. *Out of their league.* New York: Paperback Library, 1971.

Merton, R. *Social theory and social structure.* New York: Free Press, 1957.

Michener, J. *Sports in America.* New York: Random House, 1976.

The *New York Times,* November 27, 1977.

Novak, M. *The joy of sports.* New York: Basic Books, 1976.

Parsons, T. *The social system.* Glencoe, IL: The Free Press, 1951.

Pleck J. The male sex role: Definitions, problems, and sources of change. *Journal of Social Issues,* 1976, *32* (3), 155–164. (a)

Pleck, J. My male sex role–And ours. In D. S. David & R. Brannon (Eds.), *The forty-nine percent majority: The male sex role.* Reading, MA: Addison-Wesley, 1976. (b)

Pleck, J., & Sawyer, J. (Eds.), *Men and masculinity.* Englewood Cliffs, NJ: Prentice-Hall, 1974.

Scott, J. *The athletic revolution.* New York: Free Press, 1971.

Shaw, G. *Meat on the hoof.* New York: Dell, 1972.

Talamini, J., & Page, C. H. *Sport and society.* Boston: Little, Brown & Co., 1973.

Tannenbaum, A. J. *Adolescents' attitudes towards academic brilliance.* Unpublished doctoral dissertation, New York University, 1960.

Turner, R. *Family interaction.* New York: Wiley, 1970.

BEST YEARS OF MY LIFE

DONALD F. SABO, JR.

What is it like becoming a football player? In my case, the process began in 1955 when I was eight years old. At the time, and these feelings still take possession of me, I felt uncomfortable inside my body. Too fat, too short, too weak. Freckles and glasses too! I wanted to change my image and changing my body was the place to begin. My parents bought me a set of weights, and one of the older boys in the neighborhood was solicited to demonstrate their use. I can still remember the ease with which he lifted the barbell, the veins popping through his bulging biceps in the summer sun, and the sated look of strength and accomplishment on his face. This image was to be my future.

That fall I made a dinner-table announcement that I was going out for football. It was a rather inauspicious beginning. There were initiation rites. Pricking the flesh with thorns until blood was drawn and having hot peppers rubbed in my eyes. Being forced to wear a jockstrap around my nose and not knowing what was funny. Then came what was to be an endless series of ways of proving myself. Calisthenics until my arms ached. Hitting hard and fast and knocking the other guy down. Getting hit in the groin and not crying. Striving to be a leader. Ten thousand Hail Marys later, having revelled in moments of glory and

---

Author's note: The inspiration for this essay came from Michael Eugene Luzny, former teammate and friend.

endured hours of shame, my grade school football days were over. The postseason banquet was like all the others. The men made speeches and the women cooked and served tables.

By the time I reported for my first high school practice as a "Crimson Crusher," I already knew what was expected of me. The object was to beat out the other guy. I already had it in my head that the way to succeed was to be an animal. Coaches took notice of animals. Animals made the first team. Being an animal meant being fanatically aggressive and ruthlessly competitive. If you saw an arm in front of you, you trampled it. Whenever blood was spilled you nodded approval. It's no wonder that, of all the friendships formed in those years, only two survive—a married country club manager in my hometown and the other with a hippie silversmith in California. Friendships with other males were always tempered by competition. A friend today could rob you of your position tomorrow. The idea was to slap backs, but not get too close emotionally.

As for friendships with women, they were virtually impossible. Necking and petting were always in the foreground of any interaction, and the cheerleaders were the most sought-after coeds. On the sidelines and in the stands the boys, and probably the men, watched the girls' breasts bounce and waited for cartwheels.

I was eventually elected captain of the football team, had a good senior year, and hoped and prayed for a college scholarship. A football scholarship in Johnstown, Pennsylvania, in 1965 meant going to college and not the steel mills. This was the alternative that pounded my adolescent eardrums. I was recruited by several schools — going the round of dates, drunks, and interviews with star athletes and coaches. I felt important but, beneath it all, damned insecure and afraid.

By this time, my body had undergone a thorough met-

amorphosis. My hair was short and my biceps were eighteen inches around. My chest, which I measured periodically, pressed through tight T-shirts. I held my belly in, especially when women were nearby. The tenderness and sensitivity that lay scrunched inside me was carefully hidden. It was like living inside a tank. The structure was formidable, but oppressively rigid.

College football was both a joy and affliction. It was a great feeling to run for hours without tiring, to see myself responding to split-second situations with nimble alacrity, to drink in those sweet moments in which body and mind danced as one. But then there were the broken noses, fingers, toes and teeth; torn muscles, bruises, bad knees, and busted lips; and the back problems that are with me to this day. Parents, fans, and supportive teachers or administrators were always there with congratulations and encouragement. Though I didn't realize it then, I know now that their approval stemmed from the fact that I was verifying a way of life they held sacred. When we ballplayers, clad in fiberglass armor, made our triumphant entrance into the stadium, they would cheer and feel that their values were still intact. America was still the beautiful. Young men still clamoured against one another. Competition reigned supreme. As for myself, I always held "the fans" in contempt. They worshipped a game they knew little about. I can still hear their high-pitched voices yelling "Kill 'em, Sabo!"

Perhaps the saddest thing that happened in college was that the game became a job. Just being an animal didn't work anymore. Technical expertise was the new goal. As the coaches put it, "You have to make sure your body is in the right place at the right time." Game plans were devised, studied, and executed as assiduously as corporate annual reports. Coaches monitored our movements on and off the field. No staying out late. No bars. No long

hair. No marijuana. No lovemaking forty-eight hours before a game. No involvement in New Left politics because
this didn't fit the all-American boy image. They even told us
what to say to the press. What we felt or thought didn't
matter. Good public relations meant a large box office. As
long as your body functioned well on the field, coaches
and alumni were "behind you." Bad injuries meant ostracism, social obsolescence, and in some cases no more
scholarship. We were flattered and paid to "do the job." We
played not for ourselves but for others, and talk about team
spirit was publicity hype for the fans. Very often, I felt like I
had ended up in the steelmills after all.

I was elected captain in my senior year and played
"the last game" at Boston University on astroturf. When the
final whistle blew, I dropped my helmet on the sidelines
and burst into tears. Not tears of joy. I cried out of a sense of
release—from a form of bondage I didn't yet understand. I
vowed never to allow anyone to relate to me as a jock
again. I dieted and lost forty pounds, stayed to myself, and
began to make friends in the counterculture. Five years
passed before I could bring myself to do something competitive—play a game of checkers with an eight-year-old
boy.

My father often tells me, smiling gently, that my college years were the best years of my life, that I would live
them over again if I could. I always reply "No. I'd do something else." He never quite believes me: To be honest, I'm
not sure I believe myself. The image of themselves as star
athletes burns brightly in the hearts of many boys and
men. The stars' world is a "promised land"—full of notori-
ety, women, sex, and status. I walked in its gardens and
tasted its fruits. The fruits were sour. However, had I never
"made it" in athletics, had I never gone through the grist-
mill of the experience, seen through the myths and em-

braced the actualities, I wouldn't be the same person
today. I might still be chasing the kind of masculine ideal
athletic success held out to me. It feels good to be out of the
race.

THE UNIFORMS

JEANNE FOSTER HILL

The uniforms inside his closet
are not blind the way clothes should be.
When you open the door,
they look back at you.
They breathe.
The white satiny track shorts
with the yellow stripe
invite themselves to be stroked
where they still hold the curve
of a buttock,

the t-shirt marked Rochester
placed above them,
as though the person that wore them
were still in them,
the little pointed teeth of the track shoes
turned upward on the floor.

On another hook,
like an old man's underwear,
a cotton pair of shorts.
A baseball glove.
Five broken tennis rackets,

Jeanne Foster Hill is a poet. Her works have appeared in both journals and magazines.

one strapped with the Diaries of Kafka back-to-back
for added weight during shadow strokes.
The shorter handled racket for paddle ball.

And the tennis shirt with its alligator,
rust spots where it was hung up wet,
still smells of salt.

A towel,
a stiffened jock strap,
a pair of socks.
The tennis shoes, unlaced, still hold the arch of the foot.
The one good racket leaning against the wall,
the handle ribbed with his hand
and darkened with sweat.

All the young men he's been still live
in the closet.
The yellow belt and karate outfit
together on a hanger.
As the door swings open, their muscles ripple.

All the young men poised in the moment of applause.

He is afraid of the loss,
so afraid of the loss.

THE BLACK ATHLETE
AS SUPER-MACHISMO SYMBOL
ROSS RUNFOLA

Sports are American society's primary masculinity rite,
measuring the ability of boys to become men by their aggressiveness in the pursuit of victory. Although sports reflect all the contradictions of American life, including widespread racism, blacks are no more immune than whites to

the myth that sports are the most democratic area of society. It should come as no surprise, therefore, that many black parents who have been victims of discrimination on a personal level in business, government, and education turn to athletics as the most important gateway to manhood for their sons.[1]

In a capitalistic society, masculinity is defined largely in terms of power. If black men have few opportunities to prove their manhood in the social, political, and economic realms, is it any wonder that much is made of their supposed prowess in the two areas left open to them, the sporting arena and the boudoir?

Cultural stereotypes of black athletic and sexual supermen abound. The myth is fed by television, where a sea of black faces gives symbolic rather than substantive proof of the black athlete's success, and by the movies, where Superfly is an oh-so-cool, superstud.

Such folklore allows O. J. Simpson to juke a white defensive back and Superfly to score with his lady while avoiding The Man, but it contains no tales of powerful black men commanding armies or corporate empires. Dreams must in some way reflect reality and, given the formidable impediments to black achievement woven into the rest of American society, the black athlete, much like the black pimp, has emerged full-blown as a super machismo symbol.[2]

In Black Rage, psychiatrists William H. Grier and Price M. Cobbs use case studies of individual psychopathology to reveal the full dimension of the struggle of black men to achieve manhood in America. They find that, whereas the white man is assured of his masculinity as an ordained right, one that comes by virtue of the possession of a penis and a white skin, attaining any portion of manhood is a continuing struggle for black men.[3]

On the surface, it appears that black men have suc-

ceeded admirably in sports. Blacks comprise about 12 percent of the United States population, yet over 20 percent of
professional baseball players, more than 30 percent of professional football players, and almost 80 percent of professional basketball players are black. The dominant role the
black athlete plays at all levels of competition has led fans
and sportswriters alike to view the black man as a special
physical specimen compared to his white counterpart.[4]

There have been many attempts to explain black domination of certain sports in terms of race-linked physical
characteristics. For example, Martin Kane, in a 1971 article
in Sports Illustrated, based the case for black athletic superiority in part on the theory of natural selection. (Black athletes were the descendents of Africans who were tough
enough to survive slavery.)[5]

Kane's highly speculative article is dangerous in that
its Darwinistic tone suggests that the black athlete, and
therefore the black race, is separate from the rest of society.
The catch-22 in praising black's physical supremacy over
whites is the tendency to flip the coin and say whites are
mentally superior to blacks. In a rigorous scientific disputa-
tion, sports sociologist Harry Edwards questioned the sam-
pling method employed by Kane. Edwards pointed out that
historical records of life on plantations indicate that the survival of slaves was due as much to their shrewdness and
their ability to think as to their physical prowess.[6] The domination of the black athlete in sports is not biological. It is
derived from a complex nexus of historical, psychological,
and sociological forces surrounding the hope that sports
can provide an escape from the ghetto.

Walt Frazier, of the Cleveland Cavaliers, sums up the
situation this way:

> There is no physical difference between the
> races. If there are more blacks in sports, it's be-

> cause we're hungrier than whites. Sports isn't an
> escape, it's a necessity for black kids. Guys from
> the ghetto want it more. White middle-class kids
> have more options. My father had no money. I
> had to make it.[7]

For every Walt Frazier who makes it, however, there are
10,000 black kids living with the false hope that they too can
"play it cool in the NBA." The stable of woman, clothes, and
cars Frazier has appears a more realistic goal for a ghetto
kid than the manly symbols that naturally accrue to the
power brokers of society like David Rockefeller. To my
knowledge, no one ever called Rockefeller a fag because
he couldn't dribble a basketball.

The dominant white culture today uses sports as an
opiate for the black masses in much the same way the
white slavemasters used religion and a sense of dependence to keep slaves in their place. As Eldridge Cleaver re-
minds us in Soul on Ice, whites, in order to justify slavery
and, later on, to justify segregation, elaborated the myth
that the black man was a "mindless supermasculine
menial."[8] As a corollary to this pervasive cultural assumption, white society has systematically cut off access by
black men to the intellectual, political, and economic centers of power where manhood is really defined in America,
and encouraged black males to prove their worth by "making it" with their body. Even within the athletic realm, however, blacks are segregated into specific playing positions
reflecting the "supermasculine menial" status ascribed to
them by white coaches.

Dr. Jonathan Brower of the University of California at
Fullerton finds that there are "constellations" of positions
for whites and blacks in professional football, with the
former getting those requiring intelligence (such as quar-

terback and punter) and the latter getting those requiring instinctual reactions (such as cornerback and punt returner).[9]

In sports, as in the plantation system of the Old South, the overseers are white and the workers are black. Nowhere is this more clearly evident than in professional baseball, where Frank Robinson was appointed the first black manager in 1975, nearly three decades after Jackie Robinson broke the color barrier.

Jackie Robinson was selected to break the color line, of course, not because he was the best black ballplayer (remember Satchel Paige?) but because he fit all the standards of acceptability to whites and would not rock the boat. College-educated and articulate, Robinson was trained by owner Branch Rickey to be a "good nigger" and maintain Waspish self-discipline in the face of a torrent of racial abuse.

The ability of a team's owners to choose their "niggers" has lessened considerably since the 1940's. However, the assertive black athlete who does not fit the image of a mindless machismo symbol or who has the audacity to date a white woman often finds himself in trouble with the sports establishment.[10]

Much of the conflict is the result of a cultural clash between the traditional and often authoritarian values of white coaches, who demand childlike respect and devotion from all athletes, and the reluctance of black players "to perform the subservient role and thus perpetuate behavior that has been demanded of blacks throughout the history of the United States."[11]

In Confessions of a Dirty Ballplayer, Johnny Sample, who was blackballed by the NFL for his militant attitude, attempts to define the social and psychological forces that affected his life as a ballplayer. In so doing, he offers a key to the extraordinary pressures many other black athletes experience in balancing team goals with their individual sense of self as a black man:

> Growing up as a child in Virginia and seeing what was done to black people had a profound effect on my life . . . as a football player. . . . The agony and embarrassment that I've seen black people suffer put a hardness in me that made me what I am. And it's still there. I saw so many black people get pushed around I swore to myself that no man, white or black, would ever take advantage of me. White people don't understand the feeling that swells up inside a black man who struggles to get out from under your heel. . . . These things molded my life as much as a coach teaching me how to block, run, or tackle. . . . That's why I always stood up for what I believed in.[12]

Unlike the militant Sample, most athletes exhibit an almost childlike dependence on their coaches, who act as surrogate fathers. The late Vince Lombardi, like many of the most successful coaches, was a master of the not-so-subtle psychological game of keeping his players so insecure that they were constantly trying to prove their manhood. As Dave Meggysey reports in Out of Their League, even an All-Pro football player can be reduced to a whimpering mass of flesh by a coach who calls him a "pussy."[13] Thus all-time-great defensive end Willie Davis, who spent many years with Lombardi's championship Green Bay teams, had this to say about what motivated him and his teammates to win the NFL championship: "We went out and we whipped them good and preserved our manhood."[14]

All male athletes, especially conforming types like Davis, get caught at certain times in the macho traps laid by patriarchal coaches. Empirical evidence amassed by Edwards, however, proves that successful black athletes are generally more conforming in their attitudes toward fulfilling their role expectations than whites. It would appear that there is much more pressure on the black athlete to prove his manhood on the playing field, especially when his very essence is defined by white coaches almost solely in physical terms.[15]

Professional sport in the more recent past has not been without its share of black athletes, such as Dock Ellis, Curt Flood, and Muhammad Ali, who have set out to "prove their manhood" by revolting against established athletic ideals that reflect traditional white middle-class values.

The concern of the white sports establishment with control over the black athlete and the sexual anxieties that are intimately linked with the macho element of sport was most graphically displayed in 1973 when Dock Ellis, then of the Pittsburgh Pirates, was a center of controversy because he wore hair curlers for his afro. The curlers had no intrinsic effect on Ellis's athletic performance, but they were a symbol of black militancy and emasculation to the racist and sexually uptight baseball world. Curt Flood also tested the assumption that athletes were chattels, and for his arrogance was exiled from the national pastime. Apple pie, baseball, and "bad niggers" don't mix.

It was Muhammad Ali, however, more than any other black athlete, who put the entire question of the black athlete as a super machismo symbol in its proper perspective. Joe Lewis was a "credit to his race" because he fit the role of a noncommitted disposable machine in a mindless body.

Ali was an "uppity nigger" since he was a black nationalist who was a champion not only for himself but for his people.

Grier and Cobbs find that many black men continue to exhibit psychological emasculation and inhibitions that have their origins in slavery. They explain the attention and adulation blacks give athletes such as Ali as a vicarious expression of inhibited masculine drives.[16]

Ali came on the American scene during the time of black ferment in the 1960s. As a symbol of unbridled aggression and assertiveness, he personified for young blacks the ultimate symbol of manhood. He was able to combine ghetto skill at rapping with principles that would not be compromised. Ali, especially if he "whupped" a white fighter, struck down the subtle racist forces that thwarted most young blacks' pursuit of victory in the outside world.[17]

As it turned out, a black Muslim heavyweight champion was too bitter a pill for white America to swallow since the boxing arena, even for unathletic men, is the ultimate symbol of manhood. Thus Floyd Patterson, the symbol of the subordinate Negro, became the White Hope in 1967.

Americans like to think of themselves as belonging to one nation. The truth is that we are the "Two Nations" John Dos Passos wrote of in U.S.A. In the final analysis, the Patterson-Ali fight was transformed from a sporting event into one of far-reaching social significance, sucking many Americans into the vortex created by the question of the place of the assertive black man in white America.

What Patterson and others could not do in the ring was done by the boxing commissions that stripped Ali of his title for three and one-half years for refusing to make war against other Third-World peoples. His title was returned to him only after the black rebellion of the 1960s became a faint memory.

Ali today is the darling of the sports world. The Black Hope was absorbed by the white sporting establishment he challenged. He was counted out by white America when he came to understand that the true macho men toil on Wall Street, not in Madison Square Garden.

FOOTNOTES

1. Ross Runfola, "Sports: Opiate for the Black Masses," *New York Times* (February 27, 1977), sect. 5, p. 2.
2. Mark Naison, "Sports and the American Empire," *Radical America* (July–August 1972), pp. 95–120.
3. William H. Grier and Price M. Cobbs, *Black Rage* (New York: Basic Books, 1968), p. 59.
4. There is ample social-scientific proof that despite their large representation in sports, black athletes are victims of racism. See, for example, Harry Edwards, *The Revolt of the Black Athlete* (New York: Macmillan, 1969); A. H. Pascal, and Z. A. Radding, "The Economics of Racial Discrimination in Organized Baseball," in A. Pascal, ed., *Racial Discrimination in Economic Life* (Lexington, Mass.: Heath, 1972), pp. 119–56; Donald W. Ball, "Ascription and Position: A Comparative Analysis of 'Stacking' in Professional Football," *Canadian Review of Sociology and Anthropology* 10 (May 1973): 97–113; N. R. Johnson, and D. P. Marple, "Racial Discrimination in Professional Basketball: An Empirical Test," *Sociological Focus* 6 (Fall 1973): 6–18; Aaron Rosenblat, "Negroes in Baseball: The Failure of Success," *Transaction*, 5 (September 1967): 51–53; N. R. Yetman and D. S. Eitzen, "Black Athletes on Intercollegiate Basketball Teams: An Empirical Test of Discrimination," in N. R. Yetman, ed., *Majority and Minority: The Dynamics of Racial and Ethnic Relations*

(Boston, Mass.: Allyn & Bacon, 1971, pp. 509–17; and Barry D. McPherson, "Minority Group Involvement in Sport: The Black Athlete," *Exercise and Sport Science Review* 2 (New York: Academic Press, 1974): 71–101.

5. Martin Kane, "An Assessment of Black Is Best," *Sports Illustrated* 34, no. 3: 72–83.

6. Harry Edwards, *Sociology of Sport* (Homewood, Ill.: Dorsey Press, 1973), pp. 193–202.

7. Interview with Walt Frazier, February 1977.

8. Eldridge Cleaver, *Soul on Ice* (New York: Dell, 1968), pp. 90–95 and *passim*.

9. Jonathon J. Brower, "The Racial Basis of the Division of Labor Among Players in the National Football League as a Function of Racial Stereotypes," Paper presented at the Pacific Sociological Association Meetings, Portland, Oregon, 1972.

10. See LaVerne Barnes, *The Plastic Orgasm* (Toronto: McClelland & Stewart, 1971).

11. Jonathon J. Brower, "Culture Clash: The Inappropriateness of the Black Subculture in the White World of Professional Football," Paper presented at the Pacific Sociological Association Meetings, Scottsdale, Arizona, 1973.

12. Johnny Sample, *Confessions of a Dirty Ballplayer* (New York: Dell, 1970), p. 3.

13. Dave Meggyesy, *Out of Their League* (Berkeley, Calif.: Ramparts, 1971), p. 202.

14. Quoted in Jack Scott, "Sport: America's Masculinity Rite," undated essay, Institute for the Study of Sport and Society, Oberlin, Ohio.

15. See Chapter 7, "The Athlete, Black and White," in Edwards, *Sociology of Sport*, pp. 175–236.

16. Grier and Cobbs, *Black Rage*, pp. 68–69.

17. Naison, "Sports and the American Empire," pp. 95–120.

HOMOSEXUALITY AND MACHISMO SPORT:
A GAY JOCK SPEAKS OUT

DAVID KOPAY AND PERRY DEANE YOUNG

. . . *My story—and, through it, the story of thousands of others still living the way I once thought I had to live—was about to become public knowledge.*

Why I did it is a question that seems to bother everybody but me. I'm sure I don't have all the answers but I do know that it had to do with images—the way people see athletes and the way people see homosexuals. Of course I didn't have to talk about my sexual preference in public. Of course taking on any label is self-limiting and wrong. But that's not the point. Because of my homosexuality I can't get a job as a coach. Unless certain attitudes change there's no way for me to function in this society doing what I want to do. If some of us don't take on the oppressive labels and publicly prove them wrong, we'll stay trapped by the stereotypes for the rest of our lives.

Basically I am an honest person—maybe that comes from my religious upbringing. It has seemed to me at times in the past that I was lying just by walking down the street. People would see me and say, "Hey, you look like an athlete. What do you do?" I would say I used to play professional football. There would follow a lot of talk about the Redskins and Packers and other teams I've played for. I could just see their minds working on the same old stereotypes, which I think are just as unfair to athletes as they are to homosexuals. Being a homosexual does not mean you are a silly person; being an athlete does not mean you are a dumb jock. Homosexuals, like athletes, often have little more in common than coffee drinkers do.

I was caught between my own self-image and what I knew people were thinking about me. I know I have always been homosexual. I also know I am a very good athlete. While I was never any kind of superstar, I do have the credibility of having played ten years in the National Football League.

I kept making the teams year after year, although the coaches once told me I was too slow to make it as a running back. I loved playing. I think I was good for another two or three seasons after I was cut the last time. I loved being part of a team, part of a family. There was acceptance there based purely on what I could do. As long as I was able to play I never minded being relegated to the special teams or "suicide squads" sent in for punting, punt return, kickoff and kickoff return, field goals and extra points. I think it would be wrong for anybody to seize on some psychological interpretation of my enjoying those years on the special teams. It was not a case of the guilty homosexual relishing the extra punishment these squads took. In fact, I had no real choice. I either played on the special teams or not at all. But I was happy making my contribution even there.

Recently I've come to the conclusion that a lot of my extra drive came from the same forces that brought black athletes out of the ghettos to the forefront of professional sports. They were out to prove—among other things—that they were not inferior because of their race. I was out to prove that I was in no way less a man because I was homosexual. It is also true that during most of my athletic career the physical outlet of the game was a kind of replacement for sex in my life. My teammates nicknamed me "Psyche" because I would get so "psyched up" for the games. They also called me "Radar" because I could always find somebody to hit. . . . The [Washington Star] story implied that I should have been hired at the university but was not because of my homosexuality. If that was true I knew this prejudice wasn't restricted to the University of Washington. I was qualified to be a special teams coach or a backfield coach and I had applied for positions I knew were available on five different teams. Only Bart Starr of the Green Bay Packers acknowledged my application.

After telling about my problems getting a coaching job, the interview described my first sexual experiences with another man. We were fraternity brothers and we loved each other. But we were always drunk when we had sex and the next day we could never talk about it.

I also talked about my brief marriage: "I loved her, but I was very mixed up. I'd gone through a very bad depression dealing with the problems of recognizing my sexual preference. And I kind of thought this was the way out of it." I did not mention that an analyst while I was under hypnosis had convinced me to get married. But the more time I spent on this doctor's couch—listening to him say I only liked women—the more I came to accept the fact that I truly preferred sex with men.

My apprehensions about the future came through in [the] interview: "Kopay worries what effect his disclosure will have on his business interests, his family and his friends. 'It's been such a difficult trip,' he says, 'and I'm sure it's just begun.'"

The next day the story was reprinted or quoted in nearly every major newspaper in the country. I put in a call to an old friend who had confessed to me about his homosexuality a few months earlier. He had been general manager for one of the NFL clubs. A man in his fifties now, he has never had sex with another person. But he finally acknowledged that his long association with football had everything to do with the sexual attraction he felt for men.

The only difference between him and a lot of other coaches, owners, administrators in sports is that he is being honest about his feelings.

"How about letting me know when you're going to drop the next bomb," he said, laughing. He was nervous about my story—worried, I'm sure, about what it would mean for him and others who feel they have no choice but to stay secret about their sexual preference. But he was also very supportive of me and what I was doing—sharing, vicariously, in my liberation. Maybe what I am doing will help create some space so that people like my friend won't have to hide anymore.

My friend's laughter and support were in stark contrast to my parents' reaction. Nothing could have prepared them for what I did; nothing could have prepared me for their reaction. Apparently a reporter in Seattle had called them to get their reaction—and that was the first they knew of my talking publicly about homosexuality. I had told them four years before about my preference and they had never accepted it. That was why I hadn't called them before I did the interview. I knew they couldn't understand. I knew I had to make the decision on my own. . . .

[Eds.' Note: The material that follows was written by Co-Author Perry Deane Young.]

One can only begin to understand the parents' shock over Kopay's homosexuality when one considers how deeply the mythology of masculinity is embodied in the sport of football. Kopay's parents accepted the myth as gospel. When he spoke out about his homosexuality, they took it to be a flagrant refutation of all they, and their neighbors, had admired in him.

Anthropologist William Arenes has written in Natural History *that the football uniform itself "is not an expression* but an exaggeration of maleness. . . The donning of the required items results in an enlarged head and shoulders and a narrowed waist, with the lower torso poured into skintight pants."

As in no other area of our society—except cloistered monasteries—females are generally excluded not only from playing the sport but from any involvement with the players prior to a game. As Kopay says, "If a boy performs badly during practice in high school, coaches are likely to harangue him about 'spending too much time with the girls.' Professional coaches say one reason they locate their training camps outside of the big cities is so the players can't get to the women. But many of the players develop friends and sex partners in these small towns where the training camps are. Still the coaches make a habit of not announcing nights off until the last minute. I remember that there were some college coaches who would even forbid their players to marry and many others openly discouraged it.

"From grade school on," Kopay says, "the curse words on the football field are about behaving like a girl. If you don't run fast enough or block or tackle hard enough you're a pussy, a cunt, a sissy." And Jim Bouton in Ball Four tells about his teammates, grown men in the major leagues, taunting each other with "Hey, sweetheart. Where's your purse, you big pussy?" And, "He'd lisp at me when I was going in to pitch. 'Is she going out and try it again today? Is she really going to try today?'"

Homosexuality in this setting is considered such a taboo the coaches and players not only feel free but obligated to joke about it. To be homosexual is to be effeminate, like a girl. "Cocksucker" becomes the ultimate insult. On one level they would insist on the complete absence of homosexuality among them. On another they are confirming its presence—in their minds, at least—by the endless *banter and jokes about it. Billy Clyde Puckett, the fictional running back and narrator of* Semi-Tough, *uses the word "fag" twenty-two times in Dan Jenkins' short novel. David Kopay's story raises the question not how could he emerge from this super-masculine society as a homosexual, but how could any man come through it as purely heterosexual after spending so much time idealizing and worshipping the male body while denigrating and ridiculing the female.*

Football surely represents one of the most rigid subcultures in America. In few other areas will young men be found willing and anxious to obey commands no matter how unreasonable they are. The coach is not only dictator and king but God (or a direct conduit to Him) as well. To question the coach in high school is to violate the first rule of the sport: obedience. To question the coach in college or professional football is to invite expulsion and fines. It is no coincidence that many of the more successful players and coaches in football are products of authoritarian Catholic backgrounds—as [is] *Kopay. . . .*

"There were few real choices later in my life," David Kopay says. "I had early decided on football as the way I would fit in and express myself in this society. I gave little or no thought to what I would do after I could no longer play football. The absolute physical expense of the sport was sufficient in itself. It also provided a convenient way for me—and who can say how many of my teammates?—to camouflage my true sexual feelings for other men."

Similarly, Bill Tilden, in Frank Deford's biography of him, is quoted as telling his court-appointed psychiatrist: "Sex has never been important in my life; I have had an outlet through athletics."

"I know from my experience that football is a real outlet for repressed sexual energy," Kopay says. "And to the extent that there's no other outlet—except in irrational vio-

lence toward innocent people—I think it's a healthy thing for the players and for the fans.

"The whole language of football is involved in sexual allusions. We were told to go out and 'fuck those guys'; to take that ball and 'stick it up their asses' or 'down their throats.' The coaches would yell, 'knock their dicks off,' or more often than that, 'knock their jocks off.' They'd say, 'Go out there and give it all you've got, a hundred and ten per cent, shoot your wad.' You controlled their line and 'knocked' em into submission.

"Over the years I've seen many a coach get emotionally aroused while he was diagramming a particular play into an imaginary hole on the blackboard. His face red, his voice rising, he would show the ball carrier how he wanted him to 'stick it in the hole.'"

The sexual allusions help explain a player's passionate commitment to the game, as well as his difficulty in talking about it afterward.

TOWARD A NEW MALE IDENTITY: LITERATURE AND SPORTS

ROSS J. PUDALOFF

Can literature, usually perceived as elitist in origin and audience, provide alternatives to traditional models of masculine behavior through the description and examination of sports? And if so, how? The answer to the first question must be that literature, by its very nature, takes all fantasies seriously enough to both describe their benefits and criticize their defects. Superficially there would appear to exist an inverse relationship between writing and reading

Ross J. Pudaloff is a member of the English Department at Wayne State University in Detroit, where he teaches American literature and composition.

and modern sports, a distinction between solitary, reflective, withdrawn, and culturally feminized activities and
mass-based, socially approved, aggressive, and masculine ones. René Maheu has argued that art and sport are
"at opposite poles" because they "create beauty, but in
completely different ways. Sports is immanent beauty,
identified with the act which creates it. Art . . . is an act of
disassociation, [it] creates a universe which, at one and the
same time, competes with the real universe and withdraws
from it."[1] The dialectical nature of art allows writers to
immerse themselves in sports and then create standards of
judgement that are independent of the athlete and his
world. Literature and sports are further linked because
both discover and value the presence of fantasy and desire
at the center of the social and ordinary world.

Literature, by which I mean not so much texts but
rather the active relationship of authors and readers, is
permitted (because it isn't "true") to display in full the codes
and conventions by and through which we recognize each
other and our society. It goes almost without saying that
this is an implicitly critical position, a point of privilege that
literature shares with sports in our society since neither is
counted as part of the "real" world. Sports and literature
are metaphoric equivalents. Each creates enchanted
realms;[2] each seeks to capture an audience; each provides
a sense of community (spurious?); each allows us to lose
ourselves with the certainty that we shall find ourselves
once again; each changes nothing outside its own world
while insisting on the overriding importance of its rules
while the game is being played out; and each mirrors, distorts, and re-creates the self and world it has left. Each is, in
Hans Magnus Enzensberger's telling phrase, part of the
"consciousness industry" and thus part of the way in which
our lives are organized; but each also represents an irre-
ducible statement of our needs, wishes, and desires, which

the system must take into account even as it manipulates them.[3]

Writer and reader, athlete and fan, all share an essential bond. In the quasi-religious worlds of literary response and athletic admiration, we surrender part of ourselves in order to permit the spectacle to work. Coleridge's "willing suspension of disbelief" does not conclude with literature, but more and more is the key to understanding sports in modern America. Thus it is not surprising, given the self-conscious and self-reflexive qualities of modern literature, that it has been attracted to sport as subject, metaphor, and symbol.

The crucial issue in the literature of sports and in sports themselves, even beyond the vexing and important question of winning and losing, is control. Whether it is manifested in the grace of the athlete, the powers of the writer, or the reaction of the fan or reader, no other quality is more essential to the male role in America. The bravery and skill of such mythic figures as Natty Bumppo, Daniel Boone, and John Wayne can be and sometimes are forthcoming in a losing cause. The author, who is after all passive, weak, and withdrawn, demonstrates his or her control over the strong and the brave by placing them in a plot that determines their actions. More than Natty Bumppo and Daniel Boone we admire Huck Finn, for his ability to manipulate the world from a position of weakness; even more fascinating and frightening is Melville's Ahab, simultaneously a monomaniac and thus out of control and yet able to dominate a ship and a crew who are an emblem of the world.

Opportunities to develop and display control over the world have diminished since the closing of the frontier, but the need to seek such contol remains a culturally induced desire and element of the male role. The rise of an industrial, capitalist, and urban society leads to the rise of sports as an embodiment of cultural fantasies, archaic in the sense that the control they promise is possible nowhere else in our society except in literature.

Others have made these points before me, perhaps none so eloquently and cogently as Thoreau, in *Walden*. If we remember anything from the book, we remember his statement that "the mass of men lead lives of quiet desperation." But we forget that he continued almost immediately to locate the desperation most poignantly and dangerously in our leisure activities: even sports and games he points out, "have become desparate."[4] Yet Thoreau's prophetic perceptions, brilliant as they are, have three weaknesses that are of critical importance because of the way Thoreauvian perspectives dominate a major radical tradition in America. These weaknesses are the seeming irrelevance of the uncompromising and total individuality he champions for those who live in the flood tide of a mass society; the fact that he, like most writers enshrined in the literary canon, is addressing males and is concerned primarily with the fate of men; and finally the fact that his renunciation of society and his analysis of problems as socially induced depend on a perception of history as an "old woman who lives under the hill" ready to devour and cripple her male children should they let their self-control slip.[5]

These attitudes haunt the world of sports and the world of literature concerned with sports; apparently opposing traditions mirror each other in their sexism, repression, and definition of individualism. Men, writing about and for other men, struggle to achieve the power and wisdom of Thoreauvian insights, but often they can do so only by enclosing author, narrator, character, and reader in realms where freedom and identity seem to demand isolation, withdrawal, dominance, and sexual relationships seen as contests to be won or lost.

The pastoral moment and place of *Walden* pond have now been replaced by the pastoral enclosed space of the

*arena and stadium. Thoreau would not have been sur-
prised to learn that, the emptier our lives become, the more
we admire those whose actions have consequences—even
if they matter only in the fantasies of sports and the literature about it. Nowhere is the power of sports and the athlete
granted more significance than in Bernard Malamud's* The
Natural, *a novel that claims the status of serious literature
even though it is about baseball. As many readers have
already noted, Malamud mixes Freudian symbols and theory with the Grail legend so that his hero, Roy Hobbs, may
perhaps redeem the Wasteland.*[6] *His failure to do so is in no
sense a critique of the role of the athlete as redeemer but is
due, rather, to flaws in his character, especially his reluctance to take his role as knight and deliverer seriously
enough. In the novel, Malamud uncritically joins potency
and performance sexually and socially. Thus Roy's last act,
burying Wonderboy, his now-broken bat, and disappear-
ing into the mass of men, has gloomy implications for the
male reader seeking other definitions of masculinity.*

*A pastoral setting, masculinity, and sexuality are at
the center of Mark Harris'* The Southpaw *as well.*[7] *The story
is told by the title character, Henry Wiggen, a consciously
updated Huck Finn who finds himself succeeding at baseball but risking failure in his personal life. Harris ultimately
allows him to succeed at both, thus the baseball field and
his sexual relationship and marriage become the modern
equivalent of Huck Finn's territory, an ending simultaneously sentimental and evasive, for it fails to resolve the
issue of whether boyish freedom and adult sexuality can be
united. Henry achieves, with no introspection and without
much difficulty, what Huck could not—mature sexuality
and childlike innocence—and is attractive only because he
is unattainable.*

*Henry is interesting for the reader in one other particu-
lar; like Huck he is telling his own story, though both are*

trustworthy narrators only insofar as they remain unaware of the potential of language to deceive the self. The ambivalence about language that does surface in The Southpaw *is neither accidental nor unique. Henry's description of sportswriters as lacking the "guts and gumption to get out there and play ball theirselves" finds an echo in almost all serious and some not-so-serious books about modern athletics.* [8]

Since the primary issue in sports is presumably skill and ability rather than guts and gumption, Henry's comments appear to reside in the wrong text at the wrong place. Actually they are perfectly relevant in two ways. First, writing about sports has, at least since the 1920s, stressed character as a desired and desirable result of athletic participation, obtainable almost nowhere else in our society. Sometimes it seems that the sports field is about the only place a boy can learn to be a man. Harris' attack on sportswriters resolves itself into an assault on this credo, and he makes Henry unwilling and unable to fight physically. This "defect" excuses him from the military draft and leads him to refuse to join a goodwill tour of the Korean front, one organized by a sportswriter.

Second, if doing is what matters from men, then words can only be, at best, a pale reflection of reality and, at worst, a distortion of the truth. Henry's criticism of sportswriters follows in the tradition of a long line of American heroes who disdain and distrust language as either an instrument of deceit or a vehicle of betrayal, usually by women. Indeed, by and large our male heroes have been inarticulate by choice. Their bias against language has been particularly prominent in the two literary and cultural genres impossible to imagine without America: the western and the mystery. Classical American males from Wister's Virginian to Bogart's Sam Spade indicate by their silence and stoicism that glory, achievement, and identity for men come at the cost of the expression of emotion to others. Other roles, do exist besides that of the silent and taciturn individual who fears betrayal by women, language, and affect, but they are both trap and escape. American society also admires and treasures the fast-talking manipulator and confidence man. Constance Rourke pointed out over forty years ago that our humor depends upon the assumption of a mask; and Captain Simon Suggs, one of the early comic confidence men in our literature, believed "IT IS GOOD TO BE SHIFTY IN A NEW COUNTRY."[9] We admire the individual who can win because he uses his verbal or physical skills to reconstitute the world and who is not punished because he is so good at what he does. For every humble Lou Gehrig there is a dissolute, badly behaved Babe Ruth whose exploits off the field are excused or disguised by those on it. He gets away with it for us in our double roles as spectator and reader. He mocks the mythology of character building without losing potency in any arena; unlike Malamud's Roy Hobbs, Robert Coover's Long Lew Lydell gains power and fame when he mixes sports and sex in the rape/seduction of Fanny McCaffree in the dugout.[10]

The linguistically and sexually facile hero dominates sports literature for two reasons. First, his language—more brutal, more sexual, more direct, and more picturesque than that of ordinary discourse—allows the fan/reader to enjoy what he himself is not permitted. Second, language is a means of revenge for the spectator upon the hero because its importance insists that experience doesn't truly exist until it is translated into language. Heroes such as Henry Wiggen admit, by their fear of and distaste for the sportswriter, that such a possibility exists.

Some writers do hint a defect in their position, but their complaints about the limits of language end with a justification of their own use of it. They are like Jacob Horner, the antihero of John Barth's *End of the Road*, who remarks that language is "always a betrayal of experience, a falsification of it, but only so betrayed can [experience] be dealt with at all, and only in so dealing with it did I ever feel a man, alive and kicking."[11] The writer, although he distorts the world, also makes it possible for the world to exist and, as Horner indicates, gains a male identity still protected from affect and femininity. Through the writer the reader and spectator can advance the same rationale for their weakness: it would not mean anything, not even exist, without me, the audience. I am truly a man because ultimately I control the action by controlling its existence.

Serious writers have been so attracted to sports not only because of what the games mean as cultural and psychological phenomena, but also because of what they are—fictions, and thus in the special category of illusions, through which a society may escape some of its grimmer aspects. Sports reproduce important conflicts in settings that allow for a complete and successful resolution. A tie score is like kissing your sister, a fact that reveals the critical importance of the game as fiction in providing a clear and definite sense of an ending and also illustrates the link between sports and male sexuality. To the victor belong the spoils, which in masculine mythology almost always include sexual conquests.

In *The Great Gatsby*, Tom Buchanan's brutality and selfishness are found, not by accident, in a man who will never achieve the pinnacle of success and identity that he reached at twenty-one as a member of the Yale football team. Fitzgerald labeled this "an acute limited excellence" and condemned Tom; but Tom's brutal, masculine force enabled him to disguise a murder,[1] led to Gatsby's death, and let him recapture Daisy as his sexual trophy.[12]

Actually, Tom does win partially because both fiction and sports are, in order to be anything else, systems of language; that is, they provide the rules of discourse, which govern what can and cannot be said and felt. As Michel Foucault, the most perceptive interpreter of social institutions as systems of language and discourse, insists, discourse is "a violence that we do to things."[13] Sports do violence to men because masculinity exists and makes sense only in terms of contests and victories; sports do violence to women because they are not part of the action and thus cannot be represented except as objects and trophies or seducers and betrayers. Fiction, even and especially that concerned with sports, takes a critical stance toward the valorization of strength, rationality, power, dominance, and control as the elements of masculinity because the game is always seen as part of yet another game, the discourse in the terms of yet another discursive system.

At the same time both ordinary and literary language are sexist in content; to be a man is the end of a long and difficult psychological and social process for boys, but a status easily achieved by entering a game: "Pick up your man," cries the coach. Even a false language, untrue to the self and the world, gives an athlete, a character, and a man power in the world. Ring Lardner's classic story of men in love and baseball, "Alibi Ike," explores this fact. The title character has gained his nickname because he is incapable of admitting the true reasons for his actions on and off the field. This in no way hampers his performance either as an athlete or as a lover. Ike incorporates the values of American men, and this is most apparent in his refusal to admit to his friends his feelings about the girl to whom he is engaged. When she overhears him denying these feelings, stating that the engagement is the result of pity, she breaks off with him. The consequences are disastrous for Ike; his facility at both language and baseball desert him. His tongue, his bat, and his penis all lose their agility, and he recovers his potency only when he is able to *get the girl back without admitting the truth.*[14] *As Henry Wiggen was to put it in* The Southpaw: *"If you ever wish to torture your average ballplayer to death simply tape up his mouth. He will not die from the lack of food. He will just go mad from the silence."*[15]

The connection between sexuality, language, and dominance is highlighted in the conversations recorded by Roger Kahn in The Boys of Summer, *in which Kahn overcomes the gap between writer and athlete by emphasizing language rather than ability. Neither Kahn nor his admirers were disturbed at the way in which competition, both verbal and athletic, became the test of masculinity. Kahn writes: "When Leo Durocher, then married to the Morman actress Larraine Day, shouted at Jackie Robinson, 'My dick to you,' Robinson backed out of the batter's box and cried, 'Give it to Larraine. She needs it more than I do.' On another occasion, Durocher, who was coaching at third, removed his cap and scratched a bald scalp. 'Hey, skinhead,' boomed a voice from the Brooklyn dugout, 'put on your hat before somebody jerks you off.'"*[16] *Such anecdotes are witty enough to deserve retelling on that score alone; still, their presence and prominence in Kahn's text reveal the extent to which he perceives sexuality and competition functioning to establish control and through that, masculinity.*

These expressions are, of course, fantasies, a status clearly indicated by their occurrence within sports and within literature. But we should not underestimate the power of sports to encourage fantasy. Kahn retells the story of Joe Black, a pitcher for the Dodgers who reached his senior year in high school still hoping for a major league baseball career only because he had repressed the knowledge that negroes were banned from organized ball. The moment when he was forced to confront the reality of racism was one of great shock: *"The private hope on which his* life was built stood stripped, not merely as boyish fantasy, but as stupid boyish fantasy."[17]

The danger of confusion between fiction and reality and between play and competition is expressed clearly in Robert Coover's novel, The Universal Baseball Association, Inc., J. Henry Waugh, Prop. The consequences of this confusion become apparent in the story of Henry, a lonely accountant whose real emotional life is spent playing an imaginary baseball game with dice and precise statistical odds. The game gives rise to a complete world peopled with characters more vivid and alive than Henry himself. Henry unknowingly identifies his own problem when he says, "You know, Lou, when Jim Creighton died, the boys crowned his grave with a fantastic monument. It had crossed bats on it and a baseball cap and even a base and up on top a giant baseball. Or maybe it was the world. They probably no longer knew the difference."[18] It is Henry who no longer knows the difference, and when, against highly improbable odds, the dice decree that his favorite rookie pitcher be killed by a hit ball, he fixes the game to gain revenge upon the "villain." The irony is that Henry, who has gained his emotional life and his identity from his control of the game, loses his powers as narrator once he has broken his own rules, and the last section of the book is told as if he no longer exists.

The significance of Coover's ending cannot be overemphasized in the metaphoric world of sports literature. The sons have broken free of the father and live in a realm outside the control of the father-narrator. How rare this freedom is can be understood if we compare it to the happiness imagined and imaginable by Philip Roth's Portnoy. He finds that quality only in his youthful fantasies of baseball. The idyllic and pastoral center of both Portnoy's life and Portnoy's Complaint is titled "IN EXILE," and it is a memory of the softball games the neighborhood men play while

Portnoy and his father watch, for once united and happy together. The boy thinks, or the man thinks the boy thinks, "How I am going to love growing up to be a Jewish man!"[19] *The horror is, for Portnoy and the reader, that to be a man is a fantasy within a fantasy, something possible only within the matrix of memory, desire, sport, and literature, and impossible for Portnoy to reach in his adult, sexual life.*

Portnoy's experience, as well as that of Malamud's Roy Hobbs, seems to qualify and perhaps criticize the seemingly more optimistic endings offered by Coover and Mark Harris. The latter, especially, would seem to agree with Allen Guttman's conclusion in From Ritual to Record:

> *"Despite imperfections and false emphases, modern sports hold forth the possibility of a realm of relative if not absolute freedom. . . . In sport we can discover the euphoric sense of wholeness, autonomy, and potency which is often denied us in the dreary rounds of routinized work that are the fate of most men and women.*[20]

Guttman is trying to have it both ways by asserting that "modern sports" can give to the mass audience what they do indeed offer the star. His statement follows a section on sports literature, and the liberatory possibilities he writes of are indeed available for the literary character and reader, but not for the fan and spectator. In The Southpaw *Mark Harris has Henry Wiggen dismiss Ring Lardner because Lardner lacked sufficient interest in the game itself and persisted in writing about its connection to the rest of an athlete's life.*[21] *Yet Harris uses his novel to criticize American militarism in the Korean war, to expose the negative aspects of hero worship in sports, and to promote racial integration and harmony. (Henry is first white player to accept and welcome blacks and is the first to have a black* roommate.) Being on the side of the angels doesn't obscure the fact that Harris wants things both ways. He insists on athletes and games as complete and perfect in themselves, but also presents them as models and metaphors for the rest of us.

The doubled nature of sport, and for that matter literature, has its historical nexus in the transformation of baseball occasioned by the Black Sox scandal of 1919 and the influence of Babe Ruth in the 1920's. Before then, argues Leverett T. Smith, Jr., in The American Dream and The National Game, baseball was and wanted to be perceived as the "mirror of a commercial world, a competitive jungle," played by professionals and best exemplified by Ty Cobb. Afterwards sport became in metaphor, and therefore in appeal, "a community which sees itself as authoritarian and above commercial concerns," symbolized by the figure of Babe Ruth, "a child exercising his talents out of love for the game."[22]

Throughout, no hope is offered for the male who wishes to be a man without assuming an identity and a role traditionally linked with aggression, winning, and dominance, and who also wishes not to remain a narcissist, gaining vicarious gratification from a fantasy world. Others have already described new forms of sports and play we can adopt that do provide genuine choices. But there is a problem of consciousness as well as one of social role, and here literature can both protect and liberate us. We all know the story of the little boy who implored Shoeless Joe Jackson, a major figure in the Black Sox bribery scandal, to "Say it ain't so, Joe," as if the words of the hero would be sufficient to deny the facts of the matter. Nothing more clearly indicates Bernard Malamud's skepticism about the liberatory possibilities within American culture and his traditional attitudes about the male role than his use of the story to close The Natural. *In Malamud, as in the legend, no answer is given.*

Yet the little boy, potentially but not yet a reader as well as a fan, is devastated only insofar as he has confused fantasy and reality. Both the fan and the reader are returned to infancy to some extent, as is the hero, by their participation in roles where they live solely in the realm of desire. Not for nothing did nineteenth-century moralists link reading and masturbation and warn the unwary about the danger of reading novels. But if such activities and roles entail a risk of narcissism and regression to infancy, they also bear witness that the essence of identity is in the desire for something better than the "routinized" world Guttman believes we can never truly leave.

Literature is fascinated by and attracted to sports because both allow desire and then subvert the faith they initially stimulate—and in literature, the blow can be taken without devastation. The jock may have a tragic fate, but, appealing as that may be esthetically, the reader seeks to survive—with new ideas and a better sense of his or her identity. We are able to live without the belief that condemns Frederick Exley to insanity in A Fan's Notes. While Exley is in a mental hospital, a woman friend asks him why he doesn't despise Frank Gifford and the world of sports stardom Gifford represents. At this point Exley can only answer, "He may be the only fame I'll ever have!" We may find our own fate in Exley's. By the end of his narrative he is better, though not, to be sure, well. If he is not yet a success in his eyes and the world's, he at least understands and accepts difference and separation as the basis of his identity, while yet insisting to the reader and himself that "one has to live the contributive, the passionate, life."[23] He is out at last from the shadow of his father, the athlete, and from fandom as identity. Would that we all might do so well in life as we can in literature.

FOOTNOTES

1. "Sport and Culture," in George H. Sage, ed., *Sport and American Society: Selected Readings*, (Reading, Mass.: Addison-Wesley, 1970), p. 396.

2. This point is more fully developed by Roger Caillois in *Men, Play and Games*, trans. by Meyer Barash (London: Thames & Hudson, 1962).

3. Although Enzensberger does not write directly about sports and the male identity, his work is essential to an understanding of life in mass culture. See his *The Consciousness Industry: On Literature, Politics and the Media*, selected by Michael Roloff (New York: Seabury Press, 1974).

4. Henry Day Thoreau, *Walden* (New York: Harper & Row, 1965), p. 7.

5. One source of Thoreau's antifeminism and antisexuality was his struggle to establish his identity in a family dominated by women, especially his mother. He was especially affected by his brother's early death. All this is developed from an Eriksonian perspective in Richard Lebeaux, *Young Man Thoreau* (Amherst: University of Massachusetts Press, 1977). More important, in my view, is the "feminization" of American literature and manners in the nineteenth century described and analyzed by Ann Douglas in *The Feminization of American Culture* (New York: Knopf, 1977). The celebration of manhood and manliness in such writers as Cooper, Emerson, and Thoreau was, in part, a reaction to and defense against the increasing influence of women and "feminine" values in literature and society.

6. *The Natural* (1952; rpt. New York: Dell, 1971).

7. *The Southpaw* (1953; rpt. New York: Charter Books, 1962).

8. Harris, p. 125.

9. Constance Rourke, *American Humor: A Study of the National Character* (New York: Harcourt, Brace and Jovanovich, 1931); Johnson Jones Hooper, *Some Adventures of Captain Simon Suggs* (Philadelphia: H. C. Baird, 1850), p. 12.

10. *The Universal Baseball Association, Inc., J. Henry Waugh, Prop.* (New York: New American Library, 1971), pp. 112–15.

11. *End of the Road* (1958; rpt. New York: Avon, 1960), p. 119.

12. *The Great Gatsby* (New York: Scribner's, 1925), p. 4.

13. *The Archaeology of Knowledge*, trans. by A. M. Sheridan Smith (New York: Pantheon, 1972), p. 229. See also Foucault's *The Order of Things: An Archaeology of the Human Sciences* (1966; trans. New York: Vintage, 1973).

14. The story is frequently anthologized. I have used the version in Ring Lardner, *Haircut and Other Stories* (New York: Scribner's, n.d.), pp. 35–56.

15. Harris, p. 154.

16. *The Boys of Summer* (New York: Harper & Row, 1972), p. 91.

17. Kahn, p. 277.

18. Coover, p. 89.

19. The quote is from *Portnoy's Complaint* (New York: Bantam, 1970), p. 275.

20. *From Ritual to Record: The Nature of Modern Sports* (New York: Columbia University Press, 1978), p. 157.

21. Harris, p. 34.

22. *The American Dream and the National Game* (Bowling Green, Ohio: Bowling Green University Popular Press, 1975), pp. 191 and 207.

23. *A Fan's Notes: A Fictional Memoir* (New York: Random House, 1968), pp. 232, 385.

VIOLENCE, SPORT, AND MASCULINITY

INTRODUCTION

Within varying historical periods and sociocultural settings, men have displayed a respect and a predilection for violence. As Irving Louis Horowitz observes, "Pacifism [becomes] a symbol of decadence while violence [becomes] the supreme symbol of virility."[1] In America today the wedding of violence and masculine virility is particularly manifest in sports. "Except for war," Robert Kennedy remarked during his tenure as Attorney General, "there is nothing in American life—nothing—which trains a boy better for life than football."[2] Few males would disagree with this statement. Partly through sports, boys learn early that a capacity for violence is part and parcel of the adult male identity. The machismo ethos of sports promotes the belief among both athletes and fans that the experience of violence is a "mythic prerequisite of men's self-esteem."[3]

The real and assumed propensity of males for violence, reinforced by sports, does much to legitimate and enforce male dominance of other social institutions. Theodore Roosevelt neatly capsulized the ideology of domination by the phrase "Walk softly and carry a big stick." When the social world is repeatedly portrayed as threatening, filled with a potential for violence, it is but a short step to argue that strong men are better equipped than weak men or women to deal with it. Men of power, therefore, rule in part by imposing their ethics of aggression and violent weltanschauung upon the minds of the masses. Through their glorification of male virility and physical violence, and their equation of the two, sports do much to convince men that combative struggle is unavoidable and women that their subservience to males is necessary for survival. In this way sports help to ensure that the existing political and sex hierarchies remain stable and intact.

Violence in sports is a mirror image of violence else-

113

where in society. Spectator sports adjust constantly to the changing social and psychological needs of those who watch them, especially working-class males.[4] Mass spectator sports were fostered by the conditions of life in modern American industrial society. At the turn of the century, they provided an outlet for the frustrations of the urban working-class men who toiled daily in factories. Later, as workers became more alienated from their labor, play took on all the importance of work and the more violent sport of football replaced baseball as the chief national pastime. Collective violence in sports (spectator violence) cannot be understood apart from the social setting in which it occurs. It is the fans' frustration with their place in society at large that manifests itself in hostile, antisocial outbursts at sporting events. Though such unstructured violence appears to be a spontaneous response to events, it originates in the same kind of societal problems that led to the urban riots of the sixties.[5]

The Superbowl in particular and big-time football in general are viewed by Eugene Bianchi as mirrors of the most destructive characteristics of American culture, including physical brutality, commercialism, and an authoritarian/military mentality. For Bianchi, however, sexism is the most critical element contributing to the development of violence in American society, since it encourages boys to be aggressive and domineering in their relationships with one another and with women. The male mystique not only drives men to seek "impossible and dubious goals at the top of the competitive heap," but it encourages "the concentration of power in the hands of a dominating few." Thus it is antithetical to our fundamental American political values as well as to the Judeo-Christian tradition of sharing resources and minimizing destructive aggression.

In "Violence and the Masculine Mystique," Lucy Komisar examines the ways American Society enculturates the values of aggression and dominance in males. As well as attaining widespread legitimacy in sports, these twin values have been expressed in the actions of such disparate individuals as Jesse James, Richard Nixon, Ernest Hemingway, Norman Mailer, and Eldridge Cleaver. After laying bare many of the connections between violence and masculinity, Komisar calls for an end to the masculine mystique, which constitutes a major obstacle to the development of a new society based on equality, compassion, respect, and humanity.[6]

Perhaps the most distorted picture of man and his values in sports is offered by the violent game of hockey. A report commissioned by the Province of Ontario on violence in hockey in Canada found "that there is a conscious effort in hockey to enrich a small group of show business entrepreneurs at the expense of a great sport, not to mention the corruption of an entire generation's concept of sport. . . ."[7] The most disturbing part of the commission's report is their conclusion that, in the end, young hockey players are the ultimate losers, since it is they who watch mayhem on the ice and then emulate the violent role models offered by professionals.

In contrast to the socially inappropriate violence of crowds, individual acts of violence by hockey players are normative. In fact, sociologist Robert Faulkner has found that players view violence as a "personal and occupational resource."[8] The final selection by Edmund Vaz supports this conclusion, as well as the findings of the Ontario commission. Vaz suggests that aggressive and sometimes violent behavior in the junior professional ranks is normative, institutionalized behavior that is positively sanctioned by both players and coaches. The informal obligation of young hockey players to routinely engage in fighting and rough *play is, of course, exacerbated by the aggressiveness expected of all young males.*[9]

FOOTNOTES

1. Irving Louis Horowitz, *Radicalism and the Revolt Against Reason: The Social Theories of Georges Sorel* (London: Routledge and Kegan Paul, 1961), p. 118.

2. Nancy Gager Clinch, *The Kennedy Neurosis* (New York: Grosset & Dunlap, 1973), p. 266.

3. Marc Feigen Fasteau, *The Male Machine* (New York: McGraw-Hill, 1974), p. 157.

4. David Riesman and Reuel Denney, "Football in America: A Study in Cultural Diffusion," *American Quarterly* 3 (Winter 1951): 309–19.

5. Ross Runfola, "Violence in Sport: Mirror of American Society?" *Vital Issues* 24, no. 7 (1975): 1–4; Michael D. Smith, "Violence in Sport: A Sociological Perspective," *Sportwissenschaft* (January 1974).

6. Sullivan points out that the glorification of the "physical man" in pro football is achieved at the expense of the more important human qualities of justice, sensitivity, and intelligence. See William J. Sullivan, "The Pro Football Mystique," *America* (Dec. 16, 1972), pp. 515–18.

7. William McMurtry, "Investigation and Inquiry into Violence in Amateur Hockey," Ontario Ministry of Community and Social Services (1974), pp. 17–18.

8. Robert K. Faulkner, "Respect and Retribution: Toward an Ethnology of Violence," *Sociological Symposium* 9:17–36.

9. For a view of how one young athlete attempted to fit into the world of legalized mayhem known as college football, see Gary Shaw, *Meat on the Hoof: The Hidden World of Texas Football* (New York: Dell, 1972).

THE SUPER-BOWL CULTURE
OF MALE VIOLENCE

EUGENE C. BIANCHI

A few years ago I wrote an article[1] claiming that big-time football mirrored in a ritual way some of the worst characteristics of our culture. I argued that the roots of America's penchant for domestic and foreign violence could be found in symbolic and reinforcing ways in the great national sport that preoccupied a significant percentage of our population. My analysis of professional football underlined four qualities that linked to drive the American violence machine: physical brutality, profit-maximizing commercialism, an authoritarian/military mentality and sexism. Of course I was focusing intentionally on the destructive elements of that game; I was not condemning sport in general.

But after two years of reflection I would make only one important change in the earlier perspective: that the fundamental evil from which the others flowed is sexism. The way by which males in our culture establish their sexual identities within themselves and against women is a prime source for exaggerated aggression in the interpersonal, economic and political realms. The problem can be put as follows: How are we conditioned as males in society to value ourselves as persons? What are the criteria of self-worth and social acceptance among American men? I would like to explore these questions in the context of major social institutions and patterns. I am convinced that the answers to the above queries manifest a close relationship between violence and sexism.

Let me enter a brief preliminary word about my use of

"The Super-Bowl Culture of Male Violence" from Eugene C. Bianchi and Rosemary R. Ruether, *From Machismo to Mutuality* (New York: Paulist Press, 1976), pp. 54–69.

117

the terms "violence" and "sexism." I will employ the words "aggression" and "violence" to mean not only destructive conduct towards persons and property; these words also refer to the more subtle types of violence, called avoidable injury or institutionalized violence, that deprive people of rights and resources. By "sexism" I am talking about a learned pattern of relationships among men that creates an adversary and domineering style between males and towards females. These distinctions should become clearer in the examination of concrete social structures and mores.

The American family is the first conditioning agency for the self-identity that leads to aggression. The boy learns very soon that to set out on the journey to real manhood he must perform and compete better than girls, at least physically. It is a tragic experience for a male child to be thought a sissy. He is schooled to muscular and psychic aggressiveness with toys and in games and other exploits denied to girls. He understands from the start that social acceptance of him as a man depends on his being dominant towards and protective of females, while being successfully competitive towards males. . . .

The polarization of the sexes is fixed in these childhood activities. Males learn to focus on definite challenges and to overcome them; females begin their schooling in passivity and dependence. Because male-dominant culture needs subservient women, girls are conditioned to suppress their mental and physical potential. Young girls are capable of developing physical expertise and bodily confidence far beyond what they are permitted. Moreover, girls are usually superior to boys of the same age in the mental and verbal skills that could enhance their early physical development. But to form women physically adept and strong would be inconsistent with the derivative functions they are destined to perform in society. As students they would cease being careful but docile notetakers and would exercise critical abilities. As adults they would endanger the structures of patriarchy by expecting to hold leadership positions. Thus the psychosomatic power to challenge must be drilled out of the young girl.

A dual form of subtle violence is at work in these sexist patterns of childhood. Girls are deprived of their rights to develop their psychophysical qualities; later this will breed resentment against male society whether the resentment be consciously articulated or remain an unconscious source of animosity. Secondly, violence is done to the male child by demanding that he conform to the code of toughness and competition. A lifetime of·competition among men is destructive to themselves and to other men because it generates self-hatred and an undercurrent of violence in male relationships[2] Men find it very hard to cultivate a peaceful and accepting self-love in a culture that drives them to achieve impossible and dubious goals at the top of the competitive heap. In an environment of intense competition to dominate in order to establish one's personhood, men must constantly be on guard against their fellows and try to manipulate them for self-advancement.

Another way for children to learn violence in the family is to observe it in father/mother relations. An overt form of violence of men toward women in the home is not a universal phenomenon, but it is a sizable social reality. In addition to wife-beating there are threats of physical force or of abandonment. The last is especially menacing to a woman whose socialization has left her without an independent means of support. She may be punished by being ignored or by having her circle of friends and her movements limited. The young boy observes and incorporates into his own personality these control patterns that can later be used against women. He sees that his father has some power and a public life while his weaker and subordinate mother is confined to submissive and secondary roles. This *experience also creates a potentially destructive tension in the male psyche. He may value the unconditional love of the mother while rejecting or even despising her for being reduced to a derivative and dependent status. Later his own desire for position and adventure in the world may cause him to suppress the affectional (mother) dimension in himself to seek power among males. . . .*

Society thus emphasizes that female happiness consists of women subordinating their hopes and ambitions to a husband's career, housework and child care. This cultural indoctrination has been all-pervasive and remarkably successful. A sign of its effectiveness is the amount of guilt that women feel when they transgress social norms directing the proper feminine way. Another indication of the success of the training to suffer is the perverted sort of rejoicing in hardship, misery and self-negation that many women manifest. They look for and stress the negative in interpersonal and national happenings as an extension of their own self-negation. Too much happiness depresses them. Yet this widespread cultural style among women also nurtures destructive sentiments that simmer beneath the conventional conduct. The atmosphere created by these resentments becomes one of latent hostility in the family. These unresolved contradictions stimulate superficial and dishonest forms of communication in the household. Joined to feelings of being used or abused, this ambience becomes one of enmity, envy, suspicion and manipulation. These families of noncommunication and inequality provide children with a training ground for violent interactions.

Such a climate can incline a young man to violence by fostering in him a sense of impotence or lack of self-worth because he is forced to exist in a milieu of psychic impotence. The roles and expectations of family members degenerate so that no one can realize personal potential or empower others. When a family becomes a school for impotence it lays the groundwork for violence in a young man. Sociological and psychological studies have related low self-regard to antisocial, aggressive behavior. A sexist family structure can also foster violent leanings in a youth by impairing his power to empathize with others. As a survival mechanism the child may have to deny the reality of hostile and dominative parental relations. Yet such a denial of reality makes it very difficult for a youth to get in touch with his own feelings and wants. The quality of empathy requires the ability to sense our own real feelings for perceiving any pain and hurt we may be causing to others. Persons who commit violent acts against others lack this ability to feel compassion for the pain and terror of the victims.

The fundamental violence-prone sexism of our culture that demands that males compete fiercely to dominate is furthered in school and peer-group relations. What the family began the school promotes in more sophisticated ways. Athletic events, academic grades and examinations are geared to fashion children, especially males, into socially acceptable achievers and competitors. An illuminating corollary to male success is education in Matina Horner's study about student women who program themselves to fail in order not to abandon the accepted image of femininity. A humanely competitive attitude is not an inducement to violence. But schools indoctrinate young men with a deadly serious spirit of competition. It is not just a rivalry that helps a person enjoy the contest for the pleasure and skill involved in it; rather it's a confrontation with others in which a man's self-identity, self-respect and public acceptance is at stake. He can hardly afford to lose. Winning is all even if it means trampling on one's fellows. Hostility and violence are instruments for removing obstacles on the road to the top. . . .

The middle- and upper-class male peer group is also a milieu for sexist development. Fraternity hazing is a rite that demands the inflicting of pain to produce real men who can get ahead. This practice declares that for males toughness, not tenderness, must be paramount. The other side of this mentality manifests a proneness to see draft resisters as "faggots" because they refused pain and aggression as an introduction to manhood. Here we are also touching on the terrible fear of homosexuality in a male who is torn between the cultural demand for potency in heterosexual performance and his own fears about his sexual adequacy. The passion for fast cars with unnecessary horsepower is a phallic extension for youths who need reassurance about their sexual manhood. The problem is not that young men are sexually insecure, rather the difficulty and peril consists in the domineering and violence-oriented sexuality that is advocated as a cure to this insecurity. He is encouraged to "score" with girls, to "make" women. The male in this common vision is the individualist hero-hunter who sets out to make a kill, to dominate his prey. It is a sexuality of conquest, of trophies that shine from the inner mantelpiece of his ego.

I affirmed at the outset that the sexism in football was symbolically fundamental to the other evils of our culture. It is also worth noting that in a culture that encourages people to admire and revel in aggressiveness sports of intended brutality gain the highest appeal both at the box office and on television. A prototype of such sport is prizefighting; recent additions to popular games of mayhem are ice hockey and roller derbies. The well-calculated appeal to direct physical abuse in these sports points to the well-instilled need in our people to be entertained by violence. Much of the responsibility for propagating violence-teaching programs rests with the sponsoring corporations that use such programing to sell their products. Yet the high point of violent symbolism in sport is reached in football, which draws the passionate attention of millions. We can focus on that great national pastime as a transition from the male violence among peers to the crimes of men.

Big-time football manifests and reinforces the ideal of masculine identity through its aggressive ethos. The real man is aggressive and dominant in all situations. The weekend trek to the arena is not an escape from the world of corporate America; rather it is a weekly pilgrimage to the national shrines where the virtues of toughness and insensitivity can be renewed. This is especially true in the man/woman relationships. In the football spectacle the role of woman in our society is clearly defined against the masculine criteria of value. The important action is male-dominated; women can share only at a distance in a man's world. They can shout and squeal from afar, but their roles are accessory to the. male event. Ultimately they are his "bunnies," his possessions for pleasure and service.

Yet for all its chest-thumping bravado the game also portrays the anxieties and contradictions of aggressive sexuality. Football, by its very calculated violence, makes sensitive attunement to one's own body hard to achieve. The vicious body contact is the opposite of gentle touching and loving gesture. Moreover, the kind of sexuality implied in the game manifests a fearful displacement of the challenge of sustaining authentically interpersonal sexuality. It is an extension into adulthood of the latency phenomenon of young boys pummeling each other and avoiding a more mature relationship with women. Thus the sport depicts an unhealthy polarity toward women. In one way social canons urge the male to be dominant and aggressive towards women. Yet in a culture geared to aggressive attainments men demonstrate a deep fear of delicate, equalitarian sexual relations. Unsure about sexual potency in a milieu that demands—even in sex—a kind of technological efficiency and performance many men are unable to shake off these cultural imperatives and relate to women in sex as full equals. With equals there is no need to control the other or to succeed according to external prescriptions.

Violent crimes in the United States are a particularly male phenomenon. Crimes committed by women, however, are on the rise, although these actions are usually not crimes of direct assault. A combination of new opportunities for women in the public sphere plus the persistence of male patterns of competitive gain in the marketplace may partially explain this increase. Because the statistics on serious crime in our land are appallingly high in comparison with other nations, we need to ask whether the formation of the sexist male psyche is involved. The word "crime" usually conjures up in our minds violence to property (theft) or persons (assault, homicide). Often, however, we are not subtle enough in imagining the forms of theft and assault that are peculiar to those in positions of wealth and power. Watergate and the Pentagon Papers have helped to cure this weakness of the imagination. But for the purpose of my theme, rape provides an unusual way of joining theft and assault while at the same time pointing to the sexist underpinnings of much violent crime. Rape combines a taking away of freedom and other rights as well as the threat or actuality of physical violence. . . .

Rape represents a compulsion to dominate and harm women; it also tells us about the mechanisms to perform that obsess men. Rape, often accompanied by physical brutality, manifests a need to control and force a woman to do her attacker's will. This impulse to overpower and coerce is probably stronger than the actual sexual attraction of the act, although the latter is sometimes heightened by the struggle to dominate. The rapist may be venting a rage against his victim that he consciously or unconsciously feels against society or possibly against other women in his *life. In this distorted way he is trying to establish his inner sense of power and selfhood against a society that brought him to repeated failures to perform according to its rules and myths. It was Eldridge Cleaver who graphically confessed that in the act of rape, which he later saw as dehumanizing to self and victim, he was striking out against a repressive social order. The rapist may also be demonstrating by displacement an unresolved hatred of, or conflict with, another woman in his life. . . .*

Overt corporate crime is socially harmful behavior by corporations for which the law provides penalties. Many of these activities revolve around the violation of laws governing restraint of trade, anti-trust arrangements, misrepresentation in advertising, fair labor practices, rebates, financial fraud and similar categories. Even a cursory reading of the history of corporate crime indicates how vast and pervasive this phenomenon is in national life. These white collar crimes, usually committed by men, are often not discoverable without extensive investigation, whereas the misdeeds of the poor are found out quickly and publicized. Moreover, the resources of corporations make it possible for them to afford the best legal protection. These imbalances in our system of justice stand out starkly in contrast to the heavy penalties imposed on overt, physical acts of violence and the light sentences handed down for convictions concerning white collar crimes of privileged citizens. These reactions of the courts are partially explained by the intense fear inspired by crimes of direct physical violence, whereas the "clean" crimes of respectable businessmen and politicians generate less emotional response in the populace. But the matter of unfair treatment in the courts is further complicated by racism, dislike for the poor and a willingness to treat kindly men who conform to respectable middle-class conventions. Yet such men of the corporate marketplace are more easily corrupted by the difficulty of assuming personal responsibility in a collective situation. The corporation diffuses responsibility among many persons so that actions are separated from conscientious decision. The result of these crimes in male-dominated corporations is violence done to the environment and the general welfare of the people.

This male marketplace of injustice and inequality that oppresses the many and benefits the few is a breeding ground for violence. The concentration of economic power in relatively few super-corporations means that a very small group of stockholders and managers will accrue vast profits and be in a privileged position to influence public policy. The largest corporations—banks, insurance companies and utilities—are not only able to control competition, they also use their great potential for lobbying and for other forms of political influence to neutralize government regulatory agencies originally established to moderate these massive businesses. Often enough the regulatory agencies themselves become servants of private privilege rather than of the common interest. The power of special interest groups over the state is especially evident in our unjustly regressive tax system. Persons at the lower end of the income scale pay a far greater proportion of their earnings in taxes than do those at the top. Capital gains, depletion allowances, tax shelters and many other deductions favor the rich, while the poor and those of modest incomes are saddled with a cluster of regressive taxes. . . .

When women struggle for or attain equal financial standing with men, men feel castrated. On the flip side of this economic scenario, males have protected their money/identity prominence by using women as cheap labor while mouthing their self-serving ideology about mother and home. The first step towards wisdom would be to own up to the intrinsic rapaciousness of an economic system that serves male power needs (not the healthy and *humane growth of men) while it keeps women in a deprived and subservient position. There is little chance that we will reform seriously our all-controlling economic system unless we dwell and act on the awareness that it is permeated with a sexist violence. The system demands that women be "scripted" for nurturing and support roles while men be destined to realize their worth through money and power. Unfortunately, it is also a structure that keeps men from fostering lives of intimacy and community, and it even prevents them from finding real pleasure in work itself.*

More women now perceive the importance of attaining some economic independence from men. This freedom allows them to overcome the frustrations of an adult constrained into childlike dependency. It also promotes maturity and self-determination in making choices about the disposition of one's own resources. Some critics of woman's newly achieved economic independence claim that it will simply lead them into the same destructive paths of capitalist competition that afflict men. While the danger of such entrapment is real, women must live in an economic system that will not readily change for the forseeable future. It is in that milieu that women are destined to benefit from whatever self-determining potential such financial independence can give. If women in pursuit of monetary self-sufficiency do not jettison the humanizing qualities learned by their gender over the centuries they may avoid the worse aspects of male economic violence and may bring a new and less avaricious spirit to the marketplace. Male critics of economic independence for women also fear the challenge to the traditional masculine ego of the provider. But men need not suffer ego loss if they learn to look at the positive benefits to them of female economic independence.

The education of the male mind through . . . social institutions [such as sports] has prospects on the political level that are frightening for our national political structures and also for human survival. The familiar slogans of not negotiating on our knees in Vietnam, of not turning tail, of being Number One, of not presiding over the first American defeat are the proud shouts of little boys who learned that winning was all. The culture of the "fastest gun" and of Bonnie and Clyde has a ready penchant for the quick trigger finger. No one has ever lost his job on the National Security Council for being tough—only for being soft on enemies. This code of toughness views the international political scene as a game board for power manipulations, for keeping control, for placating the male psyche.

At home the code of toughness decrees that men should attain power by any means available. This is the real message of Watergate. Notice also that Watergate was a male-only-phenomenon. When a woman finally appeared among the conspirators, she was a secretary who bungled a tape-recorder. But the ethic of Watergate is that it's all right if one doesn't get caught. It's also the individualist ethic of the American hero/hunter: power for our side means there's something in it for me; I will become more important through this power-grab. Yet this power of violence destroys the power of democracy that depends on justice and open consensus. Again the lesson is that the Watergate lads (and they are symbols for many others) are living in fundamental contradiction to the best in the American heritage. But such men are acting·in full accord with their training in the super-bowl culture of male violence. . . .

The American male mystique is not only opposed to the best elements of the Bill of Rights and the Declaration of Independence, it is also a rejection of the core ethos of the Judeo-Christian tradition. For our future national destiny, the violence-prone male mentality promises constant opposition to qualities that promote the common welfare of justice, equality and community. In the Western religious tradition the masculine mystique is a denial of essential biblical perspectives. I would like to contrast these opposed orientations without further elaboration in this presentation.

The Gospel way stresses the building of trusting life-supporting communities; the male mystique emphasizes individualist self-aggrandizement through the domination of others. The Scriptures advocate the sharing of resources, the hero/hunter mentality nourishes itself by amassing and quantifying things for the self or its immediate extensions. The biblical way points to a democratic communion of persons who share their gifts with one another; the super-bowl psyche inclines men to concentrate political power and decision-making in the hands of the dominating few. Finally, the male mystique is geared towards overt and hidden forms of violence, whereas the Judeo-Christian ideal evolved toward an ethic of minimizing destructive aggression. Unless we are willing to see and deal with these contradictions we continue to live with a false conscience that is psychologically and spiritually damaging. It would be a purist mistake to think that any of us can live in this society without some complicity in its evil tendencies and actions. It is quite another matter to blind ourselves to hypocritical contradictions and even claim that they are glorious virtues.

I have intentionally reviewed the male mystique of violence in the context of our social/cultural conditioning. My purpose is to emphasize that spiritual growth and theological reflection are intrinsically related to the worldly process of becoming freer of personal and social oppressions. The focus of Hebrew and Christian Scriptures is the process of liberation from bondage, from the powers of *death that diminish our humanity. The prototype of our enslavements is the oppression of women. From this primal distortion of the male mind proceeds the oppression of other "lesser people." The conquering needs of the violence-prone masculine psyche drives us to racism, colonialism and other types of imperialism. These oppressions are extensions of the male/female pattern by which we project the dark side of ourselves on to the other in order to use and abuse our fellow for our own selfish aggrandizement. Of course, women, too, can imitate the same life style and reproduce its oppression, but this would demand a greater and more difficult rejection of qualities that women have long preserved in our culture.*

At root, male chauvinism is a denial of our co-humanity with others and also a rejection of the masculine (animus) and feminine (anima) within all of us as individuals. My intention in affirming this is not to berate men but hopefully to aid them to see that the male mystique is also the instrument of our own bondage. It keeps us from realizing our full personhood because the oppressor is also oppressed. As American men we are deeply conditioned from the cradle to value ourselves as persons according to the hero/hunter myth of aggressive individualism. How can we change the basic myth by which we live? How can we begin to sense our self-worth according to another model, that of affectionate, nondominative, sharing communal men? On our own answers to these questions depend the survival of humanity and the restoration of our own personal humanity.

FOOTNOTES

1. Eugene Bianchi, "Pigskin Piety," *Christianity and Crisis* (February, 21, 1972), pp. 31–34.
2. Joseph Pleck, "My Male Sex Role—and Ours," *WIN* (April 11, 1974), pp. 8–12.

VIOLENCE AND THE MASCULINE MYSTIQUE

LUCY KOMISAR

"We will not be humiliated," President Nixon declared in his speech to the country after the invasion of Cambodia. "It is not our power but our will and character that is being tested tonight." Agonizing over the spector of an America that acted like "a pitiful, helpless giant," he vowed that he would not see the nation become "a second-rate power" and "accept the first defeat in its proud 190-year history."

Nixon's resolve stiffens (masculine) and he sends troops into Cambodia so that we are not forced to submit (feminine) to a peace of humiliation. The big stick hasn't changed much since Teddy Roosevelt, only now it's a stockpile of missiles and bayonets on rifles and bombs that plow gracelessly into a womb that burns with napalm.

The United States of America is "the clear leader among modern, stable, democratic nations in its rates of homicide, assault, rape, and robbery, and it is at least among the highest in incidence of group violence and assassination," declared the National Commission on the Causes and Prevention of Violence. Most of those violent crimes are committed by males between the ages of 15 and 24; a majority of them are poor and a disproportionate percentage are black.

"Violence is actually often used to enable a young man to become a successful member of ghetto society," reported the Commission. "Proving masculinity may require frequent rehearsal of the toughness, the exploitation of women, and the quick aggressive responses that are characteristic of the lower-class adult male." The report

Lucy Komisar, "Violence and Masculinity," *The Washington Monthly*, (July; 1970). Reprinted with the permission of the author.

called ghetto life a "subculture within dominant American middle-class culture in which aggressive violence tends to be accepted as normal in everyday life. . . . An altercation with overtones threatening a young man's masculinity, a misunderstanding between husband and wife, competition for a sexual partner, the need to get hold of a few dollars—these trivial events can readily elicit violent response."

The only thing wrong with that is the Commission's assumption that its observations apply only to the lower classes. What it has described, in fact, is the "masculine mystique," a conception of manhood so central to the politics and personality of America that it institutionalizes violence and male supremacy as measures of national pride. The masculine mystique is based on toughness and domination, qualities that once may have been necessary in a time when men felled trees and slew wild animals. Now they are archaic and destructive values that have no legitimate place in our world but continue to exist as idealized standards for some lofty state of "masculinity." The mystique has characterized many nations, but it is particularly dangerous in contemporary America because of our distinctively high levels of internal violence, our "Bonnie and Clyde" tendencies toward its glorification, our enormous capacities for mechanized warfare, and our virtual obsession with being Number One.

A quote from a man I know: "When I was a little boy and had come home crying after a beating from some local bully, my mother would push me out and lock the door, demanding that I go back to give as good as I had gotten. She said boys who didn't fight back were sissies."

/ Little boys learn the connection between violence and manhood very early in life. Fathers indulge in mock prize fights and wrestling matches with eight-year-olds. Boys play cowboys and Indians with guns and bows and arrows proffered by their elders / They are gangsters or soldiers interchangeably—the lack of difference between the two is more evident to them than to their parents. They are encouraged to "fight back," and bloodied noses and black eyes become trophies of their pint-sized virility.

Little Men

The differences between boys and girls are defined in terms of violence. Boys are encouraged to rough-house; girls are taught to be gentle ("lady-like"). Boys are expected to get into fights, but admonished not to hit girls. (It is not "manly" to assault females—except, of course, sexually, but that comes later). Boys who run away from fights are "sissies," with the implication that they are queer. As little boys become big boys, their education in violence continues. The leadership in this country today consists of such little boys who attained "manhood" in the approved and heroic violence of World War II. They returned to a society in which street and motorcycle gangs, fast cars, and fraternity hazing confirmed the lessons of war—one must be tough and ready to inflict pain in order to get ahead.

The phallic/power symbol of our age is, of course, the automobile. The World Health Organization says that traffic accidents are the most common cause of death among young males in highly motorized countries. Often cars are stolen not to keep or sell, but for the joy of the ride and the sense of power and controlled violence it offers. Madison Avenue contributes its influence by selling cars as if they were magical potency potions. Chivalry's knight on horseback has become man on "horsepower"—even modern terminology substantiates the metaphor.

A young philosophy instructor at a Catholic men's college in New Jersey, who leads a "consciousness-raising" group for some of his students, says most of them have grown up with the same conception of what it takes to prove one's manhood: "You have a car and 'make' as many girls as possible. It's very important to have an impressive car; the freshmen all believe the ads that if you've got a Dodge Charger, you're going to get laid more." The system militates against tenderness, he says. "No physical display between men is acceptable except to fight, and the only acceptable response when someone questions your manhood is to fight. Most freshmen think there's something faggoty about being a draft dodger."

He adds, "Some guys are so obsessed with their manhood and masculinity that they can't make love: they feel it's effeminate to be sensitive or affectionate."

Boys are introduced into "manhood" through innocent pastimes like boxing, brawling, and football. And not-so-innocent pastimes like war. Consider phrases like "The manly art of self defense," "Join the army, be a man" (variation: "The army will make a man out of him"). Gene Tunney's autobiography is called simply A Man Must Fight. Men who have been brought up in this tradition, and whose memories of war, real or imagined, have bolstered their self-respect during years of bringing home the bacon, are traumatized by the young men (students and peace marchers) who refuse to accept pain, mutilation, and death as initiation rites into manhood. . . .

The Soft Battlefield

The ultimate proof of manhood, however, is in sexual violence. Even the language of sex is a lexicon that describes the power of men over women. Men are "aggressive" as they "take" or "make" women, showing their potency ("power") in the "conquest." Women, on the other hand, "submit" and "surrender," allowing themselves to be "violated" and "possessed.' Havelock Ellis declares the basic sado-masochism of such a concept to be "certainly normal." He says: "In men it is possible to trace a tendency to inflict pain on the women they love. It is still easier to trace in women a delight in experiencing physical pain when it is inflicted by a lover and an eagerness to accept subjection to his will."

Sadism cum virility is offered the fans who flock to James Bond films to see their hero play out their fantasies alternately in sensual embraces with women and bloody combat with men. In "Goldfinger," for instance, Bond has his arms around a chorus girl when he sees the reflection of an assassin in her eye. He wards off the blow with her body, a consummation which seems as satisfying to his manhood as the one he originally had in mind. There is as little tenderness and as much brutality in the sexual encounters as in the fight scenes. If homosexuality were in fashion, it is likely that James Bond could make love to the men and beat up the women without changing his sentiments toward either.

Chivalry was an early example of the worship of masculine violence tied in with sexual dominance. Then and later, duels were fought to protect the honor of women and wars waged to uphold the honor of states. In the latter endeavor, the women were raped instead of honored. Both traditions have been proudly continued, and in both the women have been objects to conquer and to parade as the validation of someone's manhood: they have no honor of their own.

Rape on foreign battlefields has always been met on the homefront with shrugs about men having certain "needs" and the "tensions" that build up in wartime. So soldiers get penicillin along with their K-rations, and they express their "manhood" by forcing women to submit to them. Those that lie with prostitutes are participating in rape in just as real a sense—they are enjoying the bitter fruits of the rape of a country that forces its citizens to choose between death and degradation.

In 1966, an American patrol held a 19-year-old Vietnamese girl captive for several days, taking turns raping her and finally murdering her. The sergeant planned the crime in advance, telling the soldiers during the mission's briefing that the girl would improve their "morale." When one soldier refused to take part in the rape, the sergeant called him "queer" and "chicken;" another testified later that he joined in the assault to avoid such insults. When one country ravages another to avoid being called "chicken," how unusual is it that soldiers follow suit? Both in the name of that elusive "manhood."

According to Seymour Hersh, some of the GIs who conducted the My Lai massacre raped women before they shot them. The day after that "mission," an entire platoon raped a woman caught fleeing a burning hut. And a couple of days later a helicopter door gunner spotted the body of a woman in a field. She was spread-eagled, with an Eleventh Brigade patch between her legs. Like a "badge of honor," reported the gunner. "It was obviously there so people would know the Eleventh Brigade had been there."

Machismo and the Don Juan cult, modern versions of chivalry, are brushed off as Latin oddities. Spaniards and Italians defend their honor with "passion killings"—and everyone winks. But they are not the only men who regard women as trophies in rape or seduction or who think wife-beating is a joke (literally, as in "When did you stop beating your wife?"). How different are those passion killings from Southern lynchings conducted in the name of white womanhood and against the imagined sexual onslaughts of black men? It is not a coincidence that white supremacy in the South organized the "Knights" of the Ku Klux Klan. That was an assertion of masculinity in the face of humiliation by other men; it was as much male supremacy as white supremacy.

The writing of Eldridge Cleaver epitomizes the way in which many black men, too, hold violence equivalent to masculinity, fully in the American tradition. "The boxing ring is the ultimate focus of masculinity in America,"says Cleaver in Soul on Ice; "the two-fisted testing ground of manhood, and the heavyweight champion, as a symbol, is the real Mr. America.". . .

Hemingway and Mailer:
the Bulls of Literature

Alan Sillitoe, author of Saturday Night and Sunday Morning, writes: "An intellectual obsession with violence is a sign of fear. A physical obsession with it is a sign of sexual impotence." Interesting, then, that Ernest Hemingway, who composed hosannas to manly brutality, took his own life with a gun and that Norman Mailer, one of America's most self-conscious "machos," once stabbed his wife and has been in more than one barroom and cocktail party brawl.

In 1927, Hemingway published Men Without Women, a collection of stories which I expect reflect his conception of ultimate manhood. The stories are variously written about a bullfighter, a boxer, several soldiers, some hired gunmen, etc. Women are represented as unwelcomely pregnant (in a story pointedly titled "White Elephants"): as prostitutes, as deceivers, or as fools. Ultimately, Hemingway's answer is to eschew women for more "masculine" pastimes—fishing, for example:

> I lay in the dark with my eyes open and thought of
> all the girls I had ever known and what kind of
> wives they would make, It was a very interesting

thing to think about and for a while it killed off trout-fishing and interfered with my prayers. Finally, though, I went back to trout-fishing, because I found that I could remember all the streams and there was always something new about them while the girls, after I had thought about them a few times, blurred and I could not call them into my mind and finally they all blurred and all became rather the same and I gave up thinking about them almost altogether. ("Now I Lay Me")

Critic Leslie Fiedler thinks Hemingway's concern with violence reflects a pathological inability to deal with adult sexuality. If, as Sillitoe says, obsession with violence is a sign of impotence, trading women for fish is one way to avoid that embarrassing confrontation.

Mailer is more extravagant than Hemingway in his exaltation of violence: "Men who have lived a great deal with violence are usually gentler and more tolerant than men who abhor violence," he says. "Boxers, bullfighters, a lot of combat soldiers, Hemingway heroes, in short, are almost always gentle men."

What romantic drivel! My Lai, cauliflower ears and broken roses, slit throats, cement blocks splashing into Mafia cemeteries, guts spilling out of gored intestines—do the actors in such violent dramas radiate the compassion and understanding Mailer attributes to them? Not to mention the Chicago police Mailer himself has had occasion to describe without recourse to adjectives like "gentle" or "tolerant."

If Mailer's ideal man of the world is described in such incredible terms, what about his man in bed? Sex is conquest, a contest, an opportunity for domination. Mailer compares the "event" in bed to the bullfight. Sometimes he sees himself as the matador, sometimes as the bull. He calls his penis "the avenger" (For what "crime" or "insult" does he avenge himself against women?) and he recalls how he "threw her a fuck the equivalent of a 15-round fight."

In Sexual Politics . . . feminist Kate Millet devotes an entire chapter to an analysis of Mailer's obsession with violence, showing how his equation of violence and masculinity masks an overriding fear of homosexuality as well as a contempt for women. Beginning with The Naked and the Dead, Mailer could barely speak either of sex or violence in terms that did not include the other. Millet cites a speech by Sergeant Croft:

> All the deep dark urges of man, the sacrifices on the hilltop, the churning lusts of night and sleep, weren't all of them contained in the shattering, screaming burst of a shell . . . the phallus-shell that rides through a shining vagina of steel . . . the curve of sexual excitement and discharge, which is after all the physical core of life.

Mailer equates the opposite of violence—pacifism—with the opposites of maleness—femaleness and homosexuality—both of which arouse his contempt. The logical outcome of this ideology, says Millet, is war and violence, the only protection against the pacifism he labels "unmanly." And the violence that Mailer venerates is the logical extension and proof of the aggressiveness this society considers an innate part of the truly masculine personality. "Men are aggressive, women are passive," says the conventional wisdom. "Men are dominant and venturesome: women are yielding and receptive." The dictionary definition of passive is "inactive, but acted upon; offering no resistance, submissive; taking no part, inert." That sounds more like a vegetable than a human being of any sex.

An End to the Game

Violence and male supremacy have been companions in the course of civilization. The domination of women by men has been the prototype of the control men have tried to exercise over other men—in slavery, in war, and in the marketplace. Bernard Clark, professor of government at the London School of Economics, speaks glowingly of "the fierce masculine joy of striving for possession according to some more or less acknowledged rules of a game." That is the game that President Nixon play[ed], the game that wins acclaim from Hemingway and Mailer, the game that enshrined Jesse James as a national hero, and the game that spills buckets of human blood and guts on battlefields at home and abroad.

That game says that to be a man one must possess, control, dominate—and that domination must be assured by force and violence. Masculinity is interpreted to demand male supremacy. Ironically, now in the black community, men are calling on women to step back so that they can "assert their manhood." The "masculinity game" can't have a winner unless it also has a loser. The rules of the game require that the losers be reduced to humiliation and powerlessness—to the classic status of women. Such was the "emasculation" of black men under slavery and segregation. And consequently, they know that the reassertion of that kind of "manhood" requires the suppression of their women.

John Wayne is the quintessential player in The Game. His role in The Green Berets would be an embarrassing parody if patriotic zeal were not immune to wit. Wayne is tough-fisted, hard-talking, and never walks away from a fight; thanks to providence, righteousness, and his rugged, muscular frame, he never loses. But it never happens in real life like in the movies. They probably wouldn't like the metaphor, but the "hard hats" constitute a Greek chorus to masculinity—they extol it through physical labor, vulgar comments at passing women, and patriotic fervor for "our brave fighting men in Vietnam." Sometimes the defense of their manhood, otherwise largely expressed through applauding someone else's violence, forces them to beat up people who disagree with them.

The enemies of national "virility" are called "effete," a word that means "sterile, spent, worn-out" and conjures up the picture of an effeminate pantywaist—the inveterate 90-pound weakling who is always getting sand kicked in his face, probably by a burly construction worker. More to the point, effete comes from "out" plus "fetus"—exhausted by bearing.

Perhaps we are "exhausted by bearing"—tired to death of bearing up under the super-masculine mystique that is a national neurosis and that sets a country to counting bodies the way it counts touchdowns—and cataloguing both as a measure of its manhood. . . .

The beginning of a challenge to the masculine mystique of violence and domination comes now from those who were its first victims: women. Today women are demanding new definitions of masculine and feminine that do not require the dominance of one sex over the other. We have rejected all the myths about masculine aggression and feminine passivity and we seek to replace them with values that encourage human relations based on equality, compassion, and respect.

Today the masculine mystique is no longer just a matter of concern for the women who have suffered its ill effects most universally. The caveman mentality outlived its usefulness when technology made the hunter obsolete, and its extension into national and international politics now threatens to destroy everything men and women have built since then.

Today men need a kind of courage that is only exhibited by those who have no doubts at all about their manhood—and that is the courage to assert their humanity.

THE CULTURE OF YOUNG HOCKEY PLAYERS: SOME INITIAL OBSERVATIONS

EDMUND W. VAZ

Because young hockey players undergo a recurrent set of relatively common experiences there develops an occupational culture, a system of values, rules and attitudes that helps guide the behavior of players. Although the value system of the larger community tends to subsume the "official" rhetoric of the Minor Hockey League, the informal values, attitudes and customs of the League fit more easily into the general value system of the lower socioeconomic strata. Moreover, boys who remain in Allstar Minor League Hockey likely come from lower socioeconomic levels; this facilitates their adaptation to the role of hockey player, and the acceptance of its values, attitudes and practices.

Older Allstar players (seventeen to nineteen years)

Edmund W. Vaz. "The Culture of Young Hockey Players: Some Initial Observations" in Edward Taylor (ed.), *Training—Its Scientific Basis and Application*, (Springfield, Ill.: Thomas, 1972). pp. 222–34.

Note: This study was aided by a research grant from the Canada Council for which I am grateful. I am also indebted to Mr. Barry Boddy, my assistant, who helped collect much of the material.

often face a conflict between academic and hockey obligations. Problematic academic success, the improbability of a university education, the lack of clear occupational goals, plus the increasing likelihood of being selected for the Junior professional ranks make a professional hockey career appear meaningfully realistic for these boys.

We suggest that physically agressive behavior is normative, institutionalized behavior, and is learned during the formal and informal socialization of young hockey players. This kind of behavior becomes an integral part of the role obligations of older Allstar players. Intense competition, the injunction to use increasingly aggressive means, and the strong motivation to be chosen for the Junior professional ranks are structural conditions which help generate, and differentially account for physical aggression in the league, i.e., among players on higher level teams. These conditions are less applicable to younger boys.

This is a working paper based on my first impressions of data collected during the first stage of a research project among boys aged 8 to 20 engaged in Minor League Hockey[1] in a medium-sized town in Ontario. Our interest is in the occupational culture of young players, their socioeconomic status, the process of their professionalization, with special consideration given the use of illegal tactics and physical aggression in their role as hockey players. . . .

Occupational Culture

Most groups that play together and work together develop a common set of norms (both formal and informal) that helps guide the behavior of their members. There emerges also a set of relatively common values and sentiments that underlies group norms, strengthens group solidarity, and often helps members overcome their everyday occupa-

tional anxieties and problems. This is the occupational culture—the group heritage that is transmitted to members. And research has revealed the occupational cultures of boxers, medical doctors, pickpockets, professors, even pot smokers. There is also the occupational culture of young hockey players.

Part of the culture of an occupation is its charter, the more or less formal statement of rhetoric of its objectives and ideals. This resembles an official version of meanings directed towards the representation of a specific image or impression of the group and what transpires within it, and is necessarily couched in abstract terms. It relates the group to the general values of the total community in which it operates, and in turn the group receives the blessings of the community.

In general the rhetoric of Minor League Hockey tends to emphasize the following objectives: to provide exercise, health and recreation for young people; to develop respect for the spirit and letter of the law, to develop sportsmanship and fair play; to develop the qualities of self-discipline and loyalty, and also to develop emotional maturity, social competence and moral character in young boys. This is an imposing list, and any community concerned about its young people would find it hard to reject a group that espouses and publicizes these virtues.

But we know that things are seldom what they seem. Good intentions and purposes are one thing, what transpires in the dressing rooms and on the ice is something else. In the course of reaching objectives and realizing goals social change occurs: original intentions are forgotten, meanings are transformed, short-term goals subvert long-term objectives, strategy replaces ideals. For example, the conceptions of sportsmanship and fair play have different meanings for different age groups. Youngsters think of it as shaking hands after the game and being a good loser. Among older experienced boys on the higher level teams the practice of shaking hands often leads to violence.[2] Similarly the qualities of sportsmanship and fair play are differentially emphasized in the system. Once boys reach the Bantam level (thirteen or fourteen years) these virtues are nearly dead letters.

Similarly, at the higher levels the value of success, i.e., winning the game, rapidly takes precedence over other considerations among coaches and managers as well as players. Little attention is paid to developing respect for the "spirit and letter" of the normative rules of the game. In fact, at an early age youngsters learn the institutionalized means of violating certain rules, and this becomes routine practice. They learn that there are "good" and "bad" penalties; the former are tolerated even encouraged, the latter are deplored.

Although the values of the larger community tend to subsume the purposes and ideals of Minor League Hockey, in fact what occurs in the dressing rooms and on the ice, and the informal codes and tactics by which players are controlled and the game conducted, reflect a narrower perspective. Many of the attitudes and values common to Minor League Hockey seem to fit neatly into the general value system of the lower socioeconomic strata. We know that there is a relationship between body-contact sports and socioeconomic levels; body-contact sports are correlated with the lower socioeconomic strata.(1) Within Minor League Hockey body contact is a much proclaimed and highly cherished virtue of the sport; it is alleged that to eliminate or seriously reduce the amount of body contact would irreparably damage the sport of hockey.

One of the most closely guarded privileges of the professions is their right to determine the proper training and education for entry into a profession, i.e., before full professional status is granted. Whenever, and in whatever manner, the professional education and training is acquired it may be viewed also as part of the recruit's socialization. Learning the expectations and obligations of the role of hockey player is the process of socialization, and it is an integral part of learning the culture of the occupation. A major function of the socialization of Allstar hockey players in the Minor Hockey League is their preparation for the higher professional ranks. And the standards according to which this training takes place reflect the considerable influence of the higher professional groups on the socialization of young players.

An important subject matter of rules is establishing the criteria for recognizing a true fellow worker, or in this case, a true hockey player. Although technical skills and competence (especially skating and shooting) are necessary features of the role of hockey players they are not sufficient. Justification for the violation of formal rules, such as tripping, elbowing, fighting, use of one's stick in a fight, besides one's attitudes towards courage, toughness, the ability to endure pain, among others, are vital aspects in recognizing the developing professional hockey player. These are not technical skills, but qualities that mirror the internalization of cherished values and the success of the professionalization process.

If the middle-class ethic tends to value the cultivation of patience, the inhibition of spontaneity, self-control and the regulation of physical aggression, then the working class tends to emphasize the spontaneity of behavior; it praises courage, stamina, physical strength and resiliency, and rewards those who "never back down from a fight." Toughness is considered a virtue, and within the working class fighting is often recognized as a moral and legitimate activity in settling disputes. This suggests that the working class both supports the sport of hockey and is supported by it through the relatively common attitudes and general system of values that they share. This overlap in values between the working class and hockey suggests that hockey is likely considered a prestigious occupation and is acceptable to both working-class boys and their fathers. This differential evaluation of occupations will likely influence some individuals to select hockey as a career.

Socioeconomic Status

All socioeconomic strata are likely represented among the youngest age groups that volunteer to play Minor League Hockey. Although the majority of boys will come from the lower socioeconomic levels, the sons of professionals will also be found. But I believe that the data will show that the majority of boys who remain in Allstar Minor League Hockey until seventeen or eighteen years come largely from the working and lower middle classes. Boys from the higher socioeconomic levels drop out of hockey. This implies that the National Hockey League is comprised largely of players from working-class levels.

We know that there exists a strong relationship between the years a boy remains in school and his family's socioeconomic status; sons of the most favored families stay in school longer and more often attend university. Children of less favored families drop out of school earlier, and fewer enroll in university.(2) It may be that as a career hockey becomes a meaningful occupational choice to those boys who comtemplate dropping out of high school, or who are doing poorly in school and/or who do not envisage a university career—boys generally from the lower socioeconomic strata. Furthermore, as a career hockey will likely fall within the range of preferred occupational choices of working-class boys, but not those from the higher socioeconomic strata.

An area of particular interest is to study the variables that influence a boy's decision to select hockey as a career. Although a number of variables will operate, such as parental influence (which is apt to be encouraging), a boy's hockey "talent," family tradition, and available alternative work opportunities, there are a number of structural features that strongly corral working-class boys toward a professional hockey career.

By sixteen or seventeen years of age a boy who remains in Allstar hockey has reached the Midget level of the league where the competition becomes intense. It is precisely at this level that boys are scouted and evaluated for advancement to the Junior professional ranks. At this point they identify strongly with their team and are strongly motivated to play in the higher ranks, but the increasingly heavy emphasis on size, toughness, physical strength, aggressiveness and the ability to withstand pain makes conformity to role obligations especially difficult to achieve. Their efforts to conform to these expectations, the intense competition, the risk of being "dropped" from the team, and their desire to reach the Junior professional[3] ranks comprise a major structural source of anxiety.

At the same time these boys are still in high school where the work is becoming difficult, and successful examination results critical for academic promotion. The conflict of academic expectations and increasingly stringent hockey obligations is a further structural source of strain.[4] Under these circumstances many boys will experience academic problems; in any case (and this is important) few boys will envisage a university education. Yet they have now reached a point where they must at least begin to consider their future careers. But academic success is problematic, a university education unlikely, and many will not have any clearcut occupational goal. Moreover, at this time they are continuously preoccupied with hockey and faced with the possibility of being chosen for Junior professional teams. It is at this juncture that hockey as an occupational career will appear more meaningful and attractive to them, precisely because it has become a realistic possibility. Once they are selected for the Junior professional teams their professional ranks are greatly enhanced.[5]

Fighting and Physical Aggression

Where fighting is found to be a relatively recurrent activity,[6] differentially distributed in the system, and assumes much the same form, the sociologist will suspect that it is attributable to some structural condition of the system itself. Explanations that focus on personality defects, faulty control systems or the debilitating childhood experiences of individuals are apt to be bypassed.

Sports have traditionally been considered a means of controlling violence. Yet the "routinization of violence" has never been complete. Violence has persistently erupted in the form of rough play and dirty tactics. But this behavior is not necessarily an uncontrolled, spontaneous outburst of physical aggression. Fighting, rough play, and dirty tactics may be normative, expected forms of conduct. I suggest that the larger amount of physical aggression, especially fighting, that occurs at the Midget and Junior professional levels is normative, institutionalized behavior; it is learned during the socialization of the youngster, and it is part of the role expectations of the player. Under certain conditions failure to fight is variously sanctioned by coaches and players. The bulk of fighting can be accounted for according to structurally produced strains within the system itself.

If boys are to succeed in professional hockey they are expected to demonstrate hockey "potential" no later than the Bantam level (thirteen or fourteen years).[7] It is at this *level that the criteria for player evaluation gradually undergo change. There is an increased emphasis on body contact ("hitting"); players must be continuously aggressive; physical size becomes a major factor in the selection of players ("a good big man is always better than a good small man"); there is the expectation that a boy "play with pain," and still greater emphasis is placed on winning the game. The ideals of sportsmanship and fair play are soon ignored.*[8]

The influence of the mass media, the selection of professionals as role models, and the formal teaching of coaches are major sources of learning in the socialization of the developing player. As boys progress from the Bantam to Midget ranks (fifteen to seventeen years) the cultural value of winning increases even more. Less attention is paid to the legitimate rules of success. At the Midget level teaching concentrates on the technical aspects of "playing the man" and the subtler methods of "hitting" the opposing player and "taking him out." It is perhaps no exaggeration to say that the implicit objective is to put the opposing star player out of action without doing him serious injury. Illegal tactics and "tricks" of the game are both encouraged and taught; rough play and physically aggressive performance are strongly encouraged, and sometimes players are taught the techniques of fighting. Minimal[9] consideration is given the formal normative rules of the game, and the conceptions of sportsmanship and fair play are forgotten. Evaluation of individual performances (whether deviant or not) is according to their contribution to the ultimate success of the team. Of course certain rule violations are normative, expected. Under such conditions playing the game according to the "spirit and letter of the law" seems meaningless.[10] *By the time boys reach the Midget and Junior professional levels dominant role expectations of the hockey player include toughness, aggressiveness, physical strength and* size, and the ability to endure pain.[11] Gradually the team is molded into a tough fighting unit prepared for violence whose primary objective is to win hockey games.[12]

Simultaneously, competition intensifies for selection to the Junior professional ranks, and the boys are made patently aware of the spartan criteria for advancement. The obligation to "produce," i.e., to perform in an unrelentingly, physically aggressive manner becomes normative, routine, and substandard performance is not tolerated. The sanctions of being "dropped" from the team or "benched" become a reality. As competition intensifies so does the structurally generated pressure in attempting to meet these difficult standards.

The major structural conditions which generate the amount and differential distribution of fighting and violent behavior among players in the league, i.e., at the Midget and Junior professional levels, comprise (a) the strong motivation of these players to advance to higher level teams (and thereby improve their opportunities for a professional hockey career),[13] (b) the considerable competition for a limited number of positions on Junior professional teams, and (c) the informal injunction to employ increasingly aggressive and rough means in the performance of their role. Because these boys are highly motivated to learn and incorporate the appropriate attitudes, sentiments and behavior of the role, they are thereby constrained to conform to the demands of the role they admire and wish others to identify them with. These attitudes and sentiments, and their role performance coincide with those groups that comprise their reference groups and with others to whom they look for encouragement and validity for their conduct. . . .

We can now ask the question, why is there much less fighting and physical aggression among players (aged eight to twelve) on the lower level teams? If we are correct the major variables that help account for fighting and violence among higher level teams should be less important to these youngsters.

As a career hockey has little real meaning for younger aged boys. Unlike older boys their futures do not yet require serious consideration nor decision making. Although they aspire to play hockey professionally their ambitions are "fantasy choices," rational considerations are not yet involved in their selections. They are not yet seriously oriented towards the Junior professional ranks and there is less competition for advancement.

At this age conflict between academic expectations and hockey obligations is minimal; school work is easier, examinations less important and hockey obligations less demanding. These boys are too young to be scouted and evaluated for their professional potential which eliminates another source of pressure. While they are strongly motivated to play Allstar hockey, conformity to role expectations does not as often require toughness, physical aggressiveness, nor courage. These are not yet major role obligations, which greatly reduces the amount and quality of violence in their performances. Youngsters receive little or no instruction in fighting, in fact fighting is strongly discouraged at the younger age levels. Although some illegal tactics are already institutionalized, these kids generally believe in the normative rules of the game and in the "official" virtues of sportsmanship and fair play. This is reflected in the formal practice of shaking hands with opposing players at the end of each game—and these youngsters believe that this practice is an important sign of sportsmanship. Finally, fighting and physical aggression accomplish little for these youngsters; it gets them a bad name; it interferes with their performance since it is not expected of them and it jeopardizes the good name and ideology of the league. Briefly, there are few structured sources of pressure towards fighting and violence; their training strongly discourages violence and there is little common motivation for this kind of conduct. Fighters are not rewarded at this level.

Functions of Institutionalized Physical Aggression Among Young Hockey Players

If deviance is not contained it always becomes a threat to the organization of the system in which it occurs. At the same time under certain conditions institutionalized deviance may contribute to the vitality and operation of the system. At the higher levels of Minor League Hockey physical aggression becomes a criterion according to which rewards are distributed to those who uphold its values and attitudes, and who conform to role obligations. The player whose role performance personifies highly desired professional values and attitudes, and who conforms to behavioral expectations will rank high in the scale of evaluation.

Again physical aggressiveness reflects the success of the socialization process, i.e., the professionalization of young players for Junior professional and higher professional ranks. Players who "have guts," who "never back down from a fight," who never "give up," and who are otherwise consistently aggressive are breathing examples of the success of the prevailing system and its values and definitions of the game.

Given the accumulation of pressure, strain and discontent from daily participation in the legitimate order of the system, e.g., practices, games, (playoffs), the spartan requirements of training, school obligations, and other formal and informal controls, a certain amount of deviance (physical aggression) which is not rigorously repressed may serve to release tension. This acts as a safety valve and helps drain some of the strain and discontent off the legitimate order. The tactics used by referees in handling fights suggest this. Combatants are permitted to "fight it out." This helps insure that they will not wish to renew hostilities. In such instances the function of the referees is to prevent the interference of others and thereby control the spread of violence.

The collective meanings and definitions of young hockey players are reflected in the norms, attitudes and practices which govern their work performance. The "official" rhetoric of the Minor Hockey League does not always coincide with what transpires among its members. Although the value system of the larger community likely subsumes the official objectives and ideals of Minor League Hockey, the everyday working values, attitudes and customs of the group coincide more closely with working-class values.

It was suggested that Allstar players who remain in Minor League Hockey come from the lower socioeconomic levels of the community. This facilitates their adaptation to role obligations and their preparation for the Junior professional ranks. Once they reach a certain level in Minor League Hockey, structural conditions influence many of these boys to pursue a professional hockey career.

The principal conditions that generate fighting and physical aggression among players on higher level teams are (a) the strong motivation of players to be selected for Junior professional ranks, (b) the intense competition for a limited number of positions on Junior professional teams, and (c) the informal obligation to employ increasing aggressive, sometimes violent means in the performance of their roles. . . .

REFERENCES

Loy, John W., Jr.: The study of sport and social mobility. In *Aspects of Contemporary Sport Sociology*, Gerald S. Kenyon (ed.). University of Wisconsin, The Athletic Institute, 1969.

Porter, John: *The Vertical Mosaic*. Ontario, University of Toronto Press, p. 165, 1965.

NOTES

1. Three methods were used to collect the data for this project. First, a portable tape recorder was used throughout one season to gather material in the dressing rooms of teams at all levels in the Minor Hockey League. This involved visiting teams in their dressing rooms before a game, between periods and after a game. Second, a series of partially structured interviews was conducted with players from the Minor and Junior professional leagues. Each interview lasted approximately 1 ½ hours. Junior professional players were paid five dollars per interview. Third, a questionnaire was designed and data were collected from all players enrolled in the Minor Hockey League.

2. In more than one instance the practice of shaking hands after the game had to be discontinued because of the regular outbreaks of violence among players.

3. The term professional is used since players on Junior A and B teams are paid for their services.

4. When seemingly distinct although interrelated groups create conflicting demands on their joint members, sometimes tiny albeit deviant efforts are made by one group to help alleviate the strain. In this case coaches and managers sometimes attempt to get high school examinations postponed or special conditions arranged for their players. The status of athletics is so high and its influence so pervasive in the high schools that independent of outside pressure players are often given special treatment, consideration and privileges by teachers. This helps players remain in school, play on the team, and also helps reduce strain. In any case

at this level few Allstar players are apt to sacrifice hockey for school obligations.

5. With the slowly increasing number of athletic scholarships a trickle of boys are able to play hockey while attending university. This provides another though longer route towards the professional ranks. One question is: to what extent does playing hockey subvert their desire to complete their education once in university? Is it the university dropout who pursues a professional hockey career? Any large increase in the number of players who proceed to the National Hockey League via the university route must ultimately mean a shorter career for them since they begin later, the National Hockey League schedule is getting longer, and the game has become more physically demanding.

6. It is generally agreed throughout the league that there is more physical aggression at the Midget and Junior professional levels than among the lower level teams.

7. Some boys develop more slowly than others and scouts and coaches are alert for "late starters."

8. This reflects the influence of the higher professional leagues. These criteria are used by professional scouts and mirror the skills, attitudes and values desired by professional teams.

9. So common is fighting and rough play that the role of "policeman" is common knowledge in the league and is employed by coaches. A "policeman" on a team is a player who is recognized as being especially tough and able to "handle himself." The "policeman" is sometimes used by coaches to "get" an opposing player who is especially rough or "dirty."

10. The coaches themselves are notorious for violating at least the "spirit of the law." The seemingly innumerable methods they employ to prolong the game or

otherwise interfere with the smooth conduct of the game in order to benefit their teams are hardly commendable, nor does it set a good example for youngsters.

11. This does not deny the considerable amount of body contact that occurs among the younger aged boys. Hard body contact is strongly encouraged at the very early stages of development throughout the league.

12. Coaches and managers of higher level teams pay lip service only to the value of education for their players. At game time hockey comes first. Players who opt for homework during examination time lose favor, and are sometimes "benched."

13. We have already noted that at this level boys will give greater consideration to pursuing hockey as a professional career.

HIGH FROM THE GAME: SPECTATORS AND THE SPECTACLE

INTRODUCTION

"Sport in America," reflected columnist James Reston, "plays a part in our national life that is probably more important than even the social scientists believe."[1] American males have more money, more leisure, and more education than ever before, yet they feel progressively alienated by whirling social, political, and economic events. They turn to sports as a temporary respite from an unsettling atmosphere of increasing economic dislocation, diminishing energy supplies, and challenges from various oppressed groups.

In part, sports are so popular because they represent an ethically simplistic world where good is defined as a high batting average. The moral idealism we associate with sports is predicated on the mistaken belief that athletics is one of the few areas of our national life uncontaminated by the erosion of standards. It is unthinkable, the public consciousness seems to convey, that front-page vices, political issues, prejudice, or injustice could corrupt the virginal corridors of the locker room.

The most obvious manifestations of the insatiable appetite of American men for sports are the yearly attendance figures for sporting events and the poll estimates of the number of television fans. Turnstiles in stadiums throughout the country are clicking at a fast rate. Approximately ten million spectators, for example, attend professional football games each year. The media has capitalized on the boundless male interest in sports to build a huge listening, reading, and viewing audience. A symbiosis has developed between sports and the mass media. Sports are used to promote newspaper sales, to sell advertising space, and to win lucrative contracts for television and radio time. In turn, the media help to sell spectator sports and attendant sports-related consumer products to the public.

161

The symbiotic relationship between sports and the mass media explains the large amount of broadcast time devoted to sports. Though economic matters have a more direct impact on our daily lives, the local broadcast time allocated to economic news nowhere approaches the time spent on sports. From 1963 to 1973, for example, televised sports programming increased by 100 per cent, and the three major networks televise over 1,200 hours of sports each year. Major sporting events, and not sport news, of course, attract the largest portion of the viewing and listening public. Some 75 million Americans viewed Superbowl VIII—thirty million more than the number who voted to elect Richard Nixon president of the United States.[2]

The widespread value consensus created by sports and the almost total dependence of the sports fan on the media for knowledge of the inner world of sport make it crucial that journalists reflect the athletic subculture accurately. Unfortunately, the picture of sports transmitted to the public through the media is shaped by organizational and business considerations. Objective reporting is seldom as important as the creation and maintenance of the political economy of both sports and the media. Moreover, sportswriters are key links in a communicative chain that promulgates patriarchal values through idealized representations of male prowess, competitive dedication, and ascetic excellence.

It is not without import that social scientists and a new breed of athlete, and *not* sportswriters, first made the public aware of sexism, racism, violence, and elitism in sports. Unlike many ex-athletes and social scientists, sportswriters are dependent upon those in powerful positions for daily access to sports figures. They are also responsible to their editors and publishers, who are not about to risk losing readers or advertisers by printing controversial articles.

The reaction to Jim Bouton's muckraking *Ball Four*[3] offers perhaps the best commentary on the protective posture of contemporary sports journalism. As "America's favorite pastime," baseball is most apt to be equated to the American ideal. In the words of political analyst David Halberstam, "If you look up and find baseball virtuous, you are apt to find the country virtuous."[4] Given the provincialism of baseball writers, it is not surprising that Bouton's exposé of baseball's backstage world incurred the greatest wrath of all the militant writings about sport. Dick Young of the *New York Daily News* led the attack against Bouton for publishing his "inside" view of baseball, calling him a "social leper." Young was not concerned about the social relevance of Bouton's descriptions of the racial and sexual tensions within the locker rooms. What bothered him and other gatekeepers in the media was that Bouton had "violated the sanctity of the clubhouse."

The unholy triad of sports, politics, and journalism has created a dangerous ethical value system that distorts the fans' experience of sport itself, shapes their standards of reality, and influences their perceptions of wider social and political processes. The influence and ideology of the institutional nexus of mass spectator sports, dubbed the "Sportsworld" by Robert Lipsyte, cut across age lines as well as educational and socioeconomic barriers. Through this "Sportsworld", industry, the military, the government, and the press can manipulate the passions of Americans and "socialize us for work or war or depression."[5] The sportsmedia complex also performs two additional social functions of critical concern within the analytic framework of this anthology. It provides an ideology for maintaining the existing system of sex stratification in America, and it reinforces traditionally masculine value systems.

Sports, not religion, have become the opiate of American males, and at the same time football has displaced baseball as America's number-one spectator sport. Why is this so? One reason is the vicarious reassurance men experience through their identification with the game. Its brutal, hard-driving aspects, its accentuation of physical strength and angry struggle, give men a renewed sense of masculine pride that is hard to maintain in a society which otherwise renders them powerless and alienated.

This theme is expanded by Dr. Arnold R. Beisser, a psychiatrist who examines the connection between sport's rising importance to the American male and his waning dominance over women in the machine age. Beisser finds that as technological changes decrease the importance of physical strength in the world of work, sport becomes a last bastion of males against the female onslaught in other sectors of society.

James Wright's "Autumn Begins in Martins Ferry, Ohio," provides a poetic insight into the role played by sports in male spectator's lives. Wright describes life in an industrial town where fathers attempt to fulfill their lost dreams and relive past lives through the athletic feats of their sons. For the worker whose dreams of success have blown away like the smoke that spews from factory stacks, the beginning of every football season represents an escape and a renewed hope for the future. With metaphorical insight, Wright depicts what remains the central drama of patriarchal history—the destiny of sons to commit the sins of their fathers.

A fear of homosexuality exists in any social order that systematically subjugates women and inhibits or distorts emotional relationships between men.[6] In "The Changing Role of Homoerotic Fantasy in Spectator Sport," Edgar Z. Friedenberg examines the hypothesis that the popularity of spectator sports and the "atmosphere" that pervades them is strongly influenced by the prevalence and intensity of homoerotic attitudes in the social substrata that support each sport. He speculates that a decline of the mania for spectator sports will occur only in conjunction with a dissipation of homophobic feelings in society.

A male's view of sport is necessarily narrow, given the important void it fills in his daily life. Women, however, view sport mainly as a form of play. As a result, the female spectator; sportswriter Larry Merchant finds, is attuned to subtle nuances of sports that are missed by most men. Unlike their male counterparts, female spectators are not jaundiced by the male desire to know the strategy of the game, nor are they callous to the violence that takes away from the aesthetic beauty of athletic competition.

FOOTNOTES

1. Quoted in Joseph Durso, *The All American Dollar: The Big Business of Sports* (Boston: Houghton Mifflin, 1971), p. xiv.
2. William Johnson, *Super Spectator and the Electric Lilliputians* (Boston: Little, Brown, 1971), chap. 1; Ross Runfola, "Sport and the Mass Media: The Myth of Objective Transferral," paper presented at the Fourth Annual Meeting of the Popular Cultural Association, Milwaukee, Wisc., (May 2–4, 1974).
3. (New York: Dell, 1970).
4. David Halberstam, "American Note: Baseball and the National Mythology," *Harpers* (September 1970), pp. 22–25.
5. Robert Lipsyte, "Sportsworld," *New York Times Magazine* (Oct. 5, 1975), p. 111.
6. Phyllis Chesler, *About Men* (New York: Simon & Schuster, 1978).

THE AMERICAN SEASONAL MASCULINITY RITES

ARNOLD BEISSER

Not all of the characteristics which are attributed to being male or female are to the same degree biologically determined. Some, considered to be basic to masculinity or femininity, are determined by the culture in which one lives rather than by obvious physical differences. In our culture athletics are considered the most masculine of activities. Let us turn now to a consideration of what part sexual orientation plays in the intense interest in sports in America.

Before puberty, boys can be distinguished from girls mainly on the basis of primary sexual characteristics. When puberty is reached, biological distinctions become more apparent. At that time, with the differences in hormonal balance, the distinct secondary sexual characteristics begin to develop. Boys begin to have hair on their faces, and their bodies and become more muscular and angular. Girls become more curvaceous and develop breasts. Primary and secondary characteristics are predictable and universal: girls' hips broaden; boys' shoulders grow wider.

Beyond these physical characteristics are others which are largely, if not exclusively, determined by the society in which one lives. These can be termed tertiary characteristics and are transmitted from generation to generation by the examples of the men and women in the culture. To suggest, as Margaret Mead does, that the nature of maleness and femaleness, outside the physical characteristics, is culturally determined, may be an extreme point of view. For differences must develop just from living in a male body which has greater physical strength compared to living in a

---

Excerpted from Arnold R. Beisser, *The Madness in Sports* (New York: Appleton-Century-Crofts, 1967), chap. 16, pp. 214–25.

female body which experiences menstruation and preg-nancy. Nevertheless, it is true that many of the male or fe-male characteristics which are taken for granted in our so-ciety are determined by social custom rather than genetics. For example, up to very recently in this country, boys wore short hair and girls wore long hair, but in other parts of the world the reverse is true. Similarly, an American boy would hide in shame if he had to wear a skirt, but in Greece it is the attire worn by a particularly virile and cou-rageous group of soldiers. . . .

Tertiary sexual characteristics, such as dominance, mannerisms, dress, and speech, are often considered un-alterable, yet studies of different cultures reveal quite dif-ferent ideas about what constitutes male and female be-havior. Each culture assumes that it "knows" how a man or woman should act. The folklore is justified by a self-fulfilling prophecy, as parents transmit to children their cul-tural expectations.

To be considered feminine in Victorian society women had to be frail, passive, and the potential victims of aggres-sive, lecherous males. Yet, according to the stories of Greek mythology, women were as urgently sexed as men. In our own age primitive tribes differ grossly in what we consider basic masculinity and femininity. Among the Arapesh tribes of New Guinea, for example, studies in the early twentieth century found that men as well as women showed such characteristics as concern, giving, protective-ness, which we in America associate with mothering. Their neighbors, the Mundugumor, living only a short distance away, had quite opposite attitudes, with both men and women being strong, tough, and aggressive, like the ideal-ized pioneer male in the United States.

Another tribe in New Guinea, the Tchambuli, showed a reversal of conceptions about masculinity-femininity in another way. The male job was head-hunting, war mak-

ing, and war preparation. To carry out their plans the men congregated daily in the "men's house." The women on the other hand were charged with all of the economic responsibilities in the village, such as fishing, food preparation, pottery, basket weaving. When the British banned head-hunting and imposed a peace upon these people, the men became essentially unemployed, while the women continued their traditional activities. These women were temperamentally stable, secure, and cooperative with others, but the men, having lost their important function, became insecure, capricious, and aesthetic. Although men could no longer make war, the preparation rituals were continued. Their interest in the cosmetic arts and in creating suitable costumes, previously an important part of war, was now used instead to make themselves sexually attractive in competing through charm for the favors of the "important sex," the women. The women were tolerant of their men whom they viewed as gossipy, self-centered playthings.

Among the Manus it is the father who is endowed with what in America are considered maternal characteristics. While the women are occupied with the economy and have little time for children, the father cares for and raises them. When Dr. Mead brought dolls to the children of the Manus, she found that it was the boys who eagerly played with them, while the girls were disinterested. The boys in their play were emulating their fathers' activities.

Largely, then, the tertiary sexual characteristics of people, the ones which are most visible and apparent, are socially determined and subject to considerable change from one generation to another and from one culture to another. Sometimes, however, the roles assigned to certain members of a society are intolerable, and in order for such a society to survive and maintain stability there have to be safety valves through which those who are placed in ambiguous or deprecated positions can gain some satisfaction or status.

The Iatmul are a tribe of New Guinea natives who had such a culture. The men despised women, considered them unimportant, worthless, almost subhuman, allocating to them only the most menial and routine of tasks. Men, in contrast, were considered to be the "real human beings," strong, brave, and courageous; they, too, were head-hunters. The men were expected to be proud, the women self-effacing. Everything in this culture was either all black or all white, all good or all bad. There were no shades of gray. To be a man was to approach perfection; women epitomized all that was to be avoided. If a man showed the slightest feminine interests or characteristics, he was con-sidered to be sliding toward the subhuman. Such rigid standards of human behavior placed each man in constant jeopardy of losing his humanity. This dichotomy was hard on the women, but it was equally difficult for the men. Ad-justment in the Iatmul society was precarious: men walked a tightrope and women were scorned.

A society like the Iatmul has doubtful durability, for the tensions and resentment engendered are at an explosive pitch. This tribe's "safety valve" was the ceremony of Naven, an annual occasion in which bitterness and ten-sions were discharged in a convulsive reversal of the year's pressures. Naven was a ceremony of cultural transvestism, during which men and women exchanged not only their clothes but also their roles. Boys who had been rigorously taught the shamefulness of femininity were now contemp-tuously called "wife" by their maternal uncles. They were bullied in the same way that women had been bullied throughout the year. The women, during Naven, were given a vacation from their despised roles and identified themselves dramatically as men, wearing their clothes and assuming their actions, strutting and swaggering. They could enter the "men's house" and could even beat certain designated men. They could engage in a theatrical simula-tion of the war games that men played. The men, who had spent the year taking elaborate ritualized precautions to avoid anything feminine could relax during the ceremony. It was a great relief actually to assume, in deliberate fashion, the female role.

By the end of the ceremony the tensions and resentments accumulated during the year were dissipated. The women felt better about their position in the community and the men admired the women for having been able to assume the masculine position. For a short time the women had become human and the men could love them. Over the next year the tensions built up again and hatred pervaded community life until the next Naven.

The Naven ceremony of the Iatmul is not unique, for other cultures have similar festivals. Rome's ancient feast of Saturnalia served a related function in discharging the year's accumulated tensions between masters and slaves. In this ceremony, slaves were waited upon by their masters and enjoyed all the privileges which they were denied during the year. It is easy to understand the necessity for such rites and their vital function in preserving a culture. Beyond a certain point, tensions and resentment would destroy any community life.

The Iatmul looked forward throughout the year to their ceremony of Naven. The Romans, both slaves and masters, eagerly awaited the festival of Saturnalia, In fact, in these cultures and others with similar rites, the populace lived from festival to festival. These were the most important events in their lives. Similarly Americans, particularly many American males, mark time by their own seasonal rites: football season, basketball season, baseball season, and so on. Many men live from one sports season to the next, with sports representing the most vital part of their lives.

Iatmul men and women were in a precarious psychological position as a result of the extreme demands which their culture placed upon them. The Naven rite offered an opportunity for the expression of strong feelings which had to be disowned throughout the year preceding the ceremony. For the women it was denial of self-assertion and aggression; for the men it was denial of passivity, with no opportunities for relaxation of their facade of super-strength. Naven saved the Iatmul people from the otherwise impossible demands of their culture and thereby saved the culture from extinction.

American men, as we have seen, are also on shaky cultural ground. Their position is precarious as a result of the contradictions in their lives. To an ever-increasing degree, American male children early in their lives have close physical and emotional experiences with their fathers. Fathers share almost equally with mothers in the maternal activities: feeding, bathing, cuddling, and comforting, which were once the exclusive domain of the American female. American parents are apt to take turns in getting up with the baby when he cries at night. When either parent has a "night out" the other serves as baby sitter. If the egalitarianism is disrupted it is likely for bitterness to develop.

"Togetherness" has largely meant the diminution of the uniqueness of the female position as well as the male position in the family. Father is no longer the ultimate authority; he has become a "pal"; he is now not a teacher but a co-learner. He has an equal, but not a greater voice in the collective activities of the household than have the children and his wife. The wife, who may have a job outside the home and may make as much as or even more money than her husband, quite naturally expects him to share the housecleaning, dishwashing, and caring for the children. The roles are diffused and the differences between male and female, between adult and child are diminished.

Like the Tchambuli, American men have had a

change in status. The Tchambuli men lost their principal function, head hunting; American men have had to share with their wives their economic productivity as bread winners. Tchambuli men became superfluous; the authority and uniqueness of the American man has diminished. Previously, the main way men were superior to women was in their physical strength. Now, development of machines has caused male strength to be less important, almost obsolete. Machines are stronger than men, and the sexes are equally competent in running most machines. Dexterity has become more important than power, and women are at least as competent as men in this respect. The serious consequence is, that in their work, the new breed of factory and office workers are essentially neuter in gender.

While these changes in technology and in the family have taken place, the cultural expectations of masculinity have remained fixed as they were in pioneer days. Physical strength and agility were the qualities by which a man was measured, for then only the strong were able to survive. Obviously, such values are more appropriate to the frontier than to the office. Now, in order to fit this already obsolete image, men and· boys must engage in artificial, nonproductive displays of strength.

As the real demands for what was considered traditional male strength have decreased, the expectation of shows of strength has grown. Parents have a special concern that their boys are not aggressively masculine enough. Mothers are more apt to be concerned about passive, compliant behavior in male children than about their destructiveness. Often they are even relieved by, and subtly encourage, overt displays of aggression, for in that way, they are reassured that their sons are not "sissies." This is quite different from the concept of several decades ago that the quiet child was the "good" child.

As fathers and sons have grown closer together, an obsessive cultural concern with homosexuality has grown. In a counter move to avoid such taint, as already noted, children are pushed earlier and earlier into heterosexual relationships. The tragedy of this parental encouragement is that it is self-defeating, since the child in latency has other more important business to learn than sex appeal. In addition, his premature explorations in heterosexuality promote a sense of inadequacy within him as he recognizes his inability to perform as expected. This inadequacy, in turn, is interpreted as the "taint" and the parental efforts and encouragement towards aggression and heterosexuality are redoubled, the situation becoming a vicious circle.

Just as Naven helps to relieve the Iatmul tensions, American sports have a similar function. The first man outside the home that a boy encounters is usually a coach. In school he meets a series of female teachers who are the purveyors of morality, knowledge, and competence. The coach is not only a man among men but, more important, a man among women teachers. Boys try to model themselves after the coach and find security in imitating him. Their roles are clearer on the diamond than in the classroom, for it is on the athletic field in those seasonal masculinity rites that males become the kind of men their grandfathers were and their mothers want them to be. Strength is king; men are separated from boys, and boys, in turn, from girls. In the best tradition of the frontier, an athlete overpowers his opponent, and the sexual roles are re-established to conform with the expectancies of the culture. Male and female are relieved of their role discrepancy just as they are following the Naven ceremony. Fortunately, this can be accomplished, not only by participation, but by observation as a spectator who identifies with the players. They can both then return to the office and the home with renewed respect for the uniqueness of the sexes and the re-establishment of their own identities, until the distinction gradually diminishes and another masculinity rite is necessary.

In a subtle way, these supermasculine "frontier rites" also allow for the expression of warmth and closeness among men which society compels them to disown. In sports, players huddle together; they caress, pat "fannies," shout affectionate phrases, and engage in activities which are scorned elsewhere but are condoned in sports. In a recent heavyweight boxing match, the victor was embraced and kissed by his manager before several thousand fans in the sports arena and perhaps several million more on television. Such behavior anywhere but in the context of sports would be highly suspect. But here, with full cultural approval and without detracting from the supermasculine atmosphere, men can satisfy either physically or vicariously their needs for close male companionship like that which they experienced in childhood. In this context, physical contact, either aggressive or friendly, is applauded rather than condemned, and in the frenzy of American sports, males are purged of their femininity, and at the same time provided with an outlet for close male contact.

Among the Iatmul, Naven takes place annually, and a single festival appears to take care of a year's accumulated tensions between the sexes. Fifty years ago a single sports season, namely baseball, sufficed for Americans. Today each season of the year is occupied with a different sport. Sport seasons now fuse with one another into a continuous succession of ceremonial demonstrations. The fall rite, football, now overlaps with the spring rite of baseball and track. The vacant moments are filled with transitional rites: basketball, hockey, tennis, and golf, to mention a few.

Although the potential for wild celebration is always present, the pitch of these ceremonies is somewhat lower than the yearly Naven in New Guinea. This is consistent with the lower pitch of all activities in our sophisticated country. Very little can be termed a "special event," since we are bombarded daily with the spectacular and the overwhelming. Just as the differences between sexes have diminished, the difference between holiday and weekday has also. Activities converge into a more integrated (for the hopeful) or amorphous (for the pessimistic) mass of ongoing activities. The Fourth of July, once fraught with danger and excitement, is now closely controlled and tame. Similarly, other holidays such as Armistice Day, Flag Day, St. Patrick's Day have lost their appeal except to the most enthusiastic. Since the range of the pitch is lower, the exposure time must be increased. Thus, sports go on continuously from the beginning to the end of the year.

Among primitives, the transition from boyhood to manhood is accomplished in a single, brief ceremony—the puberty rite. A symbolic gesture, such as circumcision or knocking out a tooth, bears witness to the cliché, "Today I am a man." For American men the transition is quite different. Puberty, the time of traditional manhood when the secondary sexual characteristics appear, is now only the signal for the prolonged period of suspension between boyhood and manhood called adolescence. Biologically and sexually, manhood has been reached, but the technical complexity of our society requires an extension of many years of education and preparation before the productive work of life can begin. The preparation extends temporally toward mandatory early retirement, which advances from the other side, allowing only a relatively brief period for the adult work career.

The adolescent is thus in a state of moratorium, suspended in his choices of occupation and a wife, prohibited from sexual activity, prevented from making any firm commitment. No true idenity can be achieved in the face of such a moratorium. In the medical profession this problem *is well exemplified. A boy who decides that he wants to be a doctor must make this decision at least a score of years before his goal is achieved. If, for example, he wishes to be surgeon he may not complete his training until he is past thirty. Failure at any stage of this process would force him to seek a new occupation and a new direction for his life. With the endless series of what can be likened to initiation rites—high school, college for four years, medical school for four years, residency—it is as senescence approaches that the moratorium is over and the man can say with some degree of finality, "I have an identity, I am a doctor."*

Because of the nature of this moratorium, adolescence is a period of turmoil. Rebellion and confusion can be expected from the man who has not yet found a place for himself, who is suspended, seemingly for an infinite length of time, between his family of origin and his family of procreation.

But as we have seen, a culture with contradictions and ambiguities, if it is to survive, must have some way of relieving and integrating its tensions. Sports form an elongated bridge across childhood, adolescence, and adulthood for American males. Although the adolescent boy may have to suspend decision and commitment on most of his affairs until many years hence, he can enter athletics with full exuberance and play and work at sports with a dedication which satisfies his personality and his society. . . .

In sports, male and female are placed in their historical biological roles. In sports, strength and speed do count, for they determine the winner. As in premechanized combat, women can never be more than second place to men in sports. They can cheer their men on, but a quick review of the record books comparing achievements in sports of men and women confirms the distinctness of the sexes here.

It is small wonder that the American male has a strong

affinity for sports. He has learned that this is one area where there is no doubt about sexual differences and where his biology is not obsolete. Athletics help assure his difference from women in a world where his functions have come to resemble theirs.

AUTUMN BEGINS IN MARTINS FERRY, OHIO

JAMES WRIGHT

In the Shreve High football stadium,
I think of Polacks nursing long beers in Tiltonsville,
And gray faces of Negroes in the blast furnace at Benwood,
And the ruptured night watchman of Wheeling Steel,
Dreaming of heroes.

All the proud fathers are ashamed to go home.
Their women cluck like starved pullets,
Dying for love.

Therefore,
Their sons grow suicidally beautiful
At the beginning of October,
And gallop terribly against each other's bodies.

THE CHANGING ROLE OF HOMOEROTIC FANTASY IN SPECTATOR SPORTS

EDGAR Z. FRIEDENBERG

About 20 years ago as I recall, I was stopped by an excited bystander as I came out of the old Madison Square Garden

---

Edgar Z. Friedenberg, Professor of Education at Dalhousie University in Halifax, Canada, though not himself notably athletic, has long regarded the sporting scene with the eyes of an ardent amateur.

after watching the final evening of a National Invitational Basketball Tournament. I was still pretty excited myself; it had been a glorious, triple-decker event. A generation ago the best college teams were more graceful than professional ball teams; and, of course, younger. College students were still a relatively privileged lot and often looked it; teams included a smaller proportion of players who appeared to have overcome the disadvantages of early malnutrition by ruthless determination and grit. The teams that had been playing in this tournament were skillful, but not sheer technicians like the Celtics and the Knicks who, except for emotional players like my favorite, Tom Heinsohn, played less expressively though better than college teams.

The NIT, coming at the end of a long, dark winter, irradiated my life. I could sustain myself on it photosynthetically in my closet for months afterward. As expected, this had been a great year. Tickets had been hard to come by, and the man who stopped me had evidently been unable to get one. Either that, or he had simply bet money on the game with no interest in attending it.

"Hey," he demanded, "what was the score?"

I stared at him in amazement. It had not occurred to me to retain the information he sought, and a lofty rebuke like "I don't come here to score, fella;—it would be ridiculous" would, I felt, just have annoyed him. So I gave him two numbers that seemed vaguely correct to me; if they were wrong, he would find out soon enough, especially if he tried to collect on them.

I also recall that, at the time, I had the grace to see this encounter as comical, a grace I no longer so fully possess. At that time I thought the joke was on me—the only Secret Sharer in the house, presumably. It was years before I came to believe that my pleasure in the game was at least as legitimate as that of the other people watching it.

Doubtful as I was of my right to get off on athletic

events—in our society so nearly sacred—and reluctant as I then would have been to claim that right publicly, I was fully aware of two aspects of my feeling and interest that could not easily be disparaged. I had come to know more about basketball and, especially, track than most aficionados who could give more respectable reasons for their interest but who didn't really pay as much attention to what the young men were doing. That was one thing. The other was my absolute certainty that I never had thought, and never could think, of the young men I found attractive in the way that heterosexual convention prescribes for men watching women in socially approved places of display like cabarets and chorus lines: as a nice "piece" or a "dish" put before me in deference to my legitimate and socially sanctioned rapacity. Sentimental I certainly was, and knew it; but never impersonal or, God knows, comtemptuous. Indeed, as many subsequent accounts of the plight of athletes in the American sporting industry have revealed, I felt far more affection and respect for these strangers than their coaches would ever have allowed them to feel for themselves.

So, as I now know, I had a right to be there; and not merely on grounds of civil liberty. I had a right to be there because I got more out of the NIT and the NCAA than a fan who was primarily interested in victory. Eros is a central figure at Dionysian revels, but he is equally at home in the temple of Apollo, where he sharpens the eye and helps the observer concentrate and care and get a better feel for what is taking place. There is a much deeper issue involved here than that of sexual preference or orientation. You don't have to be gay to dig basketball or the field events at a track meet, though it certainly helps, especially as far as the latter, which lack the superficial excitement of simultaneous competition and tend to be slow-paced as spectacles, are concerned. But the presence of a strong and pervasive erotic strain in the human response to athletic spectacles is too well established by history and by art to be questioned at this time. Indeed, we would now be quite properly skeptical that any culture could institutionalize any form of public spectacle that had no strong and firm erotic basis. If the people don't get off on it, they won't come.

This is not basically a matter of the direction of erotic interest so much as of its depth and quality. There is, after all, no logical reason why either the spectators or the athletes at sporting events should be preponderantly male; that, in itself, is a datum worth examining. Rock concerts, in contrast, attract a very mixed audience, no element of which feels obliged to dampen or disguise its erotic response though the performers remain primarily, if sometimes ambiguously, male. Sporting events, too, are highly emotional occasions. Public display of emotions is encouraged there as in no other ritual of straight culture. It is apathy and boredom that are considered bad form; if the game is that bad, you're expected to get mad and boo. Fans are expected to be enthusiastic in the literal sense of the word: possessed by gods they identify with.

This audience response, however, is traditionally structured, stereotyped—even ritualized. Boundaries are supposed to be maintained and limits respected. The spectators' role in events is as distinct from that of the athletes as that of the crowd in St. Peter's Square is from that of the Pope. They may not, as individuals, impose on players as individuals without risking being labeled "jocksniffers," an ugly and derisive term that implies clearly enough that a sniff is as much as they can ever hope to get and more than they had better admit they want. The possibility of a genuine encounter is not provided for.

When boundaries are breached, and there is a genuine encounter, the event is seen as very dangerous: there has been a breakdown of identity, and that way madness is presumed to lie. In soccer and hockey, both macho sports that generate a high level of tension, boundary maintenance has deteriorated to the point that fights now break out occasionally between players and fans. What is most notable about these fights is that they arouse such disproportionate anxiety in the authorities. In Toronto, players have been brought back from the United States to face criminal prosecution for assault. The media solemnly report these incidents as evidence of the growing brutality and declining civility of urban life, though a plethora of more convincing evidence is available and the risk of being attacked by an infuriated player is far too small to be worth considering as a reason either for avoiding a game or for attending it.

Audiences at rock festivals provide an illuminating contrast, though the vogue of these events has passed, our society having proved inhospitable to them for a variety of reasons more political, perhaps, than psychological. At rock festivals, boundaries were not stressed; when they had to be established and maintained the bands usually mumbled an apology for being so uptight. Spectators were supposed to keep off the platform during the actual performance—though they often swarmed up there anyway—and to keep their hands off the expensive equipment. But they were also expected to feel that they were part of the event: this is part of the mystique that has clung to rock since before Woodstock, since the 1967 Monterey festival, the crawdaddy of them all. Rock concerts have unisex audiences but primarily male performers. The successful women performers are all vocal soloists; the intruments, apparently, really are phallic symbols and, as such, jealously guarded. Male dominance and doubtless male chauvinism are characteristics of the world of rock as well as the world of sport. But the audience response is utterly different. The audiences for team sports are overwhelmingly male; the women who do attend usually accompany a man and express their interest in the same conventional terms men find appropriate. There are exceptions; some of the younger and handsomer athletes have teenage fan clubs whose members act like groupies. But generally women spectators are not expected to express the kind of candidly sexual reaction to athletes that they may show male actors in other media. To do so would spoil their escorts' pleasure by arousing a twinge of jealousy, either of the admired athlete or of his female companion.

Rock, in contrast to sports, is polymorphously perverse; "you pays your money and you takes your choice." At concerts, being laid back, you could let it all hang out. There were few boundaries to maintain—fewer, indeed, than health and decency sometimes required. No fantasies were tabu, but fantasy did not always suffice. Clinicians may call it "acting out"; but the observable fact is that, at rock festivals, people fucked and, at Altamont, people slew, whatever they may have been feeling or thinking, if anything.

Of course, people get killed playing football, too. But it doesn't occasion outrage or threaten society in the same way. As public celebrations, sporting events and rock concerts reflect opposite ends of the axis of emotional repression. A refusal to deal in or with repression finally doomed the rock festival as a social form, partly through the ungovernable and self-righteous rage, the harassment and litigation, they evoked from conservative elements of the community. But a more fundamental reason for the decline lay in the self-destructiveness of many of the rock fans themselves. For repression, however one may dislike it, is the backbone of every civilization, however unsatisfactory.

And any young American who has been socialized enough to have acquired a hi-fi system and a set of the albums of The Mothers of Invention has surely already become a fairly hard case as far as repression is concerned. His efforts to become authentic are inauthentic in themselves; he doesn't really have a feel for what he is doing, which makes him silly and sometimes dangerous. As the Mothers themselves tell us, over and over but never enough, nothing is more distressingly phony than a phony hippie.

If every civilization depends on repression to keep itself going and relatively intact, such social forms as rock festivals must decline after serving their essential function of liberating from social structures that have grown unbearably imposing at least those people who have a little too much class, status, and power to have to suffer in silence. Rock, at its core, was always a bourgeois force, and always on the fighting side of Merle Haggard and the deerhunters; but it certainly provided, and still provides, a joyful and aggressive answer to country and western's cheerless insistence that the destiny of mankind is to be eternally screwed and get no pleasure from it (though for most of mankind this has always been true enough, which is why country and western music has its masterpieces). Such relief, whether provided by rock festivals, Dionysian orgies, or Mardi Gras makes society more stable; but it is temporary. The return of the repressed is swiftly followed by the return of repression, often stronger than before.

Sporting events operate differently. They channel feeling and awareness as cleverly as turbines, making their force the immediate instrument of further repression — psychological and, ultimately, political. They afford no real relief. The machinery runs on unacknowledged sexual tension — sometimes literally. Old-fashioned coaches used to, and perhaps still do, order their players to refrain from any sexual activity for days before a big game in order to conserve their strength. The wives of married players are not consulted about this remarkable thermodynamic conceit.

Repression is the central social function of spectator sport. Rock festivals contribute to social order by what Herbert Marcuse calls repressive desublimation—that is, by encouraging people to express their emotions and drain off their energies in activities that, despite their revolutionary pretentions, are actually self-centered and strongly supportive of the established socioeconomic system, so that apathy increases as fast as or faster than awareness. But spectator sports, though they arouse intense emotion, surround its expression with so much anxiety and such stereotypical constraints that it can be directed only into approved and conventional channels: like competition, or school or national spirit. Emotion that is stimulus-bound in this way cannot heighten awareness or respond selectively to other people as individuals rather than as teammates, buddies, or good ol' boys.

I wish to be very careful to avoid being misunderstood as oversimplifying the central issue here. I am not arguing that the emotional climate of athletic events is distorted by repressed homoerotic feeling, though this is indeed usually true. But this is far less important than the fact that sport has become institutionalized as not just homophobic but hostile to all spontaneous feeling. As a gay observer I am naturally struck by the sadness and waste of such severe and pervasive self-imposed emotional starvation in the midst of alluring plenty; but that is my problem and I can live with it. It is not, however, a simple problem when translated into broader social terms. It cannot be attacked effectively by calling for affirmative action to remedy the effects of earlier deprivation and provide a measure of equality of opportunity. For women, too, are excluded from any genuine or significant role in spectator athletic events and relegated, if they are present at all, to the peripheral and stereotypical position of booster, cheerleader, or pom-pom person. For a recent account of the determination with which the athletic establishment resists simply accepting women as competent colleagues and diverse human beings, responding to them as individuals with a variety of qualities including erotic ones, you need only read Roger Angell's dispassionate and probing account of the experiences of women sportswriters in the April 9, 1979 issue of The New Yorker. They are subjected to insulting innuendos by males who treat them as voyeuses, and who are unwilling or unable to grasp the simple fact that a reporter requires access to the event to be reported regardless of her sexual orientation. Litigation under antidiscrimination legislation has opened some doors and will open more. But the fact that such a struggle should even be necessary is remarkable in itself. Such big boys, to be so bashful, when a bash is all they seem to want to talk about when they're alone together, as they choose to be.

The citadel of maleness, once breached, may yield only emotional sterility. Macho stereotypes do not, of course, tell us what men are really like; but they provide an influential model that leaves something to be desired. Something, and doubtless, some body; but someone, some person? Loving a macho male is a fruitless exercise, for the essence of the macho posture is an utter disbelief in one's own lovability and right to be loved. If a man believes that gay men are contemptible, and women are inferior, precisely because they love people like him, his opportunities for friendly intercourse would seem pretty limited, and his prospects for satisfaction in life sharply reduced.

Some men have, indeed, been made so malevolent by being ridiculed or punished whenever, as boys, they showed any feeling or need for affection that they do scorn broads and hate faggots as much as they say they do. For most men, though, these declarations serve a quasi-declamatory function as ways of swearing allegiance to the male pack. They like to be loved and, given a little privacy, they might even like to be taught how to love themselves, in both senses of the phrase; they may even know how already, as long as they don't have to show it in public. This, indeed, is the tragic paradox: that one of the most compelling and universal forms of dramatic display known to man—the athletic spectacle—which seems clearly designed to display human strength, vigor, and ardor, should so systematically and consistently find itself crippled and transformed by anxiety into a competitive and dehumanizing assertion of individual male supremacy. No beauty is acknowledged, except that of technique; a beautiful play is still recognized, but not a beautiful player or team. Women, who cannot be expected to see things quite this way, are given no role in the spectacle; their events, when included at all, are separate and unequal and seem to have achieved artificial prominence in recent years in response to political and ideological pressure. Male officials and athletes become awkward when faced with female colleagues; they're athletes, so you can't attack them with whistles and wolf-calls during the event; but they're women, so you can't take them seriously or put them on the same team with men. Women, when present, are either segregated or treated as neutral particles, nonparticipants, like neutrons among the charged particles in a magnetic field, that obey rules of their own.

The conventions of sport thus deal with heterosexual tensions by acting as if women were not there, though the persistence of repression becomes obvious enough in the anger that is released upon women who insist on making their presence known and felt. But homosexual tensions cannot be as neatly set aside; the bodies are there and, lurking within them, the ever-present threat of hearts and minds. There is, in my view, no significant difference in the intensity of repression directed against heterosexual and homosexual feeling in the sporting arena. But the young men arouse feelings because, like Mount Everest, they are there; they cannot, in the circumstances, be banished; their bodies are indispensable to the event.

Homoerotic tension is therefore a relatively constant component in athletic events; and the ways it is usually dealt with are useful indices of the level of erotic repressiveness operating in the society at large. Until the 1920s—the jazz era, if you will, and the time that psychoanalysis emerged into popular consciousness, introducing the concept of repression as a problem—there were no sports in which the body could be candidly displayed, not even swimming. The American national sport, baseball, seemed the essence of nineteenth-century propriety. The game was slow-paced, and the players voluminously garbed; body-contact played no part in it. Such eroticism as it aroused was mostly oral; baseball fans chant at players in a peculiar tone that sounds like the echolalia of small children, at ease in the bath. But the players don't touch one another except, rarely and symbolically, with the captured ball—and that touch is fatal, it causes sudden death. Touch isn't even an issue in baseball; nor, across the Atlantic, in cricket, a sport about which much the same observations can be made. The cricket bat, however, did become an instrument for bodily contact in the friendlier beatings that older boys used to inflict on younger ones in British public schools; when real hostility was intended, they used a cane. American society, at any given time, is usually more direct and less repressed than British Society. People here are sometimes attacked with a baseball bat, but never, to my knowledge, as an act of love.

One of the most disgusting, as well as revealing, aspects of our culture is the way in which it defines behaviour as acceptable if it is unmistakeably and officially hostile but indecent if it is playful or loving. A schoolteacher who is caught slapping a boy's bottom is a felon if his intent is affectionate; if he is merely trying to hurt the child in the course of his official duties as he defines them, he enjoys the protection of a U. S. Supreme Court verdict.

In sport, something similar seems to have happened in the case of boxing, the first sport to abandon the tank-top shirt (boxers did wear these in the nineteenth century) and expose the male body above the waist. There is almost a maximum of body contact in boxing, and not all of it is aggressive. A clinch is the closest, sweatiest embrace young men in our culture are ever permitted—however briefly—to enjoy. What makes this acceptable to the audience is the formal context of violent, though regulated, hostility; they can't be loving each other, look at them. Boxing shorts are baggier than those worn in any other sport.

Assuming my general hypothesis, one would expect that as sexual repression changed in intensity throughout society with the passage of time there would be corresponding developments in spectator sports. The rise of basketball, I would suggest, illustrates just such a development. A less uptight society is ready for a thinly clad sport and the advantages in speed and mobility it affords. One might almost say that basketball, with its sudden shifts in fortune and enormous but unstable scores, mirrors the attractions of a dynamic economy. It reflects the busyness and ethos of twentieth-century commercial life uniquely in being the only sport in which it is considered legitimate to break the rules—and accept the penalty, like businessmen bribing third-world government officials—for the sake of the ensuing real advantage; as when a player commits a foul in order to gain possession of the ball late in the game. But basketball is also peculiar, and I think revealing, in its regulations concerning body contact. In other team sports it

simply has no place, as in baseball and cricket; or it is legitimate unless it is used to inflict deliberate injury, as in the
various forms of football and in hockey. But in basketball
body contact is ritually avoided and penalized; violations of
the ritual, and the exaction of the penalties thus incurred,
are an integral part of the game. The rules are enforced,
but they are nevertheless not meant to be obeyed. It's like
courtship; the players have to do what they are forbidden
to do, or nothing would finally be accomplished. The condition is even officially recognized; there are kinds of fouls
that go too far and are gross; these the players really aren't
supposed to commit, and they bring no possible advantage. They're called deliberate fouls, and when they occur
the aggrieved team retains free possession of the ball after
the free shot. Basketball is a marvelously evocative game;
it's also very middle-class, and the fact that it is now dominated by black players is one of the more solid pieces of
evidence that blacks are really getting somewhere in the
United States. You can't pick this game up on the streets; it's
a different, and a classier, hustle.

What is happening with the heavier team sports is
harder to figure out because the factors involved are
harder to analyze. I think it reflects decreasing sexual repression, but at the cost of much greater impersonality. The
net result is a clear erotic loss. Management seems willing
to exploit erotic interest in their players' bodies; even baseball uniforms are knitted rather than flannel, now, and
football pants and jerseys fit. But those bodies are now capitalized at hundreds of thousands of dollars each and are
too expensive to risk. The torso has the outlines of a slightly
lumpy Superman, but not a person, while the headgear
now totally conceals facial expressions. When I was a
small child—really small, less than five years old—the
players on the college football team in the town where I
lived were as familiar to me as the gods must have been to

a little boy in ancient Greece—more so, since I got a set of photographs of them, in uniform, every year and you could see their faces, which were visibly the same as the faces they played in. My father would take me to one or two out-of-town games each year on special football trains—a dozen or so ancient day-coaches, jam-packed with people who were at least smart enough not to try to drive in the condition they would soon be in. We weren't allowed in the players' car, but they would walk through ours, friendly and avuncular. Their exploits, off the team as well as on, were legendary but homely, making them again like Greek gods. They didn't need knitted football pants for me, then; my fantasy fed on the whole of them.

Erotic repression is likely, on the whole, to continue to abate in the interests of a consumer-oriented society; and if it does, the emotional climate at sporting events is likely to get healthier for everybody. The trend, though it may certainly reverse itself whenever American society develops a bad case of Ayatollah, has been fairly consistent for years. When I was a child, basketball was for college kids and sissies; it took the promise of violence implicit in football to keep homoerotic anxieties at bay. Prancing thinclads would have been too much for a mass audience to accept and identify with. That has changed. Violence is as welcome as ever; but life is tamer, and competition even when it is nonviolent, is known to be powerful enough to vanquish the threat of tenderness. All social classes now attend basketball's ballet and enjoy it with little obvious discomfort. Whether or not the Cosmos' sexier new uniforms are doing as much for the wives in the stands as expected, the younger spectators at least are bringing their wives, instead of greeting the players with jeers and catcalls. The next step—and it would be a giant one, though the Giants are hardly ready to take it—would be the sexual integration of teams in sports women are qualified to play. Having watched the list of jobs women were assumed to be physically incapable of doing well, or too nervous to perform, or whatever, grow shorter and shorter under the relentless eye of truth for half a century, and recognizing that the rules of sports also change to accommodate—indeed, as I have been arguing, to reflect—the changing values of a society, I would be most reluctant to say that any sport must, be its very nature, remain closed to them. Could a woman play for the New York Jets? It may sound strange today, but I feel sure that a woman might even become president of the Ford Foundation.

How would gay men react to the spectacle of women being included on previously all-male teams? With tremendous relief, if we really understood what was happening. But the shifts in social psychology that would have to underlie this development are not only great, they would threaten the whole structure of spectator sport itself; and the institutionalized obstacles to this change would clearly be enormous. For ultimately, there is something dehumanizing and pornoscopic about the institutionalized division of spectators for participants, regardless of the content of the fantasies that are thereby promoted and marketed. Even though I didn't think of the players who delighted me as sexual objects to be viewed impersonally and contemptuously like a burlesque show, I used them without ever really getting to know them or giving them anything of myself except what filtered down from the price of a ticket. That's a little degrading, though the degradation is not explicitly sexual. And as an obese and private youth I never played a body-contact sport; I only watched. I don't know what I missed, but it probably wasn't what I imagine. But even when I grew up, sports were already serious business. There wasn't much place for amateurs.

Today, in fact, there would be more place for people like the boy I was; there is more support for intramural athletics both relatively and absolutely. Purely recreational sports like boating and skiing, in which competition plays a much smaller role—and which, in their recreational form, include both men and women—are growing much faster than spectator sports, which are probably declining. Indeed, the direction of the thrust that maintains the structure of spectator sport may be shifting. Whereas institutionalized spectator sports used to weld the populace into good, working-model Americans by the force of the message they implicitly conveyed, today they seem to be maintained primarily to carry explicit commercial messages. There is a big difference between using football to make millions of young Americans feel like the kind of people who would be unmanned if they didn't have the kind of car Marshall McLuhan used to call a mechanical bride and keeping the sport going on TV in the wistful hope of drowning out Ralph Nader during the commercial breaks.

Whether the future of sport will be marked by a decline in the spectator's role and a marked, sustained increase in participation, and hence, become both a richer and a more diverse fantasy tempered by more frequent reality-testing and yielding, ultimately, greater satisfaction, depends, I suspect, largely on whether catering to this consumer demand can be made more profitable than producing TV sports spectaculars. This is still a consumer- and profit-oriented economy, with a political structure to match; and repressive desublimation is not liberation. But it isn't as heavy as old-style repression; it is, literally, more diverting. And it does leave more room for a wider marginal differentiation of taste and much more heterogeneous and varied forms of participation. Things should, at least, get a little friendlier, though the millenium is not at hand, and won't be for another twenty years. The lion will not lie down with the lamb, nor the Leaf with the Flame.

TWO VIEWS: MEN ATTEND, WOMEN COMPREHEND

LARRY MERCHANT

Philadelphia. Franklin Field. Eagles vs. Steelers. Sun-dappled day in September. Field plush-green. Yard-stripes and sidelines chalked yellow.

She: They look like dandelions.

He: No, love, the Eagles and Steelers.

She: Dandelions. Look.

He: The dandelions, love, play in Detroit.

She: I mean they look like dandelions: running around, blowing in the wind, the colors.

The Eagles were green uniforms with green helmets. The Steelers wear yellow with yellow helmets. On that green-and-yellow field. . . .

He (to himself): Good grief, I'm looking for trap plays and zone defenses and she sees more of what this is all about than I do.

And that is petrified truth. Women generally do see more than men at football games. Which is why it is imperative for men to take their wives, girls, mistresses, mothers or daughters to games. Men's heads are cluttered with so much nonsense that they frequently miss the best part of the show. They need womenfolk as guides and interpreters.

On a day when the home team is losing on merit or when the weather is bad, for instance, the men dismiss the quarterback as a spastic and question the ancestry of the coach. The women look around for amusement, and find it. The players—boys rolling in the mud—huddle on the side-

---

193

*lines in parkas that women may see as the height of mascu-
line chic. Perhaps an emotional lineman stands uncovered
shaking a fist at the fates, his hair sensationally unkempt:
God, she says, or thinks, the size of the neck of him, and the
bulge in those calves. Sex can be the name of the game
too. The scoreboard, blinking its magical mystery code,
may be too mysterious for her to decipher, but she knows
the half is coming to a close because the band stirs and
then groups behind the end zone. Unconsciously she has
hooked into a quarterback's wave length: "I aim for the
tuba," says Don Horn of the Denver Broncos, explaining
how he throws the ball out of bounds when his receivers
are covered. . . .*

*The grimmer nonsense of the pro football mystique
narrows men's field of vision to the line of scrimmage. It
ranges from the pretense of being able to forsee or understand strategy that is often obscure to the players themselves, to the illusion that being able to spout jargon and
spot the difference between an X and an O in a meaningless play diagram qualifies you as an expert. This is like
being distracted from a psychedelic light show by examining a fuse box. The male of the species is cursed by a compulsion to know how things work and when it's over-done,
as it is in football, it undermines the primary sensual pleasure of watching the game.*

*There are three basics to football: the spectacle, the
violence, the forward pass. Men see about three-quarters
of one of them, on a good day. Women, their antennae
more receptive and their field of vision as wide as the stadium, see a lot more.*

*College football games are our most colorful sports
spectacles because students can be hip, zany and creative
in their enthusiasm. Crowds at pro games tend to be hu-
morless and when the home team hasn't been winning*

enough lately, which usually is the case, they can get sullen and mutinous, as a coach once said. Still, pro football can give us a spectrum of fine madness, from insane traffic jams to the sound and fury and the fustian and wham and back to the traffic jams. As for the half-time shows, they're likely to be two-touchdown underdogs to a chorus of Jew's harps.

To men that is something to be endured, to be suffered for art's sake. To women it is the string of pearls on the basic black dress.

Women see and sense the violence of football for what it is too, and, bless their sweet hearts, they may even like it. Men have become largely callous to the violence, which is the core of the game, because their heads are into the mystique of strategy and jargon and deep-think, and the imperative of victory. "The love of violence, the dedication to violence," says Gary Pettigrew of the Eagles, "is what this game is about." Yet the bulk of the fans, the men, seldom connect to the violence directly. Their connection is indirect: the comment that this team has a good front four, that that linebacker is tough, that the blocking is lousy. Have you ever heard a fan discuss the intensity of the violence in football? It isn't likely. A woman's eyes follow a groggy lineman off the field for a second or two longer than a man's. She winces when a runner is stopped for no gain or a quarterback is nailed; he second-guesses the call. About the only time they are on the same frequency is when a pass spirals toward a moving target of fingertips. The pass, with its potential for instant rapture or despair, is a sight dug so viscerally and freely that not even strategic pretense can interfere with it. But when the receiver is throttled, she shudders; he checks the first-down chain.

Except for those rare body-hurtling collisions in an open field, the hitting blends into the grass. From a distance the players resemble so many toy boxers in a penny arcade. Most fans are too far away or too involved with the flow of the game to see, hear, smell or feel the hitting for what it really is. It is as abstract as the pain in a newspaper photo. They are looking at the romantic hurly-burly of actors on a screen.

Paul Brown has said, "I've known women who thought football was worthless and brutal. They just don't understand the sport and don't understand the nature of the male. Most of the big collisions don't hurt. The players are young and strong. Anyway the fact is that young men enjoy it."

Young men do enjoy knocking each other around— before football it was the custom at many colleges for entire classes to test their manhood on each other in free-style scrums—but while it's true that individual collisions don't always jar them, sometimes it's because they're numbed out of their skulls. The cumulative impact is shattering. Not even television, with its repertoire of closeup lenses, picks up the vibrations of the field shaking under the thundering herd, of muscles trembling and smacking. The instruments needed to record them are a seismograph and an oscillograph. "If a man doesn't get hurt," says Larry Wilson of the Cardinals, "he hasn't been playing hard enough." By the fourth quarter linemen are playing on instinct revived between shifts by smelling salts. . . .

The violence escalates to the megaton level on kickoffs, when twenty-two bodies try to knock off twenty-two heads. The incidence of injury on kickoffs is roughly eight times what it is on scrimmage plays. Stan Isaacs, sports columnist for Newsday on Long Island, New York, would make kickoff's a game alone:

For those who think pro football is the greatest of spectacular sports I'd like to call attention to a game I call "Annihilation." It's not for sissies. Annihilation is like football, but without the dull parts. It's a game of kickoffs. Each team takes turns at kicking off and receiving—and may the better team survive. . . .

Actually the general spectator insensitivity to the violence of football is best dramatized on kickoffs. Despite their glamour, their potential for a thrill, the expectations they raise, very little happens on the average kickoff in terms of yardage gained. There are nine or ten kickoffs per game, of which six or seven are returned, one or two beyond the 25-yard line. In a good year 1 out of 300 returns results in a touchdown, in a bad year 1 out of 500. But everyone follows the beautiful end-over-end flight of the ball on kickoffs, followed by a quick scamper to the 23— while a human demolition derby is taking place upfield. Demolition is the name of that game.

Each of us brings our own sensibility and neuroses to the stadium, enabling us to find whatever we want there, from fun and games to hero and scapegoat and even to catharsis and the fount of essential, infinite wisdom. Norman Mailer has found the relationship between the quarterback and the center, well, absorbing. . . . Good luck to both of them. The thing we have to remember is that none of us knows what's really going on out there, and that knowing is unimportant. Seeing and feeling are important.

Because, for the fan, if not for the coach, pro football is by yards and yards the least intellectual game there is.

A hockey crowd is a football crowd without the pretense. Strategy, shmategy. The game is a blaze of color: swift, violent, explosive. Which is more than enough to involve you.

A basketball crowd in a basketball city, pressing around the court, is aware of the game's schoolyard subtleties and strategems to a sophisticated degree impossible in football.

And a baseball crowd is geological ages ahead of a football crowd, because baseball is easier to follow and anticipate, and because the statistical records and daily exposure define athletes as athletes and personalities.

The problem in football is trying to assign individual responsibility, trying to sort out what happened from that clamor of bodies. The problem is compounded by the fact that even should you be able to determine precisely what happened, chances are that some of it was set into motion and commotion off the field. . . .

Try to analyze a simple incomplete pass. Was it incomplete because the quarterback panicked in the face of a rush? Or because he didn't get enough time? Or because he was following orders from the bench? Or because the receiver didn't go where he was supposed to go? Or because the quarterback didn't know where the receiver was supposed to go? Or because the defense anticipated his target and the quarterback didn't see another open man? Or because a speck of dust got in someone's eye or a gust of wind came along? Or did the quarterback throw away the ball deliberately because of any or all of these reasons? There are five or ten passes thrown away in every game, but only when the ball is thrown into the fifteenth row of the bleachers, or into a tuba in the band, can fans be reasonably sure that that is what's happening. And who knows, maybe the quarterback has a thing for the tuba player. . . .

. . . Gradually it may be sinking in that nobody knows exactly what's going on out there. When players talk about pride, character, emotion and momentum all the time it begins to dawn on us that perhaps we are dealing with athletes who are as confused as we are. This realization may induce a state of melancholia among many men, but think of the dividends in expanded consciousness.

WOMEN, SEX ROLE STEREOTYPING, AND SPORTS

INTRODUCTION

In her analysis of power relations between the sexes within patriarchal society, Kate Millett describes many similarities between sports and what anthropologists have called "men's house institutions." In preliterate societies, the men's houses serve as a social nexus of patriarchal association and emotion. These cultural centers of male ritual and values are the experiential theaters in which youngsters make their tenuous passage from boyhood to manhood. Shrouded by secrecy, the activities of the men's house reveal a preoccupation with power, a latently homosexual and phallic-oriented sexuality, and a general disdain for women. "While hunting, politics, religion and commerce may play a role," Millett observes, "sport and warfare are consistently the chief element of men's house comradery."[1] In order to insure male solidarity and the overall segregation of the sexes within the tribal group, any breech of house norms is met with severe censure and even social ostracism.

Like Millett, we suggest that the complex network of values and practices occurring in the locker rooms of America are a vestige of the men's house tradition of patriarchal society. Despite the growing infusion of women into athletics, sport remains a central source of masculine communal experience in our society. Feminism, the new zeal for physical fitness, and juridical mandates have fed women's expanding involvement in sport. To date, however, the status of women's athletics within the institution of sport is accurately described as "separate and unequal": "separate" because women have tended to develop *their own* distinct teams and organizations; "unequal" because women's sports and intramurals are grossly underfunded compared to men's athletics, female professionals are paid less than their male counterparts, and the media overplay men's sports. Discriminatory funding practices and the collusive camaraderie of team owners, athletes, coaches, and sportswriters preserve the athletic mythos of masculine supremacy and virility as well as the competitive and aggressive values necessary for social and economic intercourse.

Because of the interdependence of sport and other social institutions, until women overthrow the male domination of athletics they will remain subjugated and discriminated against, since sports disseminate, reaffirm, and reinforce male values found throughout society.[2] Despite the growing numbers of women athletes and the legal progress toward sexual equality in sports during the early seventies, more recent trends indicate a growing opposition to further reforms that would guarantee equal opportunity for women and men.[3] Social scientific debate on the women's sports issue is raging, political struggle continues, and many questions remain unanswered. Will women's increased participation in sport change its inherent machismo ethos? Does women's presence in the "men's house" of athletics deter the development of sex role identity along traditional stereotypical lines? Is the establishment of nonsexist sport a prerequisite for full sexual equality?

According to Marie Hart, the oppressive rigidity of sex role stereotypes in American society weighs most heavily on female athletes. Unless they are black, superior female athletes are persistently regarded as less than feminine. Hart's ideal is to establish a sports structure for women that allows each individual to strive for self-actualization within natural physical limits.

The article by Thomas Boslooper and Marcia Hayes goes a long way toward explaining why, until recently, females have been underrepresented in sport. The author's argue that most women do not participate in sports because they are playing the femininity game—being submissive and underachieving to win the love of a man. Their competitive and aggressive impulses are channeled into the female superbowl—getting married. Women are not born losers but are socialized into subservience and athletic immobility through rigid sex role stereotyping.

Opponents of equal rights for women in sports and society at large often argue that any further erosion of sex role differences will produce disastrous consequences for individuals, marriage, the family, and the social order in general. Unless traditionally feminine and masculine psychological distinctions and the traditional differentiation of female and male social roles are maintained, they assert, individual emotional instability, role confusion, and chaotic interpersonal relations between the sexes will result. Dorothy V. Harris's empirical investigation of 600 female and male college students debunks these contentions. She finds that, while female athletes exhibit more "masculine" personality traits than nonathletic women and men, they are no less "feminine" and possess high levels of self-esteem. Moreover, both males and females with "androgynous" personalities, that is, a blending of masculine and feminine personality traits, have high levels of self-esteem.

Sociologist-feminist Marjory Nelson casts a cynical eye at men's liberationists who reject the model of masculinity offered by "the jock culture." She questions whether it is possible for men to develop a nonsexist and compassionate personality in a society the *systematically* oppresses women. A man does not have to be a jock to oppress a woman, argues Nelson, since the roots of male dominance and violence are in patriarchal, capitalistic, and racist institutions. Within such a social system, the power and prestige men hold over women is institutionalized and changes in male consciousness do little to alter social conditions that subjugate women.

Nelson's cynicism is well founded in that men have been more willing to grant woman equality on verbal and ideological levels than on behavioral levels.[4] Though a more egalitarian ideology has become widely diffused throughout American society, the status of women compared to men, measured in terms of the occupations they hold, the education they receive, and the income they earn, has actually declined in the last twenty-five years.[5] While agreeing with Nelson's argument that changes in underlying social and economic conditions are a prerequisite to full sexual equality, we contend that the development of new ideologies and the restructuring of individual consciousness are also indispensible to this end. To use a recent historical example, with the emergence of modern feminism, many women attended informal consciousness-raising meetings where they explored and reevaluated their inner lives, emotions, and social roles. Having achieved varying degrees of *personal* change, these same women turned their thoughts and energies toward eliminating the social conditions they had come to identify as sources of their oppression. Because the idea of men's liberation is so new and participants in the men's movement are still comparatively few, we can only speculate that men will travel a similar passageway from intensive self-examination to collective solidarity and viable social-political action.

FOOTNOTES

1. Kate Millett, *Sexual Politics* (New York: Doubleday, 1970).
2. Harry Edwards, "Desegregating Sexist Sport," *Intellectual Digest* 3 (November 1973): 82–85.
3. Candice Lyle Hogan, "Title IX: From Here to Equality," *Women Sports* 4 (September 1977): 16, 17, 22, 24, 60.
4. William J. Goode, *World Revolution and Family Patterns* (New York: MacMillan, 1963).

5. Arlie Russell Hochschild, "A Review of Sex Role Research," in Joan Huber, ed., *Changing Women in a Changing Society* (Chicago: Univ. of Chicago Press, 1973), p. 261.

SPORT: WOMEN SIT IN THE BACK OF THE BUS

M. MARIE HART

The roles of woman and successful female athlete are almost incompatible in the United States. The woman who wishes to participate in sports and remain "womanly" faces great stress. By choosing sport she usually places herself outside the social mainstream.

Today's new movements offer little support. What does Women's Lib have to say about freeing the woman athlete? Not much. If woman is to be more than mother, secretary and Miss America, we must reward her for sports achievement instead of stigmatizing her for it.

But the struggle focuses on other areas, such as dance. "Dance is a field for women, and male homosexuals," said Women: A Journal of Liberation, which described dance as one of the few ways to escape "Amerika's sick sexuality." And we seem to see sport as a field for men, and female homosexuals. Certainly, for a woman, sport intensifies sex-role problems. In most other parts of the Western world women coexist with men in sport as accepted and respected partners. Not in the United States. A female athlete meets more oppression than most other women in the American way of life.

Norms

Being female in this culture does not necessarily mean that one is perceived or accepted as feminine. Every culture has its social norms and sex roles. In the United States these seem to be especially rigid and narrow; women in sport do not fit our particular concept of femininity and those who persist in sport suffer for it.

Why has it been so difficult for women to remain "womanly" and yet be athletes, especially in games that require great physical skill? Games of physical skill are mostly associated with achievement and aggressiveness, which seem to make them the exclusive province of males. Women are more traditionally associated with obedience training and routine responsibility training and with games of strategy and games of chance. Conditioning begins early—in elementary school a girl feels pressure to select some games and avoid others if she is to be a "real" girl. If she is told often enough at 11 or 12 that sports are not lady-like, she may at that point make a choice between being a lady and being an athlete. This forced choice may create deep conflict that persists into adulthood. Sport is male territory; therefore participation of female intruders is a peripheral, noncentral aspect of sport. The sexually separate (and unequal) facilities and organizations in sport in the United States illustrate the subordination of women athletes.

Conflict

As a girl becomes more and more proficient in sport, her level of personal investment increases and the long hours of practice and limited associations may isolate her socially. Personal conflict and stress increase as it becomes necessary for her to convince others of her femininity. This tension and conflict may increase still more if a girl chooses a sport that most regard as exclusive male territory.

Chi Cheng, a student at California State Polytechnic College at Pomona who holds several world track records for women, was quoted as saying, "The public sees women competing and immediately thinks they must be manly— but at night, we're just like other women."

Why would a woman need to comment about herself in this way and how does this awareness of stigma affect her daily life? For Chi Cheng, one solution is "to give a lot of public appearances—where I can show off my femininity."

Hair

Numerous discussions with college groups over the past few years have convinced me that our society imposes a great burden on women who commit themselves to sport, as participants or as teachers. Several married women students majoring in physical education confided at one discussion group that they had wanted to cut their hair but felt they couldn't: they simply didn't want the stereotyped image. Even when general hair styles are short, women in sport are judged by a standard other than fashion. And if the married woman experiences anxiety over such things, one can imagine the struggle of the single woman.

When young women do enjoy sport, what activities are really open to them? In a 1963 study, 200 first- and second-year college women from four Southern California schools strongly recommended that girls not participate in track and field activities. The sports they did recommend were tennis, swimming, ice skating, diving, bowling, skiing and golf, all of which have esthetic social and fashion aspects. Physical strength and skill may be components of some but are not their primary identifications.

In startling contrast is the black woman athlete. In the

black community, it seems, a woman can be strong and competent in sport and still not deny her womanliness. She can even win respect and status; Wilma Rudolph is an example.

Tomboy

Sport standards are male and the woman in sport is compared with men—not with other women. It starts early: Wow, what a beautiful throw. You've got an arm like a guy. Look at that girl run; she could beat lots of boys. *Father comments,* Yes, she loves sports. She's our little tomboy. *It would seem strange to say of a small boy,* Oh, yes, he is our little marygirl. (We have ways of getting messages to boys who don't fit the role, but we haven't integrated them into our language so securely.)

These comments carry the message of expected cultural behavior. When the girl has the message clearly she loses games to a boy on purpose. She knows that she may win the game and lose the boy.

Male performance standards and the attending social behavior have resulted in even more serious problems. In international sports events a woman must now pass a sex test of cells collected from inside of the cheek. In a normal woman, about 20 cells in every hundred contain Barr bodies (collections of chromatins). At the 1968 Olympic games, women whose tests showed Barr bodies in fewer than 10 cells in every hundred were barred from competition. Marion Lay, a Canadian swimmer said that at those Olympics a long line of women awaiting the test in Mexico erupted in reactions that ranged from tension-releasing jokes to severe stress and upset. Some athletes suggested that if the doctor were good-looking enough, one might skip the test and prove her femininity by seducing him. Many were baffled, feeling that their honesty was in question along with their femininity.

There is also the problem of the use by some women performers of "steroid" drugs, male sex-hormone derivatives that tend to increase muscle size. There have been strong and continued warnings against the use of steroids by men because of their dangerous effects, but little has been published about the negative effects of male steroids on women. They are known to increase muscle size, to change fat distribution and also to produce secondary male characteristics such as increased face and body hair and lowered voice.

Why would a woman take such a drug? Because the values are on male records and performance and she will attempt to come as close to this goal as possible.

Bar

Social attitudes that limit sport choices for women have a long history. Here's an editorial from a 1912 issue of Outing Magazine:

> Other things being equal, the man who has had the most experience in outdoor sports should be the best aviator. By the same token, women should be barred . . . Women have not the background of games of strength and skill that most men have. Their powers of correlation are correspondingly limited and their ability to cope with sudden emergency is inadequate.

In 1936 the editor of Sportsman, a magazine for the wealthy, commented of the Olympic Games that he was ". . . fed up to the ears with women as track and field competitors." He continued, "a woman's charms shrink to something less than zero" and urged the organizers to "keep them where they were competent. As swimmers and divers, girls are as beautiful and adroit as they are ineffective and unpleasing on the track."

/More recent publications such as Sports Illustrated have not been as openly negative; but they sustain sexual bias by limiting their coverage of women in sport. The emphasis in periodicals is still largely on women as attractive objects rather than as skilled and effective athletes./

Muscles

Operating alongside sex bias to scare girls from sport have been such misunderstandings as the muscle myth—the fear that athletics will produce bulging muscles which imply masculinity. The fact, well documented by the exercise physiologists Carl E. Klafs and Daniel D. Arnheim, is that "excessive development (muscle) is not a concomitant of athletic competition." They further report: "Contrary to lay opinion, participation in sports does not masculinize women. . . ." Some girl and women athletes are indeed muscular. Klafs and Arhheim explain:

> Girls whose physiques reflect considerable masculinity are stronger per unit of weight than girls who are low in masculinity and boys who display considerable femininity of build. Those who are of masculine type often do enter sports and are usually quite successful because of the mechanical advantages possessed by the masculine structure. However, such types are the exception, and by far the greater majority of participants possess a feminine body build.

Opening

Myths die hard, but they do die. Today, gradually, women have begun to enter sport with more social acceptance and individual pride. In 1952, researchers from the Finnish Institute of Occupational Health who conducted an intensive study of the athletes participating in the Olympics in Helsinki predicted that "women are able to shake off civic disabilities which millennia of prejudice and ignorance have imposed upon them." The researchers found that the participation of women in sport was a significant indicator of the health and living standards of a country.

Simone de Beauvoir wrote in The Second Sex

> *. . . In sports the end in view is not success independent of physical equipment; it is rather the attainment of perfection within the limitations of each physical type; the featherweight boxing champion is as much of a champion as is the heavyweight; the woman skiing champion is not the inferior of the faster male champion; they belong to two different classes. It is precisely the female athletes who, being positively interested in their own game, feel themselves least handicapped in comparison with the male.*

Americans seem to be still unable to apply to the woman in sport this view of "attainment of perfection within the limitations of each."

The experiencing of one's body in sport must not be denied to anyone in the name of an earlier century's image of femininity—a binding, limiting, belittling image. This is the age of the woman in space, and she demands her female space and identity in sport.

THE GAME IS FIXED:
PROGRAMMED TO BE LOSERS

THOMAS BOSLOOPER AND MARCIA HAYES

Most women are losers. Sometimes they lose through lack of opportunity; more often, they lose by choice. Even those who have the odds in their favor in terms of education, money, and intelligence—and who are competing in the most favorable feminist climate the world has seen for some three thousand years—still end up throwing the game. Women don't know how to win or how to compete, and they're programmed not to try.

These are meant to be fighting words. For if women are ever to get to a point where they can do something, really do something, to change their lives and society, they will have to learn to win and win big. Not in imitation of men, but in full realization of themselves.

A lot has been said and written recently about unreasonable sexual roles, about the arbitrary attitudes that divide masculine and feminine natures into polar opposites, like male and female electrical plugs and outlets. It's now generally acknowledged, in theory if not in practice, that women are men's intellectual equals and deserve the same career opportunities and pay.

But for all the new laws and policies, few women— even when they make it—can stand long in the winner's circle. Women have been conditioned to fear success, and to cop out when it gets too close. The cop-out can be as glamorous as living happily ever after with a prince or an oil tycoon, as sordid as an overdose of Seconal, as selfless

---

Extracts from Thomas Boslooper and Marcia Hayes, *The Femininity Game* (New York: Stein and Day Publishers, 1973), originally entitled "Cinderella Was a Winner," pp. 15–25.

as sacrificing personal ambitions to the cause of sisterhood. The first alternative will be applauded, the second pitied, the last scorned. But all are viewed as the natural outcome of feminine ambition—as, in a way, they are.

The big game is fixed. Women who don't take a dive become, in society's eyes, losers in a more basic sense: neuters who have broken the rules on their home playground—the rules of the femininity game.

All women know about this game. At one time or another most have played it. And with the possible exception of lesbians and the most dedicated women's liberationists, most still do. The goal is a man and, traditionally, marriage. The sporting equipment is charm, guile, social shrewdness, clothes, cosmetics—and underneath it all, one's own physical apparatus (hopefully 36-24-36). No holds are barred. Deception, flattery, and manipulation are all respectable tactics. The competitors are all other eligible women, beginning, in preadolescence, with Mom.

The femininity game meets the two basic requirements of other destructive life games. It is essentially dishonest having an ulterior motive, and it has a dramatic payoff.[1] But unlike other games classified by transactional analysts (the species of social psychiatrist who first defined life games and now referee them), the femininity game is not entirely voluntary. Women play it because the payoff— love—is too tempting to resist. For love, women are persuaded to smother their identities and their ambitions, channeling all their competitive and aggressive instincts into the game.

At some magical moment, usually determined by adolescent alterations in their bodies, girls are expected to trade in their tennis shoes for glass slippers. Like Cinderella's sisters, they struggle to fit oversized feet into tiny glass shoes. Usually they manage to squeeze them on and totter through a lifetime of discomfort, blaming themselves for the bad fit instead of the capricious cobbler, who had a passion for glass and triple-A size fours.

Only ladies can play the game, and ladies are supposed to be supportive, passive, unaggressive, even frail. The role and the game could be amusing as an occasional charade under soft candlelight. Unfortunately, it's taken very seriously by both sexes. Girls who don't play it will have a rough time with parents, friends, and teachers.

A basic rule of the femininity game is that its contestants must be prepared to lose all the other games. Men don't love women who win. This fact of life was illustrated recently in an episode of the family television series My World and Welcome to It. The juvenile star of the show has just finished a chess game with her father, who is accepting defeat less than graciously. Her mother calls her aside for a heart-to-heart chat. "There's a game all women play, dear," she says. "It's called getting married and living happily ever after."

"But I can beat Daddy at chess," says the girl. "You mean I have to let him win?"

"I think," says Mom, "that it would be the feminine thing to do."

Margaret Mead would call it negative reinforcement. Winning games against men elicit such a negative response that girls learn early to lose rather than face rejection—whether from boys and girls their own age, or from fathers.

"The bribe offered to the little girl by the father is love and tenderness," psychiatrist Helene Deutsch has written. "For its sake she renounces any further intensification of her activities, particularly of her aggressions."[2]

Social and parental bribes are not often subtle. At home a girl may be confronted, as was one Michigan girl, with a father who wants to exchange her baseball bat for an electric blender. Or she may beat her father at arm wrestling and be sent to a psychiatrist—which happened to the daughter of a New York YMCA executive. Or, if she goes to a Midwestern sorority-oriented school, she may find, as one student did, that "you can be a sorority girl or a track and field girl. You can't be both."

"When I was about fourteen, I was pressured into giving up sports," says Judy Mage, founder and former president of the New York Social Service Employees' Union and one-time vice-presidential candidate on the Peace and Freedom Party ticket. "I used to play street games with the boys on our block in the Bronx. But as I got older, people would just stop and stare at a girl playing, as if I were a freak. I was getting into liking boys, and wanted to be accepted. One night after a dance I got into a snowball fight with some boys. The girls took me aside later and said 'boys don't like that.' And that is when I gave up."

Betty Friedan has noted that at puberty girls drop special interests and pursue those that will appeal to boys. "Men compete for awards, and we compete for men," said a recent *Ms.* editorial.

Having been taught that "winning" means losing love, girls usually find that achievement is accompanied by anxiety. In a study conducted by Matina Horner, now president of Radcliffe College, 65 per cent of a group of women at the University of Michigan expressed anxiety over feminine success figures, equating success with a loss of femininity. At Radcliffe, students were asked to describe a hypothetical student named Anne, who is at the top of her medical school class. Nearly 75 per cent of the group pictured her as unattractive and hard up for dates. When asked what would happen to Anne when she learned about her top standing in the class, one student replied: "Anne will deliberately lower her academic standing during the next term, while she does all she can to subtly help Carl. His grades come up, and Anne soon drops out of medical school. They marry, and he goes on in school while she raises their family."[3]

No comparable study has been done on reactions to successful sportswomen, but one can assume that the negative percentages would be considerably higher. Physical prowess and the aggressive, competitive instincts that go with it are thought of as exclusively masculine qualities.

"I didn't take physical education in college, even though I love sports," says a girl who was named queen of the Drake Relays, an annual track event in the Midwest. "I was really afraid that I would be associated with the typical physical-education majors, who were definitely mannish."

The result of this kind of pressure is that "as age increases, sports prowess increases in boys but not in girls," says Dr. John Kane of St. Mary's College, London. "A girl's performance level is deflected to other, more acceptable behavior during late adolescence." And he adds: "With society's expectations of women, it's not surprising we get the kind of women we're asking for."[4]

Women's attitudes toward competition and success are established early. Infant girls are handled differently from boys—more affectionately, more protectively. And as soon as they learn to walk, girls are trained differently. Sociologists John Roberts and Brian Sutton-Smith confirmed this in a cross-cultural study of 1900 elementary-school children given a variety of psychological tests and interviews. "Boys . . . are given higher achievement training," they concluded, "while girls are given more consistent obedience-and-responsibility training. These differences in socialization correspond to the general differences between adult male and female roles over the world."[5]

It doesn't stop there. Anyone who has snoozed through introductory psych knows about Skinner's boxes and Pavlov's dogs. Behavioral training has to be reinforced to be effective. And in all cultures, games and sport serve this purpose. They are not idle play but life models—dress rehearsals, as it were, for the real thing.

Competitive team sports involving displays of power and physical skill, Roberts and Sutton-Smith found, were game models for youngsters—mostly boys—whose parents encouraged achievement and success.

Games of strategy were found to mirror childhood training in responsibility. For boys, who are trained in social responsibility, strategy games are preparation for gaining a responsible position in life; games like football, which combine strategy and physical skill, are models both for social responsibility and for power.

Finally, games of chance and fortune were the choice of two groups: those children who had been strictly disciplined in obedience (a preference shared in maturity by minority and low-income groups) and girls. Discouraged from initiative and achievement, these children could only dream that their ambitions might some day be realized by chance.

Roberts, Sutton-Smith, and Robert Kozelka followed up this research on children with polls of some 7000 adults who had a variety of occupations and income levels. (The polls were conducted by Minnesota, Gallup, and Roper.) The same game preferences were indicated.

Business executives, politicians, and other men in positions of power, for instance, overwhelmingly favored games that combined strategy and physical skill. Those in professional occupations—accountants, for instance—preferred games of strategy, like poker. Men in blue-collar jobs enjoyed games of pure physical skill, such as bowling, while women (and members of ghettoized minority groups) showed an overwhelming preference for games of pure chance, or those combining strategy and chance.

It would appear then that the battle really was won on

the playing fields of Eton. Boys train for success and power through competitive games and sports. Feminine skills and wiles are honed at the bridge table, the bingo board, and the lottery ticket window, perfected in the femininity game.

This same group of sociologists found that real-life situations have equivalents or parallels not only in games and sport but in myths. Fairy tales and other stories written to formula are really literary games which can be scored in terms of winners and losers. Ideally, they provide a way for children to experiment with winning and losing in symbolic situations.

"Desiring to beat opponents but frightened to lose," say Roberts, Sutton-Smith, and Kozelka, "the child is motivated . . . to deal with his conflict in more manageable fashion. He is attracted to a variety of expressive models. Some of these may be as vicarious as folk tales, comics, and television, and may suggest that the small participant can win . . . or that the central figure may have powers to overcome insuperable odds (Superman). . . . Through these [play] models, society tries to provide a form of buffered learning, through which the child can make . . . step-by-step progress toward adult behavior."[6]

Boys have Superman and Jack the Giant Killer; girls have Cinderella—the beautiful, unassuming, supportive drudge whose lucky number is written on the prince's shoebox. Cinderella was obviously a winner and the wicked stepsisters losers in what is essentially a vicarious game of chance. This theme—a literary form of the femininity game—pits feminine woman against unfeminine shrew, bitch, or witch. The payoff is the prince, and usually princely sums of money as well. A well-known variation is the tomboy-turned-lady plot (Annie Get Your Gun, The Taming of the Shrew), a sort of double solitaire in which both women and men win by playing their respective roles to the hilt.

Because the femininity game combines strategy and

chance, it is an attractive alternative to real life, one which mirrors early training and offers a strong incentive—love—as reward for conforming to a stereotype. The game is self-perpetuating because the payoff depends on masking real identity. Players know they are loved not for themselves but for their roles, and few have the self-confidence necessary to break away from the game.

Another sociologist, Roger Caillois, would classify the femininity game as mimicry. "Every game [involving mimicry] presupposes the temporary acceptance, if not of an illusion . . . at least of a closed, conventional and in certain respects, fictitious, universe," he has written. "The subject plays at believing, at pretending to himself or at making others believe that he is someone other than he is; he temporarily forgets, disguises; strips his own personality in order to be another."[7]

Faced with a conflict between what she is and what she is expected to be, an ambitious, competitive, athletic girl often responds by becomiing defensively aggressive and masculine in attitude. Resenting her restrictive role but lacking the self-confidence and initiative to create something else, she becomes a hostile mimic of the only success models around: men.

Occasionally, given parental support or outside encouragement, she may create a new, successful role for herself. Unfortunately, unless her mother has been an athlete or a career woman, she will find few feminine success models to imitate. At the 1972 Penn State Conference on Women and Sport, a study of elementary school students was cited in which boys listed 150 life roles they wanted to imitate. Girls could think of only 25.[8]

Most women, of course, neither rebel nor create. They play the game—sometimes pretending, sometimes even believing themselves to be something they're not. And for centuries, the game and the role requirements have been an effective way to keep women insulated from life.

Women, conditioned to the femininity game from infancy, are expected to play for a lifetime. Society thus dooms them to perpetual childhood, playing adult as they once played house as children, dependent on husbands as they were once dependent on parents, chastised for showing initiative and independence.

Full-time gameswomen will find all sorts of subsidiary contests to occupy them after the big prize has been won at the wedding: New House, Expectant Mother, Hostess—and, more and more often, Divorce and Remarry, when the original payoff palls.

The game also creates a masculinity trap for men, who feel threatened when their wives take over roles they are expected to perform. A man's independence often hinges on his wife's dependence. "When a man is thought superior because he is a man," Florida Scott-Maxwell has written, "then woman is crippled by the inferiority she sees in him."

A woman sufficiently attractive and talented may decide to play both sides of the fence, using the game as an entree to the career world. Women have often been criticized for this, for using feminine wiles to gain power. But these tactics are the only ones most women know. Their equipment is looks and charm, which tend to erode with age, so they play the game as hard as they can in the limited time available. Their power base is men. Their opponents, unfortunately, are other women.

Women who play the game successfully find, when the crow's feet begin to track the corners of their eyes, that it's a losing proposition. At forty-five or fifty, after decades of dedication to beauty and passivity, they suddenly find themselves out of the competition, with no identity or purpose to fall back on. As Freud once put it, "The difficult development which leads to femininity [seems to] exhaust all the possibilities of the individual."[9] Freud should know. He wrote part of the script.

The physical requirements of the femininity game encourage a neurotic preoccupation with physical appearance. Women are usually self-conscious rather than proud of their bodies, spending an excessive amount of time trying to improve their looks. Because men are the payoff, players tend to evaluate themselves and other women through a man's eyes. The seductively clad girls on the cover of Cosmopolitan and other women's magazines are models that women will presumably envy and try to emulate. When women meet for the first time, they size each other up in terms of attractiveness—not to each other, but to men.

This perspective also leads women to think of themselves and each other as objects, both to envy other women for qualities they lack and to despise them, as they often despise themselves, for the role they are playing. Because the financial and personal destiny of players so often rests on the payoff, one can expect to find jealousy and disloyalty affecting adult feminine friendships—attitudes often carried into the career world.

Women aren't born losers. They're brainwashed. They don't know how to win because they've been conned and coerced from infancy into believing they shouldn't try. Except for fashionable differences in dimension—from the Rubens model to Twiggy—the physical image of woman has remained the same for thousands of years. Women have succeeded in liberating their intellects, but their bodies are still in corsets. They still think of themselves as passive, nonaggressive, and supportive. And that's why, no matter how intellectually or sexually liberated they are, women continue to lose.

FOOTNOTES

1. The criteria used to define games by Eric Berne in *Games People Play* (N.Y.: Grove Press, 1964).

2. Helene Deutsch, *The Psychology of Women* (N.Y.: Grune & Stratton, Inc., 1972), Vol. I, p. 251.

3. "Radcliffe's President Matina Horner," *New York Times Magazine*, January 14, 1973. Also "Femininity and Successful Achievement," a research study conducted at the University of Michigan, quoted in *Parade*, July 9, 1972.

4. Dr. John Kane. From authors' notes at Penn State Conference on Women and Sport, August, 1972.

5. John M. Roberts and Brian Sutton-Smith, "Child Training and Game Involvement," *Sport, Culture and Society*, p. 126.

6. Brian Sutton-Smith with John M. Roberts and Robert Kozelka, "Game Involvement in Adults," *Sport, Culture and Society*, p. 253.

7. Roger Caillois, "The Structure and Classification of Games," *Sport, Culture, and Society*, p. 49.

8. From authors' notes at Penn State Conference on Women and Sport, August, 1972.

9. Sigmund Freud, *New Introductory Lectures in Psychoanalysis* (N.Y.: W. W. Norton, 1933), p. 184.

FEMININITY AND ATHLETICISM: CONFLICT OR CONSONANCE?

DOROTHY V. HARRIS

"What are big boys made of? Independence, aggression, competitiveness, leadership, assertiveness, task orientation, outward orientation. . . . And what are big girls made of? De-

---

Dorothy V. Harris, Ph.D., is the director of the Center for Women in Sport and the graduate program in Sport Psychology at the Pennsylvania State University.

pendence, passivity, fragility, low pain tolerance, nonaggression, noncompetitiveness, inner orientation, interpersonal orientation, empathy, sensitivity, nurturance. . . . (Bardwick 1971).

In today's society, if one were asked to describe the psychological and behavioral demands of competitive sports, the response would be most compatible with the description of what big boys are made of. Therein lies the rub and perhaps the biggest deterrent to female athletes. Traditionally, involvement in sports has been the prerogative of males, a laboratory for socializing males for appropriate masculine behavior in society. The behavioral demands of competitive sports reinforce what is stereotypically masculine and what men are supposed to emulate. At the same time, the psychological and physical demands of competitive sports are not generally considered compatible with society's stereotyped image of how females should behave. On the contrary, they represent the antithesis of what women are supposed to be, so that athleticism becomes a detriment to the female image.

Women in sports are both a social reality and a social anomaly. This results in considerable confusion with regard to roles and perceptions of females in sport. If masculinity and femininity are viewed as polar opposites, and if sports are largely assumed to be the prerogative of males, then any female intrusion into the domain of sport makes a mockery of the situation. Throughout history female athletes have been apologetic about their intrusion into a man's world and have compensated for their perceived lack of femininity by participating only in certain types of sports and by avoiding any serious commitment to sports. They have not only appeared to "sense their place" in sports but traditionally have promoted an ideology that has justified and perpetuated that place.

Research suggests that the reason relatively few females continue to pursue involvement in competitive sports for any length of time is the perceived dissonance or disparity between the traditional conceptions of femininity and athleticism. The long-standing notion that somehow a serious commitment to sports precludes maintaining one's sense of feminine selfhood has been perpetuated without any evidence that it is detrimental in any way. In today's culture, women are neither expected nor required to develop athletic ability, though physical attractiveness is valued. As a result, the development of strength and physical skills is relatively unimportant to girls. Whereas males discover early that their athletic accomplishments open the door to almost universal social acceptance, female athletes soon find that certain groups consider them socially undesirable.

The negative sanctions that discourage women and girls from serious participation in athletics apparently stem from two basic fears: the fear that their behavior will become masculinized and the fear that their physiques will become masculinized.

As investigators continue to examine the female and her role in society and to sort out the products of socialization from the products of biological sex, it becomes more and more evident that characteristics previously considered sex-related are actually culturally determined. The behavior of males, as well as females, is only minimally dependent on biological differences. It is much more dependent on the restricted positions of both in today's society. So long as males and females are effectively socialized to accept stereotyped roles, they can be expected to accept and demonstrate the role behavior ascribed to them. Parents and society teach children to be boys and girls by rewarding them for behavior appropriate to their sex and punishing cross-gender behavior. Marmor (1973) finds that gender roles and gender identities, although generally related to the biological sex of a child, are actually shaped not by biological factors but by cultural ones. From infancy on, a myriad of culturally defined cues are presented to the developing child that shape its gender identity to fit its assigned sex. The pattern is familiar to all. Girls wear pink with ruffles while boys wear blue with no ruffles. Girls get dolls for Christmas while boys get baseballs, and so on. Boys are encouraged to build a concept of self-esteem based on tangible accomplishments, while girls learn not to gratify impulses adults find offensive and to rely on others to determine whether they have done well or poorly in a situation. Girls learn to please, to defer, to wait for reinforcement; this becomes a big part of the "feminine role." The typical child can and will exhibit behavior that is either "masculine" or "feminine" but the adults to whom the child is exposed will reinforce only that behavior which they deem appropriate to the child's sex. In short, the psychological sex or gender role appears to be learned, to result from a multitude of experiences that are considered part of growing up to "fit" into adult society.

Many theorists studying the psychology of women feel that the real explanation of the status of females is not something implicit in their nature, but rather a manifestation of the male ego. Males have traditionally defined femininity and emphasized the importance of a feminine image. In many situations, a girl's natural desire for competitive experiences in sports may be totally stifled by male disapproval, either directly or indirectly. From an early age girls are taught to "please" males; the only show of competitiveness they are permitted is toward other females for the favor of a male. In short, their identity is related to their role and their relationship to males.

Traditionally, men and women have regarded the traits attributed to males more highly than those attributed to females (McKee and Sheriffs 1959; Rosenkrantz, Bee, Vogel, Broverman, and Broverman 1968). A more recent study by Broverman and others indicates that male and female clinical psychologists agree on the attributes characterizing healthy behavior for men and women in today's society. They also agree that these attributes are different for men and women, and that the differences closely parallel the dominant sex-role stereotypes. When characterizing the healthy behavior of adult males and adults whose sex was unspecified, the psychologists questioned used quite similar terms. However, their description of the behavior of a well-adjusted adult female differed significantly from the adult male and adult unspecified. The authors of the study concluded that, for a female to be well adjusted, she must exhibit behavior considered normal for her sex even though this behavior is considered less healthy than that expected of the average well-adjusted, competent, mature adult.

The difference in attitudes towards and acceptance of males and females in sports originates in the differences in the traits society ascribes to each sex. Kagan and Moss (1962), basing their definitions on observations and research during a study of children from birth to maturity, described the traditional masculine model as athletic, sexually active, independent, dominant, courageous, and competitive, and the traditional female was described as passive and dependent, socially anxious, sexually timid, and fearful of problem situations. Douvan and Adelman (1966), in studying female development, resort to classifying girls into three groups: feminine, nonfeminine, and antifeminine. Feminine girls are those who are other-directed, whose self-esteem is gained through helping others. They display little motivation for personal achievement and prefer security to success. Nonfeminine girls are a slow-developing group who say that they feel more important and useful when they are participating in competitive sports and games. Antifeminine *girls are those who say that they do not intend to marry. These girls are perceived as psychologically deviant. In Douvan and Adelman's study, only those girls who fit traditional roles are considered "normal"; all the others are labeled as either slow developers or psychologically deviant.*

Cheska *(1970) describes a paradox when she indicates that though the traits that are considered undesirable in females include aggressiveness, independence, ambition, assertiveness, and having goals other than being a wife or mother, these are the very traits needed by females to succeed in attaining a different role. Griffin (1972) confirms this notion. In examining how college students perceived the female's role she asked the students for descriptions of a housewife, a woman athlete, a girlfriend, a woman professor, their mother, and an ideal woman. The results suggested that the roles of woman athlete and woman professor were perceived as farthest from the role of the ideal woman.*

The *dissonance between the behavioral characteristics necessary for success in athletics and those that are considered appropriate for women can produce a real identity crisis in the young female who is struggling to establish her own identity and enjoys participating in sports. Bardwick (1971: 143) makes some pertinent comments about this identity crisis. She says,*

> If a girl has had many years in which she has been permitted to participate in what will be perceived as masculine activities, and to the extent that success in these activities, especially individual competitive ones, forms a core part of her self-esteem, it will be difficult for her to assume a clearly feminine sex-role identity and preference for the feminine role.

Bardwick also notes that

> *the motorically active, preadolescent girl will achieve status through competitive sports. Later, in adolescence, especially when teenagers are cruel in their demands, she will undergo a deep crisis. . . .*

This crisis occurs when the female athlete perceives the disparity between how she sees herself and how society expects her to be. There is dissonance between smelling sweet and being sweaty, between being rough and being gentle, between being vigorous and being inactive, between being athletic and being feminine. One cannot tolerate this dissonance too long; it must be resolved.

Traditionally, females have resolved this interpersonal conflict by withdrawing from involvement in sports. This withdrawal generally occurs during adolescence when a girl's body begins to mature and her femaleness is constantly reinforced. Society dictates that her status as a woman be increasingly linked to her femininity as traditionally defined, and she withdraws from sports to protect that status.

There are other ways, besides withdrawing from involvement in sports, to resolve the perceived dissonance between sports and femininity. Some females continue to play competitive sports but focus on "feminine appropriate" sports such as swimming, tennis, golf, or gymnastics. Somehow these sports are not considered as masculine, even for men, as team sports, so participation in them does not create the same degree of conflict. Still other females compensate for the perceived threat to their femininity by attaching feminine artifacts to their sporting attire. It is as though by wearing ruffles, pastel colors, or lacey designs and styles they are saying, "In spite of the fact that I am a highly skilled athlete, I am still feminine."

The female athlete whose behavior is farthest from the feminine stereotype causes the most concern. Such women avoid any social situation that is traditionally feminine because of their inability to cope with such a wide latitude of behavior. They are most comfortable with those behaviors that are associated with the traditional masculine orientation. The penalty for this resolution of an identity crisis is the greatest.

Fortunately, increasing numbers of females are discovering that they can cope with any superimposed conflict by adapting to the demands of the situation in which they find themselves. They are secure enough in their feminine selfhood to be capable of a greater diversity of behavior and healthier psychological functioning.

A More Contemporary Perspective

The position that has dominated the writings of social and behavioral scientists is that masculine and feminine attributes are essentially bipolar opposites. The presence of feminine characteristics tends to preclude the appearance of masculine ones. Indeed, the absence of a feminine attribute is, by definition, equivalent to masculinity. Conversely, masculine characteristics are assumed to preclude feminine ones and their absence defines femininity. In most societies, the goal of socialization is to inculcate appropriate attributes in members of each sex so that they may be capable of executing the sex-roles society has assigned them by virtue of their biological role. In fact, the link between masculine and feminine characteristics and sex-roles has been assumed to be so strong that these psychological dimensions are frequently discussed under the general sex-role rubric.

Distinctions between sex-roles is universal among human societies; males are assigned different tasks, rights, and privileges, and are generally subject to different rules of conduct than females. Males and females are typically assumed to possess different temperaments and abilities whose existence is used to justify the perpetuation of double standards of behavior. Definitive data are lacking about whether there are genetically determined differences in the temperamental make-up of males and females. However, there is abundant evidence that the human personality is highly malleable. Observed differences in the behavior of the two sexes in a given society can be shown to be strongly influenced by sex-specific child-rearing practices and by the nature and severity of sex-role differentiation.

Psychologists have tended to accept as given complex sets of sex-related phenomena and to focus attention on the processes by which individuals develop the behaviors and attributes expected of their sex within a culture. Psychologists have also been interested in the variability in behaviors and attributes among individuals and have attempted to identify the factors that promote or interfere with the development of expected and appropriate patterns of behavior. Psychological inquiries have been based on the notion that the categorical variable of biological gender is intimately associated with masculine and feminine role behaviors and presumed psychological differences between males and females. This bipolar conception of masculinity and femininity has historically been the one that has guided research. The major psychometric instruments designed to measure masculinity and femininity have been set up as unidimensional scales.

While the bipolar approach to the psychological aspects of masculinity and femininity has been the major one, dualistic approaches have also been proposed. Jung, for example, distinguished between the masculine animus and feminine anima and proposed that both were significant aspects of psychological make-up. More recently Bakan (1966) offered agency and communion as coexisting male and female principles. Agency, he said, demonstrates self-awareness and is manifested in self-assertion, self-expansion, and self-protection. Communion implies selflessness and concern for others. Both modalities are essential if society or the individual is to survive. Bakan further associated agency with masculinity and communion with femininity. Thus, according to Bakan, masculinity and femininity, in the sense of agency and communion, are two separate dimensions; however, the manifestation of one neither logically nor psychologically precludes the possession of the other.

Helmreich and Spence (1977) contend that the relationship among the various components of masculinity and femininity such as biological gender, a sexual orientation, and psychological attributes of masculinity and femininity and the adoption of conventional sex-roles, is not as strong as has been traditionally assumed. Their position reflects the more contemporary concept that masculinity and femininity represent two separate dimensions that vary independently. Helmreich and Spence have developed a new instrument, the Personal Attributes Questionnaire (PAQ), to assess masculine-feminine components of behavior. While they have maintained the psychological aspects of masculinity and femininity, they have discarded a strictly bipolar model in favor of an essentially dualistic concept.

The PAQ is composed of a masculinity and a femininity scale. The items that compose the masculinity scale refer to those attributes which are considered socially desirable in both sexes but were found to a greater degree among males during preliminary investigations. Conversely, those attributes considered socially desirable for both sexes but observed to a greater extent among females are the basis of the femininity scale. Two scores are generated, one for each scale, and an individual is classified according to his or her position relative to the scale medians. The basic classification scheme is shown in Table 1. In the lower right quadrant are those who have scored above the median on both the masculinity scale and the femininity scale; these individuals are labeled androgynous. In the upper right quadrant are those individuals who scored high in masculinity and low in femininity. Males who correspond to the typical male stereotype and females judged as cross-sex fall in this group and are labeled masculine. The lower left quadrant includes women who displayed typical feminine attributes or men who displayed cross-sex behaviors; these were labeled feminine. Those who do not fall in any of the previous three categories, that is, those who fell below the median on both the masculinity and the femininity scale, go in the upper left quadrant and are categorized as undifferentiated.

Table 1

Sex-role Classification:
Personal Attributes Questionnaire*

	MASCULINITY	
FEMININITY	*Below Median*	*Above Median*
Below Median	Undifferentiated	Masculine
Above Median	Feminine	Androgynous

*After Helmreich & Spence (1977)

Using several hundred subjects, Helmreich and Spence studied the relationship between the two scales. They found a tendency for high masculine scores to be associated with high femininity and low scores on one scale to be associated with low scores on the other scale. A bipolar conception would suggest that the sets of scores should be negatively related, so that those with a high masculine score would have a low score on the feminine scale. As indicated, this was not the case with Helmreich and Spence's sample.

In order to examine the relationship between sex-role identity and self-esteem, Spence, Helmreich, and Stapp (1975) correlated the PAQ data with scores on the Texas Social Behavior Inventory (Helmreich & Stapp, 1974), a measure of self-esteem. They found that the self-esteem of those labeled undifferentiated was the lowest, that of those in the feminine category the next lowest, and that of those in the masculine category the next lowest. The highest self-esteem was observed in the androgynous group. The differences between the means were significantly large, and the relationship between sex-role categories and self-esteem held true for both males and females. In the college population studied, approximately the same percentage of males and females was classified as androgynous, more males were classified as masculine and more females as feminine, and approximately the same percentage of each sex was classified as undifferentiated.

In summary, Helmreich and Spence's data suggest that masculinity and androgyny are related to desirable behaviors and to positive self-esteem in both males and females. These desirable attributes provide the androgynous individual, either male or female, with behavioral advantages over those in other categories. In an attempt to validate their findings, Helmreich and Spence also studied unique populations of females where the existence or nonexistence of differences in the distribution of masculinity and femininity might support a lack of congruence between these variables and the adoption of conventional sex-roles. A group of female athletes was included in the study. The data on these women suggest that females who are high achievers are more likely than their male counterparts to possess both masculine and feminine attributes without suffering any deficit in their femininity. In fact, they displayed significantly higher self-esteem than the females who were classified as feminine.

Applying the Concept to Athletic Groups

In a series of studies that began in 1976, Harris and Jennings (1977, 1978) found no evidence to support the supposed inevitable trade-off between a female athlete's self-esteem and femininity and her commitment to sports. The data generally supported the finding of Helmreich and Spence that females who succeed in areas of endeavor considered stereotypically masculine do not do so at the expense of their femininity. Again, the data suggest that women who are high achievers are more likely than their male counterparts to possess both masculine and feminine attributes without suffering any deficit in their femininity and that androgynous individuals, male or female, have behavioral advantages over others.

In the first study of 68 female distance runners (Harris & Jennings 1977), 33.8 per cent turned out to be androgynous, 27.9 per cent masculine, 17.6 per cent feminine and 20.6 per cent undifferentiated. In Helmreich and Spence's sample 39 per cent were androgynous, 31 per cent masculine, 10 per cent feminine, and 20 per cent undifferentiated.

In a second study, this time of 96 female athletes participating in a wide variety of sports (Harris and Jennings 1978) 54 per cent of the sample were androgynous, 21 per cent masculine, 14 per cent feminine, and 11 per cent undifferentiated. Among 72 nonathletic women also studied, 38 per cent were androgynous, 24 per cent masculine, 28 per cent feminine, and 10 per cent undifferentiated.

In a study of 125 males and 150 females, 22 per cent of

the males were androgynous, 31 per cent masculine, 12 per cent feminine, and 35 per cent undifferentiated. Forty-five per cent of the females were androgynous, 23 per cent masculine, 21 per cent feminine, and 11 per cent undifferentiated. Yet another study of 64 male and 92 female athletes found 51 per cent of the women androgynous, 23 per cent masculine, 15 per cent feminine, and 11 per cent undifferentiated, while 25 per cent of the men were androgynous, 34 per cent masculine, 11 per cent feminine and 30 per cent undifferentiated. Both these studies used college-age subjects, and the high percentage of undifferentiated males may reflect the slower maturation rate of males.

In all the studies reported here, females who were classified as androgynous also scored significantly higher on self-esteem. Masculine individuals, both male and female, scored the next highest on self-esteem, while those classified as feminine or undifferentiated scored significantly lower. Apparently, it is not being male or female per se or being an athlete that provides the behavioral frame of reference related to self-esteem, but the psychological attributes one possesses.

Summary

An increased understanding of human behavior and changing attitudes have made the stereotyped masculine and feminine roles no longer appropriate for socializing human beings to function effectively in society. As a result, many of the personality instruments that perpetuate stereotyped expectancies for male and female behavior are no longer appropriate.

Males and females are very much alike psychologically in many respects. Some of the ways they differ can be explained by how they have been socialized rather than by their biology. Athletes, some of whom are male and some of whom are female, appear to be more alike than different in their behavior. This suggests that a person's behavioral frame of reference must be compatible with the demands of the environments he or she seeks to inhabit.

The behavioral demands of competitive sports are less compatible with stereotyped expectations about feminine behavior than they are with the traditional male role. This explains why there has been more concern about the personality conflict female athletes may experience than that male athletes may experience. With the advent of new ways of conceiving behavior, that is, a dualistic as opposed to a bipolar perspective, male and female athletes have been demonstrated to be more similar than different in their behavior. Further, other aspects of their behavior are better explained when examined from this perspective. Attributes such as self-esteem and components of achievement motivation, for example, appear to be more related to one's behavioral frame of reference than one's gender.

There is an obvious need for more research on the possible side effects of changing the definitions of "masculine" and "feminine" that are traditionally used as the standard for rearing boys and girls. The evidence available in no way supports the notion that attempts to foster sex-typed behavior as traditionally defined will produce men and women able to function effectively.

Based on what has been learned about behavior to date, it appears that societies have the option of minimizing, rather than maximizing, sex differences through socialization. This fact is especially pertinent to the kinds of opportunities that are presented to males and females to compete athletically as well as to the reinforcements and rewards that are inherent in these competitive situations. Social institutions and social practices are not merely reflections of the biologically inevitable, according to Maccoby and Jacklin (1974). The social institution of sport needs to change many of its practices to insure that all those who seek to compete athletically maximize their potential and have the same rewards and reinforcements, regardless of their sex. For much too long females have had their "femininity" questioned whenever they made a serious commitment to competitive sport; conversely, for much too long males have had their "masculinity" questioned whenever they chose not to pursue athletic goals.

It is up to human beings to determine what behaviors must be learned by all men and women to foster the lifestyles they most value. Educators and coaches, likewise, must decide the attributes that are needed for athletes to behave effectively in competitive sports. One's biological sex does not appear to have very much to do with behavioral dispositions.

REFERENCES

Bakan, D. *The duality of human existence.* Chicago, Il: Rand McNally, 1966.

Bardwick, J. *Psychology of women: A study of bio-cultural conflicts.* New York: Harper and Row, 1971.

Broverman, J. K., Vogel, S. R., Broverman, D. M., Clarkson, F. E., and Rosenkrantz, P. S. Sex-role stereotypes: A current appraisal. *Journal of Social Issues* 7 (1972): 146–52.

Cheska, A. Current developments in competitive sports for girls and women. *Journal of Health, Physical Education and Recreation* 41 (1970): 86–91.

Douvan, E., and Adelson, J. *The adolescent experience.* New York: Wiley, 1966.

Griffin, P. S. Perceptions of women's roles and female sports involvement among a selected sample of college students. M.S., University of Massachusetts, 1972.

Harris, D. V. *Involvement in sport: A somatopsychic rationale for physical activity.* Philadelphia: Lea & Febiger, 1973.

———. Physical Sex Differences: A Matter of Degree. *The Counseling Psychologist, Counseling Women II* 6 (1976): 9–11.

———. Research studies on the female athlete: Psychological considerations. *Journal of Physical Education and Recreation* 46 (1975): 32–36.

Harris, D. V., & Jennings, S. E. Achievement motivation: There is no fear-of-success in female athletes. Paper presented at the Fall Conference of the Eastern Association of Physical Education of College Women, Hershey, Penn. October, 1978.

———. Self-perception of female distance runners. In Paul Milvy (ed.), *The marathon: Physiological, medical, epidemiological, and psychological studies.* New York: New York Academy of Sciences, 1977.

Helmreich, R., & Spence, J. T. Sex-roles and achievement. In R. W. Christina & D. M. Landers (eds.), *Psychology of motor behavior and sport* (vol. 2). Champaign, Ill: Human Kinetics Publishers, 1977.

Jones, W. H., Chernovetz, M. E., & Hansson, R. O. The enigma of androgyny: Differential implications for males and females? *Journal of Consulting and Clinical Psychology* 46 (1978): 298–313.

Kagan, J., and Moss, H. P. *Birth to Maturity.* New York: Wiley, 1962.

Maccoby, E. E., & Jacklin, C. N. The psychology of sex differences. Stanford: Stanford University Press, 1974.

McKee, J., and Sheriffs, A. The differential evaluation of males and females. *Journal of Personality* 25 (1959): 356–71.

Marmor, J. Changing patterns of femininity: Psychoanalytic implication. In J. B. Miller (ed.) *Psychoanalysis and Women.* New York: Brunner/Mazel, 1973.

Rosenkrantz, P., Bee, H., Vogel, S., Broverman, I. and Broverman, D. M. Sex-role stereotypes and self concepts in college students. *Journal of Consulting and Clinical Psychology,* 1968, *43,* 287–295.

Spence, J. T., & Helmreich, R. L. *Masculinity and femininity: Their psychological dimensions, correlates, and antecedents.* Austin, Tex: University of Texas Press, 1978.

Spence, J. T., Helmreich, R. L., & Stapp, J. Ratings of self and peers on sex-role attributes and their relation to self-esteem and conceptions of masculinity and femininity. *Journal of Personality and Social Psychology 32* (1975): 29–39.

FEMINISM, THE JOCKOCRACY, AND MEN'S LIBERATION: CRYING ALL THE WAY TO THE BANK

MARJORY NELSON

The great question that has never been answered, and which I have not been able to answer despite my years of research into the male soul—what does a man want?—has at last been resolved. He wants everything!

Men already control the economy, get the best jobs, earn the most money, and run the universities, churches, media, health-care system, courts, police, army, navy, marines, and air corps. They live in a world "created" by one male god, "saved" by another, and described by an establishment of misogynist historians and sociologists. They live in a society founded by their "Father," George, whom they want us to remember with a monumental erection. They are protected from women's aggression by male

---

Dr. Marjory Nelson is a sociologist who lives and works in San Francisco.

shrinks, welfare, police who wink at wife beating, laws that ignore rape, and movies that glorify it. Their technology has polluted the entire world: land, sea, and air. And to finish the job, in order to better "protect" us, they are now perfecting a nuclear first-strike capacity that can blow us all up many times over.

And now, what is it that they want? They want to be able to cry in public, to show us how really kind and gentle and good they are.

As I understand the men's liberation movement, its basic position is that men are oppressed by their socialization into a concept of maleness that models itself on sports and the "jock." What this means is that they are not allowed to show compassion or to cry. They are expected to be tough and competitive and to perform under any and all circumstances: to "play the game." The prototype for this kind of behavior is the football player who is shot full of drugs and sent out to play even though injured. He has a responsibility to the team, and to all men, to show that he is a man. Above all, he must not exhibit any of the characteristics—weakness, compassion, emotionality, dependency—typically ascribed to women. In the jockocracy,[1] the worst thing a man can be is womanly.

Many men of the movement reject this national hysteria over sports. They say that they want to be able to express their emotions, to be gentle, nice guys. And I, for one, approve of this, while at the same time I have a healthy skepticism about what this movement really means to women. That is why I, a radical, socialist feminist decided to write this article, not because I see any hope for my liberation from this men's movement, but because I suspect this book will be read by women who are still looking to men and to the society based on patriarchal values for their salvation.

One concomitant of those values is the belief that personal, psychological solutions are adequate responses to a vast societal oppression. This attitude is so pervasive that I'm sure there are many women, as well as men, who believe that if only men could be a little "nicer," more gentle, help out with the housework, watch the kids, then marriage might not be so difficult, then their own lives would have more meaning.

One of the products of the modern women's movement is a cataloguing of the myriad ways women are exploited, denigrated, and psychologically and physically abused in our society. A complete report of this research would more than fill this book, so I will cite only a few examples: (1) In 1974 the earnings gap between men and women was wider than it was in 1955. In 1974 the median income earned by men was 75 percent higher than that earned by women, whereas in 1955, it was only 55 percent greater.[2] Thus at a time when there are more women in the labor force, when more women than ever before are heads of families, we find that discrimination against women workers is actually increasing.[3] (2) The two most rapidly increasing crimes against women are rape and physical assault. Between 1969 and 1974 the number of rapes rose 49 percent. Reported rapes in 1974 numbered about 50,000. However, estimates of actual occurrences number ten times that amount—over half a million, or one every two minutes.[4] Conservative estimates of the number of wife beatings that same year begin at a million.[5]

Starting from this data, my real question for the men's liberation movement is this: how is it possible for men to develop compassionate personalities in a society that systematically and ruthlessly abuses women? In a society where wives who don't conform to their husband's wishes are beaten, raped, and locked up in mental hospitals where they are given shock treatments, strong drugs, and even lobotomies? When women are assaulted, ridiculed, or *fired if they try to change things? Does it make any sense to worry about abstract qualities of compassion and creativity?*

As far as I can determine, the men's liberation movement is a heuristic fiction invented by a few guys who've been battered around a bit more than they think is their due: athletes, upwardly mobile professionals, friends and husbands, or ex-husbands, of militant feminists. These men are worried because they have discovered that they are not going to get the pot of gold at the end of the rainbow; not because it doesn't exist, but because it is out of their reach. And their explanation for this (since they are already equipped with the magic male wand) is that they must have some psychological deficiency.

It seems to me that their reaction is not so very different from that of many middle-class feminists, women who grew up believing that if they just played the game, followed the rules, they, too, would be greatly rewarded. These women talk about assertiveness training just as the men talk about learning compassion. In both cases, the "problem" is dealt with as an abstraction, apart from the fabric of their lives. However, a man doesn't have to be a jock to oppress a woman. All he has to do is marry her. He doesn't even have to beat her to destroy her. The law, the isolation of nuclear families, the economy, do the rest.

The roots of violence do not lie in the male character, but in the institutions of patriarchy, capitalism, imperialism, and racism. Men, particularly upper-middle-class white men, get some real goodies from these institutions. And if their movement does not deal with this reality, it may function only to obscure, deny, or even oppose movements that have risen in opposition to these institutions: the women's movement, the labor movement, the third-world and the civil-rights movements.

My criticism of the men's movement is that it fails to

deal with the whole question of power. There is a reason for the jockocracy. The oppression of women has provided men with some very clear advantages: it has excluded women from economic competition, channeling them into low-paying, dead-end jobs; it has provided men with round-the-clock unpaid domestic labor; given them gentle, soft, undemanding sexual partners on whom they may vent their rage without fear of retribution; and given men children who bear their name, thus providing them with a form of immortality.

The oppression of women has also played an important part in the growth of capital. In addition to providing cheap exploitable labor, women have reproduced, trained, and serviced the rest of the labor force. The isolation and mystique of the family has served to diffuse and cool out some of the frustrations of exploited labor. The home is a "refuge" in a cruel and demanding world. Ever since Eve, women have been societal scapegoats. No matter how bad things get, part of the payoff for the man is the assurance that he at least is not a woman.

On the other hand, the rigid sex-role stereotyping that has been part of this system has also managed to deny the male access to the important human qualities of compassion, gentleness, and intuition—all characteristics essential to the flowering of culture and creativity. Therein lies the paradox. A man cannot be truly liberated without giving up his power. Also, he cannot do this as an isolated individual. If he wants access to female characteristics, he must look at and change the system, including the ideology that defends his power over women. That is the dichotomy in which emotion is seen as the opposite of rationality. Woman is emotional, evil. Man is rational, good. This belief is supported by the entire fabric of patriarchal thought from the Bible to Freud, which denigrates what women say as idle chatter or gossip, distorts and ignores the significance of women's contributions and serves as a rationale for with-holding power from women and letting them live at the bottom of the economy.

The contradiction here is that although a man may not have much individual power in society, he is still part of a system that treats women as a lower caste, and he still benefits from that system. This is why he is trained not to show his feelings and why, in fact, he doesn't show them. A display of emotion reveals vulnerability. It is part of the ideology of power that it is not vulnerable. If a man revealed his true feelings to the women around him, the old myth that she is dependent on him—that it is he who protects her—would begin to break down. A man benefits by not showing his emotions. For him, withholding his feelings is a function of power. One of the reasons this gets confusing is that the kind of power men have over women is institutionalized. Their privileges are protected by a whole series of interlocking social mechanisms that function continually to keep women in their place. A man does not necessarily have to assert himself to benefit from this power. It is there for him. It is built into our language, reinforced by laws, the police, religion, social customs, traditions, and so forth. It is so much a part of institutional life that most of the time it operates smoothly without anyone's conscious intervention.

Since the beginning of recorded history, we have lived under patriarchal domination. The growth of capitalism affected the patriarchal structure in important ways. The separation of production from the household changed the value of women's labor in the home, while revolutionizing the organization of productive labor. This created a new middle class and an industrial working class, but it also pitted women workers against their male counterparts.

In the 20th century, the reorganization of capitalism

into larger and larger units of production caused a relative loss of power to males of the middle class. In 20th century patriarchal capitalism, the individual father's power is woven into a class system and checked by the grandfather of us all, the federal government. Authority is both concentrated in an elite class and delegated to the big brothers who are managers, administrators, and government officials. For most middle-class men, male authority no longer comes from being head of a household or a unit of production, but from identifying with state violence and class privileges. But in order to partake of this authority, a man must continually prove that he is, in fact, a man. Thus the patriarchy, under capitalism, has become the jockocracy.

This shift in power has not meant a lessening of control over women. Under the guise of liberal reforms, state control of the family has actually increased. In writing about the state in 1931, sociologist, Robert MacIver noted that it exercised "more stringent control" over the marriage partnership than over any other partnership or association.[6] Power over women and children no longer resides in the individual husband and father alone, but also in the state and its representatives. However, there has been an adjustment in the control of women according to their class. Middle- and upper-class women have more benefits, such as control of property and children, as long as they remain within the family structure. But should they reject that structure, particularly should they become lesbians, they find their rights severely restricted. Poor women, notably those on welfare, are rigidly supervised by government agencies.

Instead of understanding Father's loss of direct authority as a result of class relations, social analysts put the blame squarely on Mom. Maggie and Jiggs cartoons popularized the new ideology. Yet it wasn't all that new. The old myth about Eve was only dressed up a bit. Woman's rebelliousness was now defined as a "sickness." The new secular religion, science, developed much more sophisticated instruments for controlling women: psychology and modern medicine. Father's power now is reinforced by the psychoanalyst and the gynocologist. The housewife is cooled out with therapy and drugs.

It is the diffusion of power, seemingly away from the individual Father, that makes the problem difficult to understand. It has been easy to put the blame on women, since the "equalitarian" family obscures the realities of patriarchal control over women. Males, meanwhile, long to fit the old petit-bourgeois ideal of the rugged individual who is directly in control of everything. Sports heroes help "feed" the fantasy that this is achievable.

Unfortunately, like everything else in our economy, sports have become big business. Just as the corner grocery store has been replaced by the supermarket chain, so sandlot baseball has been replaced by the New York Yankees. The players are owned. One of the reasons the modern male is disenchanted with sports is that they are no longer under his control, or even under the control of his local community. Some person he has never met owns his team, and the game is played strictly for profit. Under such conditions, it is easier for men to see the violence within the system. This violence has always been there, but now it seems more impersonal and therefore more offensive.

Men today have another problem too. The women in their lives are discovering that they don't really need them so much. They are even beginning to find that other women are more interesting than them. No longer will a woman sit at a man's feet listening to him, pretending to be enthralled when she can spend the time enjoying good talks with other women. No longer does a women sit home sewing clothes to save money. She goes out to get a job so that she can buy the clothes. No longer does a woman allow a man to define the sex act and lie about having an orgasm. If he doesn't satisfy her, she goes elsewhere.

Actually, the men have something to cry about, all right. All over the world the women's movement is touching women's lives. Profound social and economic changes are occurring that are getting women out of the isolation of their homes, putting them in touch with other women and with other revolutionary movements. Men can't become the leaders of this movement—even though they are forced to respond to it—and so they invent their own.

I do want to encourage men to deal with their psychological inadequacies, however, and to give each other real emotional support—the kind they automatically expect from women. But if they want real changes, they are going to have to begin giving us some support too. Men cannot liberate women. But they can take their feet off our necks. They can speak out against rape and wife beating and stop doing it! They can work for social programs that develop jobs with decent pay for women as well as for men. They can begin to listen seriously to what women are saying about them and this society. And finally, they can begin to put some of their money where their mouths are. My skepticism about men's liberation might weaken a little if the proceeds of this book were invested in a shelter for battered women, rape victims, and crazy wives—a shelter controlled by those women themselves, and not by the doctors who treat them, the church, or the state.*

*Editor's note: A portion of the royalties from this anthology are being donated to *Haven House* and *Simple Gifts*, two halfway houses designed to meet the needs of victims of wife beating in the Buffalo, N.Y., metropolitan area.

FOOTNOTES

1. Florynce Kennedy, a black feminist lawyer, invented the work "jockocracy."

2. U.S. Department of Labor, Women's Bureau, "The Earnings Gap Between Women and Men" (1976), p. 1.

3. For a fuller exploration of this subject see Louise Kapp Howe, *Pink Collar Workers* (New York: Putnam, 1977).

4. Nancy Gager & Cathleen Schurr, *Sexual Assault: Confronting Rape in America* (New York: Grosset & Dunlap, 1976), I.

5. Karen Durbin, "Wife-Beating," *Ladies Home Journal* (June 1974), p. 64.

6. Robert M. MacIver, *Society, Its Structures and Changes* (New York: Long & Smith, 1931), pp. 145–46.

ALTERNATIVES
FOR THE
FUTURE

INTRODUCTION

C. Wright Mills observes, "The uneasiness, the malaise of our time, is due to this root fact; in our politics and economy, in family life and religion—in practically every sphere of our existence—the certainties of the eighteenth and nineteenth centuries have disintegrated or been destroyed and, at the same time, no new sanctions or justifications for the new routines we live, and must live, have taken hold."[1] Within the past century, women and men's lives have undergone a marked transformation and the patriarchal sources of male and female identity are eroding. Alternative lifestyles and values are emerging but remain largely undefined. We often find ourselves threatened, confused and uneasily adrift within the sea of social change.

Women have made important strides toward redefining their role in American society. Socially, feminists have sought to forge new ways for men and women to relate to one another. They have developed an ideology through which greater equality and understanding can be secured for the betterment of all. Politically, they have agitated and lobbied for legislative and institutional change. Sexually, women's liberationists have articulated a person-centered sexual ethos intended to combat impersonality, a lack of communication, and the exploitation of women as sexual objects. In short, feminism represents a medicine with which to treat "the malaise of our time."

And yet, men's attitudes toward women and their understanding of the changing male role are lagging behind shifting social realities. Male resistance to change hinders woman's further liberation, limits self-expression and role options for men, and produces destructive relations between the sexes. Change, however, is often inevitable, and as Myron Brenton writes,

> . . . no matter how much American males may
> yearn for the simpler, more clearly defined times
> gone by, their yearnings are futile. They have the
> choice of remaining what collectively they are—a
> sex at bay—or of redefining themselves in the
> light of the changing culture.[2]

As this anthology shows, many men have begun to
seek the cure, to change society and themselves to fit and
further present egalitarian trends. Spurred by the ethos of
feminism and men's liberation, prompted by interpersonal
pressures from women, or faced with rethinking their lives
after a divorce, they are searching for a better model of
human behavior outside the restrictions of traditional sex-
role stereotypes. As we have tried to show, however, personal change without concomitant political and institutional change too often is like a sailboat without wind. The
individual and society, ideologies and material conditions,
the personal and the institutional, are inexorably interde-
pendent elements of social change. If we wish to humanize
our identities, we must also transform the society that
shapes our lives. Recognizing the interplay between the
personal and institutional dimensions of social change, we
can now present several alternatives to the present machismo ethos and structure of sport. Our proposals are not
to be considered a panacea, but merely steps toward creating the conditions necessary for sexual equality and less
stereotypically masculine socialization in athletics.

Of prime importance is a redefinition of sport that emphasizes health rather than winning, playfulness rather
than aggression, and participation rather than consumptive passivity.[3] The stoical, hypercompetitive, and combative conception of sport that is so prevalent today is an extension of our patriarchal value system that we can well do
without. Discarding it would facilitate the integration of

women into athletics and make room for an alternative athletic ideal for men to identify with.

Contributor George B. Leonard finds that the "win at all costs" conception of sport seeped into the public consciousness during the Vietnam war, as both military and corporate voices sang the praises of relentless competition in a way that recalled images of human social intercourse endemic to Hobbes and Social Darwinism. Leonard argues that a grotesque emphasis on winning and competition not only distorts the meaning of athletics and has inhumane social consequences, but it leads to blind conformism and self-defeatism in those who participate in sports. He concludes that, "To turn this society toward peaceful, humane change, we can begin with reform of sports."

In "The Competitive Male as Loser," R. C. Townsend explores the roots of his failure as a marriage partner. His autobiographical reflections reveal how the machismo ethos of athletic competition contributed to the development of a self-destructive drive for success, an impersonal and exploitative sexuality, and an inability to express emotion in relationships with either women or men. The pathos and realism of Townsend's disclosures dramatize the need for a reformulation of the meaning of sport.

Just as economic achievement is an essential hallmark of successful manhood in social life, so winning is the earmark of success in sports. Because the institution of sport is such a fountainhead of traditional masculine values, failing to do well in sports often means a loss of self-respect for males. Book and magazine writer Dan Wakefield offers the reader some thoughts about being male and failing at sports. A frustrated jogger and formerly uncoordinated youngster who couldn't quite meet the standards of masculine excellence in sports, he suggests that the increased participation of women in athletics may help dispel the notion that athletic prowess is equivalent to "manhood." Behind Wakefield's entertaining observations is a recognition that the waning of the rigid sex-role stereotyping inherent in sports will encourage new modes of self-expression and physical freedom for *both* men and women.

Sociologist and marathoner David Broad suggests that the increasing popularity of running in America signals a trend away from alienating athletic activities and toward a redefinition of sport that emphasizes health, equality, and self-fulfillment. He also contends that the history of running erodes the mythos of male supremacy and debunks commonly held stereotypes of the aged. In Broad's view the running revolution may be steering our culture toward a more humanistic conception of sport.

Co-editor Donald F. Sabo, Jr., argues that physical exercise, as it is structured by the subculture of traditional sports, bears the imprint of stereotypical masculine values. Rather than enhancing the pleasure of physical motion, the jock approach to exercise is predicated on a stoic denial of mind-body unity. Sabo introduces several exercises designed to induce new states of body awareness and to restructure male consciousness away from a traditionally masculine motif.

One element crucial to a more humanistic attitude toward sports is *complete parity* of funding for women's and men's athletics at the intercollegiate, secondary, and elementary school levels, and to this end we call for full implementation of Title IX of the Education Amendments Act. Enacted by Congress in 1972, Title IX bars discrimination on the basis of sex in all educational institutions receiving allocations for women's and men's sports. In 1972 women's intercollegiate athletic programs, for example, received only 1 per cent of the amount budgeted for men's programs. By 1978, the women's slice of the monetary pie had increased to approximately 10 per cent, which is far from the ideal of equal athletic opportunity prescribed by law.[4] Arguments against the full implementation of Title IX have come from the male athletic establishment—the National Collegiate Athletic Association, administrators, athletic directors, coaches, authors, and sportswriters.[5] Their overall position can be quickly summarized: Men's sports such as baseball, football, hockey, or basketball are major moneymakers, and profits gleaned from ticket sales and alumni donations are used to fund women's and intramural programs. Although women's programs deserve a larger portion of institutional funds than they have received in the past, complete funding parity will sound the deathknell for existing men's programs. The Department of Health, Education and Welfare, the agency charged by congress with enforcing Title IX, unfortunately has not framed any firm guidelines for compliance with the law.

As a result of the ambivalence exhibited by HEW about the controversy surrounding Title IX, fed in part by a million-dollar lobbying campaign led by the NCAA, virtually no major college or university now provides equal athletic opportunities for women. This lamentable circumstance has arisen in part because college administrators regard men's sports as a commercial rather than an educational venture. Women's athletics and intramural sports, on the other hand, are regarded as bereft of commercial value. Title IX provided for resolution of the conflict, but HEW's vacillation makes the outlook for equality of opportunity in athletics doubtful.[6]

The potential social benefits of complete funding parity for women's and men's athletics are numerous. First, the influx of money into women's programs would better their quality and make them more attractive to more women. Second, such a funding policy would help to decentralize athletic programs at *all* educational levels. Under the existing hierarchal system, the largest portion of funds goes to traditional men's sports (usually basketball, baseball, and football). Hence, a comparatively small number of "stars" receive a disproportionate amount of money while less "prestigious" sports and intramural programs with more participants suffer from a lack of facilities, supervision, and equipment. *It is important to note that a decentralization of funding would increase the number of males as well as females participating in sports.* To put it simply, the net effect would be to reduce the number of "stars" and increase the number of athletes. Third, decentralized funding might encourage a greater emphasis on participation, fun, and health rather than on winning at any cost, stoic dedication, and building teams of superstars. Fourth, any decentralized restructuring of the existing male-dominated, star-dependent athletic hierarchy would make the institution of sport more eqalitarian. This, in turn, would facilitate the growth of empathy between the sexes and end the male identification with the destructive image of masculinity inherent in the traditional view of sports. In summary, funding parity would make athletic programs at once more democratic and more humane.

In addition to restructuring the larger socioeconomic organization of sport to increase equality between the sexes, we must develop alternative modes of athletic activity free from destructive sex role stereotypes. As sociologist-anthropologist Bonnie A. Beck observes, both the historical and the contemporary impetus toward humanistic sport has come mainly from women. The masculine tradition of sport, or "ManSport," has been predicated upon the patriarchal values of male supremacy, the glorification of physical power, excessive competition, and individualism. In contrast, the ethical and political legacy of "WomanSport" has emphasized a nonelitist, playful, healthful, and cooperative athletic ethos. In impassioned prose and with analytical acumen, she describes the current struggle between ManSport and WomanSport and calls for complete "integration with equality" in all sports. If the future of sport is to move in genuinely humane directions, she asserts, women athletes must act collectively to ward off co-optation by the male-dominated athletic establishment, and male inhabitants of the athletic subculture must begin to show their sister athletes acceptance rather than ridicule, support rather than resistance, solidarity rather than separatism.

In "Creating New Sports for Men and Women," Warren Farrell offers some innovative designs for nonsexist athletic participation. He devises six new categories of sporting activities that would at once invite participation by both sexes and encourage the development of nonsexist values and behavior.

We hope that the critical analysis of the influence of athletics upon the male identity provided in this book will raise the consciousness of its male readers and serve as a complement to the preceeding recommendations for changes in the definition and institution of sport. Because sports are so close to the experiential pulse of most men and contain the earmarks of traditional male socialization, they constitute an excellent departure point for introspection and for rethinking one's life.

In summary, we have outlined several alternative aims for the future of American sport in hopes of contributing to a more humane society and transforming male consciousness and experience. We conclude our remarks with these words from Myron Brenton:

> *There is a new way to masculinity, a new concept of what it means to be a man. It has little to do with how strong the male is physically, how adept he is at ordering people around, how expensive his cars are, how versatile he is with a set of tools, or how closely he identifies with all the other ster-*

eotyped attitudes and acts. It has everything to do with how he manages his life—the way he conducts himself as a human being in terms of his wife, his children, his business associates, his friends, his neighbors, and his compatriots in the community—and with his ability to make decisions, with his courage to say no, as well as yes, with his perception into the consequences of his actions and decisions. This isn't the easy way. It could hardly be called the path of least resistance. But there's no turning back the clock. With the equality of women an inexorable trend, with the traditional male patterns increasingly losing their significance for a variety of reasons, it is—at bottom—the alternative to what may well become psychic castration.[7]

FOOTNOTES

1. C. Wright Mills, *White Collar* (New York: Oxford University Press, 1956), p. xvi.
2. Myron Brenton, *The American Male* (Greenwich, Conn.: Fawcett, 1967), p. 207.
3. For an articulation of this position see Harry Edwards, *The Sociology of Sport* (Homewood, Ill.: Dorsey Press, 1973); Dave Meggysey, *Out of Their League* (Berkeley: Ramparts Press, 1970); Paul Hoch, *Rip Off the Big Game* (Garden City, N.Y.: Doubleday, 1972); Jack Scott, *The Athletic Revolution* (New York: Macmillan, 1971).
4. For a discussion of this subject see "Comes the Revolution," *Time* (June 1978), pp. 54–59.
5. For an expert exposition of this "liberal" position see James A. Michener, *Sports in America* (New York: Fawcett, 1976), chap. 5.
6. Margot Polivy, "July 21: Deadline or Dead End?" New York *Times* (July 16, 1978).
7. Brenton, *The American Male*, op. cit.

WINNING ISN'T EVERYTHING.
IT'S NOTHING.

GEORGE B. LEONARD

In less than a generation, the prevailing sports ethos in America has shifted from, "It's not whether you win or lose, it's how you play the game," to "Winning isn't everything. It's the only thing." The current public glorification of winning at all costs came to the fore during a war we did not win. Sermons by top corporate executives on hot competition as the American way were being directed at the younger generation during a period when many of these same executives were making every effort to get around the federal regulations against price-fixing and illegal cooperation among corporate "competitors.". . .

If winning has become our national religion, the Super Bowl is its apotheosis. But the ceremony, in spite of the huge crowd, the music, the flags, the pom-pom girls, the special coin struck off in memory of the late Vince Lombardi, is somehow unconvincing. We are embarrassed when the three Apollo 17 astronauts, paraded out to lead the Pledge of Allegiance, become confused, make several false starts and look at each other to see if the right hand should be placed over the heart. And we are perhaps relieved when their ordeal ends and a disembodied voice floats out over the stadium: "Now, to honor America, let's join The Little Angels for the singing of the national anthem."

Contradictions, anomalies and grotesqueries in the current sports scene should not surprise us. A neurosis asserts itself most painfully and insistently just as it is being uprooted and cast out. The final period in any evolutionary

---

George B. Leonard, "Winning Isn't Everything. It's Nothing." *Intellectual Digest* (October 1973).

line of development—of a biological species, an artistic movement or a society—is often marked by convolution, overspecialization and other bizarre extremes. If, as many scholars have pointed out, a society's sports and games mirror its basic structure, then what we may be seeing in the current worship of hot competition and winning at all costs is the end of a particular line of social development. The Super Bowl may ultimately stand as a symbol of a culture in transformation.

Because our own sports are so highly competitive, we may tend to believe that all human beings, especially males, are born competitors, driven by their genetic nature to the proposition that winning is "the only thing." The games of many cultures, however, have no competitive element whatever. For example, the Tangu people of New Guinea play a popular game known as taketak, which involves throwing a spinning top into massed lots of stakes driven into the ground. There are two teams. Players of each team try to touch as many stakes with their tops as possible. In the end, however, the participants play not to win but to draw. The game must go on until an exact draw is reached. This requires great skill, since players sometimes must throw their tops into the massed stakes without touching a single one. Taketak expresses a prime value in Tangu culture, that is, the concept of moral equivalency, which is reflected in the precise sharing of foodstuffs among the people.

> *"The notion that humans evolved through relentless competition with nature and each other is false."*

Indeed, the notion that humans evolved only through relentless, grinding competition with nature and each other is a false one. The familiar cartoon showing the caveman as a brutish creature carrying a club with one hand and dragging a woman by the other tells us nothing about primitive life. The Stone Age peoples that survive in remote corners of the world are, until we meddle with them, usually gentle and sensitive, with a fine ecological sense. The recently discovered Tasaday tribe of Mindanao in the Philippines, true Stone Age cave dwellers, have no words for "hate" or "fight." They are cooperative and loving. The brute in the cartoon is our secret image of ourselves.

Darwin's theory—natural selection, the "survival of the fittest"—is sometimes cited as justification for hot competition. Social philosophers of the propertied, industrial classes in the late nineteenth and early twentieth centuries promoted a brutal, jungle philosophy, but it was based on Darwin's account of the predatory rather than the social animals. This social Darwinism was long ago discredited. Charles Darwin is clear on the point that, for the human race, the highest survival value lies in intelligence, a moral sense and social cooperation, not competition.

Among the English-speaking peoples, the close and inevitable relationship between sport and competition is of fairly recent origin. According to Webster's New International Dictionary (second edition), the word "sport" comes from "disport," which originally meant "to carry away from work." The first definition applied to the word is, "that which diverts and makes mirth; pastime; amusement." In a series of definitions 40 lines long, there is no mention whatever of competition and only one brief reference to sport as a "contest."

The attempt to justify hot competition as an essential aspect of human existence goes on in the face of all the evidence. There exists, for example, a common assumption that competition is needed to "motivate behavior." Yet no study has shown that competition necessarily motivates behavior any more effectively than other means—extrinsic reinforcement, for instance, or even the sheer joy of doing something well. To see the real function of competition in our society, we must look deeper.

In 1967, I collaborated with Marshall McLuhan on an article entitled, "The Future of Education." Our idea sessions ranged over a number of topics but kept coming back to the question of competition and why it is so tirelessly proclaimed, not only by coaches, but by educators and all those traditionalists who concern themselves with shaping the lives of our young people. At last, McLuhan came forth with one of his "probes"—a sudden thought from an unexpected direction.

"I know," he said. "Competition creates resemblance."

To compete with someone, in other words, you must agree to run on the same track, to do what he is doing, to follow the same set of rules. The only way you'll differentiate yourself is by doing precisely the same thing, slightly faster or better. Thus, though performance may improve, the chances are you will become increasingly like the person with whom you compete.

In this light, it is easy to see that a culture dedicated to creating standardized, specialized, predictable human components could find no better way of grinding them out than by making every possible aspect of life a matter of competition. "Winning out" in this respect does not make rugged individualists. It shapes conformist robots. Keep your eyes open during the football season. The defensive ends begin to look more and more alike. The cornerbacks become ever more interchangeable.

The final argument for hot competition all the way down to nursery school is that competition makes winners. The argument is, at best, half true. It makes nonwinners, too—generally more nonwinners than winners. And a number of studies indicate that losing can become a lifelong habit. What is more, when competition reaches the *present level, the argument becomes altogether false. As proclaimed by the more extreme coaches and sportswriters today, competition makes us—all of us—losers.*

Between 1958 and 1971, the San Francisco Giants had the best overall won-lost record in the National League. For five straight years, from 1965 through 1969, they finished in second place. To do so, you would think, they must have "won out" over many other teams. Increasingly during this period of second-place finishes, however, they came to be characterized by fan and sportswriter alike as born losers.

"Winning isn't everything. It's the only thing." And in our present-day sports culture, that means being Number One, Numero Uno, the one and only.

Take the Dallas Cowboys. For five straight years, from 1966 through 1970, the Cowboys won their division championships, then were eliminated, either in the playoffs or finally, in January of 1971, in the Super Bowl itself. And what was said of this fine professional football team during this period of unprecedented winning? They "couldn't win the big ones." They were, you see, just losers.

> "Competition makes more nonwinners than winners. Studies indicate that losing can become a habit."

When the Cowboys did at last win the Super Bowl, in January 1972, it became apparent that the players themselves had been swept up in the Numero Uno mystique. One by one they came to the TV cameras after the game to affirm that nothing had really meant anything except this victory. The champagne flowed. The players were probably happy for a moment, but their faces were not entirely unclouded. And the mask of fear that coach Tom Landry wears along the sidelines during every game when his winning record is threatened was not entirely erased. The problem is this: even after you've just won the Super Bowl—especially after you've just won the Super Bowl—there's always next year.

If "Winning isn't everything. It's the only thing," then "the only thing" is nothing—emptiness, the nightmare of life without ultimate meaning. This emptiness pursues us wherever "winning out" is proclaimed as God. I once spoke to a group of top-ranking industrialists in a seminar session and argued that hot competition is far from inevitable in the future. As my argument developed, I noticed a look of real anxiety on some of the faces around me. One industrialist finally spoke up, "If there is to be no competition, then what will life be all about?" We would probably be appalled to discover how many people in this culture have no notion of accomplishment for its own sake and define their own existence solely in terms of how many other people they can beat out.

Only through this viewpoint can we understand how a talented young athlete can let himself become what Gary Shaw in his new book has called Meat on the Hoof, a commodity to be manipulated, hazed, drugged, used, traded and discarded. And we may be able, by imagining the emptiness that accompanies "winning," to comprehend why (as David Meggyesy has revealed in his book, Out of Their League) a prototype of supermasculinity would allow himself to be treated in the manner of a eunuch, prevented at times from having sexual relations with his own wife.

There is nothing wrong with competition in the proper proportion. Like a little salt, it adds zest to the game and to life itself. But when the seasoning is mistaken for the substance, only sickness can follow. Similarly, when winning becomes "the only thing," it can lead only to eventual emptiness and anomie.

The time has come, I feel, to blow the whistle on this madness. We may not be able to turn the American sports juggernaut around overnight, but we can suggest that sports are possible without beating the brains out of the opposing team, and that it may be possible for players and fans alike to take great pleasure in a beautiful play, even if it's executed by the opposition. We can start working out new sports that are noncompetitive or less competitive or in which competition is placed in the proper perspective, as a matter of good sport and good humor. We can start looking for the larger potentialities that actually already exist in the realm of sports and games.

Our present way of life, based upon endless, ever-increasing expansion of the production and consumption of energy, is eventually doomed. And so much else is based upon that expansion—our definition of job and full employment, our inculcation and suppression of aggression our attempts to fix consciousness at a single point, our whole neurosis structure, our glorification of what we call "competition" and "winning." The present rate of expansion in the United States can go on for a few more decades, but then it comes up against the most fundamental law of thermodynamics. Even with perfectly clean nuclear energy, the final result of all our burning and wasteful consumption will be the overheating of this small planet. We must seek alternate modes of life, other ways of being on this earth.

"There is nothing wrong with competition in the proper proportion. Like a little salt; it adds zest to life."

Changes are coming. Sports represent a key joint in any society. To turn this society toward peaceful, humane change, we can begin with reform of sports. Some intellectuals have ignored this aspect of our life, believing somehow that sports are beyond serious consideration. They are quite mistaken. There is nothing trivial about the flight of a *ball, for it traces for us the course of the planet. Through the movement of the human body, we can come to know what the philosopher Pythagoras called* kosmos, *a word containing the idea of both perfect order and intense beauty. Sports are too beautiful and profound for simplistic slogans. How we play the game may turn out to be more important than we imagine, for it signifies nothing less than our way of being in the world.*

THE COMPETITIVE MALE AS LOSER

R. C. TOWNSEND

. . . Four months ago I separated from my wife. I have not the distance, nor the novelist's or analyst's talent to discover and set down in clear sentences why our relationship failed, but I can look into myself, look into my own past and ask what it was that might explain my failure in the relationship. What I want to explore is how my experience over the years with men and women, boys and girls, shaped my expectations and behavior in what should be the culmination of a male-female relationship—a marriage. Only in the negative sense was it a culmination for me. What was distorting and stultifying in moments and situations in my early life bore sour fruit in my marriage. Looking at some of those moments and situations may help me understand why I failed, why my relations with my wife were not open, vital, life-affirming. . . .

First vague memories are seemingly unrelated to my own marriage, but they are indicative of the atmosphere in which I—a boy and an only child—was first groomed for

---

R. C. Townsend, "The Competitive Male as Loser," from Alice G. Sargent, ed., *Beyond Sex Roles* (St. Paul, Minn.: West Publishing Company, 1977), pp. 228–42.

success. And being groomed for success can, I think, deprive one of the natural ability to give in a relationship. Out for oneself, one doesn't give; fearing failure, loath to admit to failure, one cannot receive. The memories that crowd upon me are of striving to succeed and of doing so in an atmosphere that was consequently lacking in opportunities to give, to fail, to take, to experience the mutual love in which a marriage must be grounded. . . .

My parents were motivated not only by their marital history but also by living in wealthy New York suburbs. It was in Rye, New York that I was catapulted into first grade; it was in Fairfield, Connecticut that I finished my elementary school education, in the Country Day Schools of both towns. The Depression figured prominently in the little of my parents' conversation that I heard. My father spoke of how a corrupt partner left him to pay off thousands of dollars worth of debts; he could always stun me with the story of how he knew the Depression had come when, sitting in a Wall Street office, he saw a body on its way to death below. More immediately, I knew that we rented a house for one hundred dollars a month in Fairfield; whereas my classmates owned their own houses, more than likely, swimming pools, and, in the case of an heir to the Reynolds tobacco fortune, a bowling alley. My mother might brag that when a friend of mine came for the night we used to fight for the honor of sleeping on the floor, but what I knew was that my friends very seldom came for the night. We had no extra bed; I usually did the visiting. My parents were older, poorer, and my mother was Armenian in a totally WASP community. She would take ritual swipes at the Turks and she would point to the fact that the first Christian church was established in Armenia, but she felt no pride. Mostly she wanted it known that Armenians were not Semitic. She wanted it known—when the warning went out to my future brother-in-law, for example—that there was no "Jewish blood" in the family. And I would have to succeed to the extent of wiping out any thought that there was.

Intended or not, I felt the pressure to defend us against a younger, more stable, wealthier, purer community. It was easy enough to get A's. It took a little more energy to stay on the honor roll while home in bed with pneumonia, but I did, and was praised. It was easy enough to play school sports. It took a lot more energy—primarily my mother's—to try out for and eventually play on the Pee Wee Rangers' hockey team. That required an hour's commute to New York City three times a week, and when Grantland Rice made a movie short of the team, some fast talking on my mother's part was necessary to get me a starring role. But she was the only mother there (the other boys knew the subways; I had to be driven in from the country), and she managed to have it that I was the representative Pee Wee, going through the paces with the Ranger's star center, Buddy O'Connor, for all the world to see. She wanted me to be a Quiz Kid and had the school fill out a recommendation; she wanted me to be a movie star. A lot of A's and a star role in a twenty-minute short were all I got, but that was a great deal and I was praised.

I was not praised enough by others for my mother's satisfaction, though: she never did forgive the school for giving the Outstanding Boy Award to someone else. I had to wait four years for that. Then I would win the Deerfield Cup, awarded "to that boy who most nearly represents the Deerfield ideal." At Deerfield I lived with boys my own age but still went to classes with boys a year older. It was not until my last year that, inevitably, I "caught up." I was, as the inscription would have it anyway, an ideal student and though my parents were miles away, I kept in touch, complying with their wish that I write once a day on one of the self-addressed postcards they gave me at the beginning of the year. And so it went; "A on the algebra test, scored three goals in practice today. All's well. Your loving son." At the ivy-league college I did the same, the difference being that my parents made it to most of the home games. And I assume that their pride, the sense that their boy was succeeding, only increased. It must have. When I was about twelve, I can remember my father positioning guests in front of a portrait of me, asking them to admire not only the face—"look especially at the eyes"—but also the prizes won up to that point. After I had graduated from college, my wife and I fended off my embarrassment and her aggravation over my father's chatter about me by referring to me as "Phi Beta Kappa, Summa Cum Laude," the terms in which he referred to me—reward, as it were, for my having called him "Sir" all those years.

The success story goes on—scholarships, graduate school, a professorship—but God knows it is not in my pride that I write. First, I write in order to bring out the tremendous pressure for success under which I labored. . . .

I felt the pressure keenly and I felt it long. Indeed, one may never get out from under it; or at least it may always be there. When I told my mother about my separation, beginning an uncharacteristically long and searching letter with the uncharacteristic opening, "all is not well," she answered in pain: "Oh, Kim (author's nickname). I always thought of you as on a pedestal!" I might have found a better place to stand: I might have realized that posing for others' momentary delight (and being encouraged to strike poses by others) is soul-destroying. But she only saw marriage as one more achievement—or, in my case, a separation as grounds for being stripped of all one's hard-earned honors.

Such was the pressure; it was only one kind of pressure the most obvious. It was, perhaps, extreme, but most young men feel it and they exert it—and the attendant pressure created by the fear of failure—on each other. Having given some indication of the pressure my parents put on me, I must go on to explore what is inelegantly called "peer pressure" and ask regarding both parental and peer pressure: What are the implications for anyone trying to establish a mature male-female relationship? What relations must one have had while trying to make one's way? What relations to other young men? What relations to young women? What did those relations do to me? How did they prepare me for my marriage? . . . .

In the classroom, at first at least, I was with young women, but at whichever institution, we were all protected from competition in its rawest forms. But it was not in the classroom that we (boys at least) were most seriously ourselves anyway. It was not there that I was most damagingly miseducated for marital life. There was—there always is—recognition of the fact that education is in part a game. Ironically, it was in games on the playing fields, and, of course, in the dormitories, that real damage could be done.

The serious business of education is soon turned into a game; in games one's life is often on the line. I was always good at sports, played successfully on many successful teams, but I always sensed that as was the case at home, one could never be quite good enough. Coaches are unrelenting parents.

I never have learned to love the violent in sport, but this was not for having been underexposed. My first memory of having failed at violence was in day school, in about the fifth grade, at football practice. Our colors were orange and black, but my parents, having seen the possibility of saving a little money, had found a cheaper version of the jerseys, something closer to yellow and black. I got into one of the few fights I have ever been in for a reason I cannot now imagine, especially as the boy I fought was one with whom I played, a boy with whom I sang in choir, a boy for whom I had vague sympathies because he was an orphan. Fights were rare at such a school. They were an educational opportunity. A group gathered; it seemed to be under the aegis of the coach, who made no attempt to stop us. I can remember being amazed by the energies that welled up in me—the confusion, the loss of bearings—and suddenly I was seated on top of the boy. He was down. I saw him there and quickly jumped off, partly in bewilderment over why this kind of thing was going on, partly in fear of what had been unleashed in me and what, therefore, might be unleashed on me, partly, rationalizing my fears, assuming that my position proclaimed me the victor. And so I jumped off, though a winner, feeling myself somehow a failure. At least that is the lesson the coach would have had everyone learn: "You see Kim has a yellow streak," he announced.

One should fight through to the end, even though one does not know why one is fighting or what the end might be. It is a lesson in manhood in our culture. I could look as if I had learned it. I continued to play well. Though avoiding fights, I looked as if I was hell-bent on winning and, for the most part, I was. But I still held back and junior year in prep school I drove another coach to public comment on the virtues of manhood. This time it was my hockey coach. I knew him for the four years I was in school. I had infuriated him once by quietly questioning the worth of serving in the military, but it is unlikely that he was vindictive about it. Again, I was someone who would rather not fight without a reason. . . . But it was actually on the ice, during a game, that I enraged him (and thus he scared me) most. I cannot remember the game, can only imagine I was not skating my heart out, but down out of the players' box he came, grabbing me to steady himself on the ice, grabbing me, though, in fury over my lack of aggression, muttering through clenched teeth, "Move! Go! Fight!"

The lesson was shouted at me for years, most impressively, of course by coaches, but also continually by teammates. And I shouted it at them. No need to cite examples, so pervasive is the competitive ethos of so-called "sports" in American life. Being a participant sharpens one's sense of the costs, but they may be felt as keenly by the spectator, as keenly even by the nonspectator who tries in vain to escape out of earshot of the calls "Win! Hit! Fight! Kill!"

Other human beings become the Enemy, far more than they do in the classroom. Thomas Hardy's famous soldier, musing what it would have been like to have a casual drink with "the man he killed" might—without too great a stretch of the imagination—have been an athlete. It was not until I played club sports in England (without coaches, incidentally) that I had any contact with an opponent. In America, after a game, you file sullenly or raucously back on the bus.

The first great cost I paid, that any "sportsman" pays, that a culture pays if it lets "sports" be so pervasive and penetrating a ritual, is that you may never relate to other men. And what followed, in my case at least, is that I could relate even less successfully to women. There was plenty of noise and contact. We were a team, pounded each other on the back, embraced each other after goals. We did what pros do on television, the kind of patting and hugging that you would get beaten up for if you tried it on the streets. But we never shared feelings. By senior year in college, I had tired of the same dirty jokes on every trip, of dropping water bombs out of hotel windows, and I took to reading. I cut myself off with some sense of the rightness of my cause, but I had also cut myself off because I had not been elected captain, because I had lost in the competition. I was, for bad as well as good reasons, "a poor sport."

Naturally, instinctively, I had tried to share thoughts and feelings with my "friends," my fellow sportsmen, all through the years, but the kind of competitive atmosphere I wandered in, the kind of machismo code I knew we all had to pay more than lip service to, made it impossible. It has been only recently—what with a separation and the attendant feelings of depression and loss—that I have been able to stop running, to share, to help and be helped. Up until now that had been made to seem weak, effeminate.

One learns to hide one's feelings early. My parents took pride in never admitting to being sick: my father collapsed rather than let on that the toilet bowl was filling up with blood from his ulcer; when he was discovered and the doctor called for an ambulance, my mother sent it back, insisting that she could get him to the hospital just as well. My parents were a great partnership, a devoted cheering section, but I never saw them touch (or fight), nor did they lavish caresses on me. When I went off to school my father informed me that from then on we would have to shake hands. Supposedly at fourteen I was a man and that was the way men expressed emotions.

There was little or no imtimacy with my contemporaries either. Inevitably I was introduced to homosexual intimacy—not surprisingly by a fellow athlete, ironically by the eventual Outstanding Boy of Fairfield Country Day School. My memory of the physical side of it is that it was pleasing, involving, as it did, my first orgasm. Indeed, it was so pleasing that I tried to transform the occasion into my first mounting of a woman, which made it awkward as well. But it was, above all, embarrassing. We certainly had no words to understand what we sought. The embarrassment was so intense on my friend's part that he told another member of our grade school backfield, and told him a version that had me as the perverse instigator of the whole affair. In that form it came back to me, an intimacy too hard for my friend to live with, too much to accept as part of young men's attempts at growing up, feared and then scorned. None of us young men could imagine or tolerate the possibility that we were attracted to each other. . . .

The competitive atmosphere that envelopes men in America is unlikely to make for intimate relationships among men themselves and, as I have suggested, even less likely to engender them between men and women. Holed away in male institutions for eight years, how could I, or anyone else in my position, learn to respect and love a woman? (And are co-educational schools in the larger male institution that is America different in kind?) Our very language (as is students' now) was filled with proof that we viewed women as we viewed each other, as strangers somehow pitted against each other, only more so. What we did was "score" against women or, as such claims were almost always false, we got to first or second or third base. A frequent question after a vacation or a date was, "Did you get much?" Women were commodities, fields on which we played, or so we assumed, never imagining how sad and foolish we might have seemed in their eyes.

We were born too soon to try to take advantage of a liberated era; we were of an age that had to frequent whore houses. It started in prep school. I never made it to Florida where most of the clique had their first such experience, but I am sure I would have remained in the car, in bewilderment, in fear, as did one friend of mine, and I would have been derided as he was. Nor did I make the New York trip from college: a run in, armed with lust and notebooks, the latter for studying purposes while one waited one's turn to satisfy the former.

But I listened with envy as well as with disgust. After one Deerfield vacation I got a ride back to school with two friends who lived in New York. I went in, spent the night in the Park Avenue apartment of one of them, and in the morning we set out, we three in the back of his car, a chauffeur driving. At our lunch stop, the chauffeur having tactfully disappeared, my two friends talked of a girl they knew in common, not only knew but, as it turned out, had successfully dated on the last two nights of vacation. How far did each get? We all had to know, but neither would say. And so it was decided that each would write down his achievement on a napkin and I, an impartial judge, would declare the winner. But it was a tie, a tie over which we could all three laugh with a sense of conquest and relief: both had written "Finger Fuck."

A woman had been almost conquered and both men had won. That was ideal, for as was not the case in the classroom or on the playing fields, we did not want to win out over each other. We only wanted it known that we were "men" on the same team. For years stories were told, exploits shared. There was this girl who let every member of one fraternity do it to her on the pool table; there was this one suite of men who had it rigged so they could watch their dates relieve themselves, so honorable a group that they vowed never to go near their mirrors when one of their mothers was involved. . . .

But reality seldom intruded. Or is it that it never intruded on my illusions? I recount a bit of the lore. I myself perceived the world and other people in the fantastic terms of the lore, but perhaps others saw beyond, could imagine what a girl felt like there on the pool table or could dismiss the tale altogether and build up a relationship with another human being physically, emotionally, intellectually, even spiritually. In thinking back on those years, I can only recall that somehow we knew there was a better way to live and that many of us started out to find thay way. I cannot say that then and there we found a way out of the male-dominated, competitive world I have described. Indeed, our record of affairs and separations and divorces does not suggest that many of us did find a way. Of eight relatively close friends with whom I went both to school and college, two never married, six did, and of them two remain married. . . .

The woman I was to marry was a WASP, went to good private schools, and lived in a nice country house. And I sensed that my parents approved. (When I asked my mother recently if the sight of such respectable money had impressed her, she scorned the notion, saying she'd seen much more magnificent estates, which hardly contradicted my sense of my parents' stake in the matter.) They did not care, but I found security in the fact that although Susan was well-schooled, she was not in the intellectual race, as it was set up by her college, at least. By the time I met her (our sophomore year), she was just getting off academic probation, and when she took courses in English in an attempt to understand what I was interested in, she did poorly. No competition there, nor, I thought, was any there in our sexual relationship. Susan was boyish, short-haired, slight, almost waiflike, and without much guilt we did everything allowed by the Victorian belief in virginity that we shared.

On the narrow grounds on which I had played up until then, there was no competition. But neither was there any voicing of our doubts and fears, so little time had been spent in warm human relationships. We were about to graduate, everyone else was getting married, our parents were clearly satisfied, and somehow it would work out. Susan's roommate announced her engagement a few months before ours and a house dinner her fiancé got up and toasted the two of us for planning to follow suit. I did not know our plans were so definite but I said nothing. Susan allowed her deep reservations about our relationship to surface only once but I quickly buried them. The occasion was grimly appropriate: an idle hour before the final hockey game against Harvard. Our training rules were lax enough to allow for visitors and while I thought of the approaching game she started to cry and said she didn't think she could go through with the marriage. But I was never to learn why, for once I knew that she had doubts. I brought to bear the pressure I felt from thoughts about the engagement party the previous December, about the wedding in June, and—not least—about the game that was soon to start. Ours was not a relationship in which we could help each other express doubts and needs.

When I took a job teaching college I was returning to even more familiar turf, literally, because Deerfield was only fifteen miles away, but most important, socially. The atmosphere could be summed up in the words of a therapist whom two colleagues of mine visited in an effort to cope with the pressures of our department. The first went on at length about the overbearing presence of the then "old man" of the department and about the ways his staff competed with, yet supported each other. When the second came, he started in on the same story, only to be interrupted by the therapist's saying, "Yes, I know—rigid informality." It was a phrase that characterized not only the department but the institution, not only this particular all-male institution, but the others I had attended as well, another place where men worked and played and competed against each other, while women played the unrespected, often unrecognized roles of grader, librarian, homemaker, mother. It was, like those institutions, a place where men, like the students they taught, like the students I imagine them to have been themselves, fended off exposure and intimacy with irony and the pose of stoic self-sufficiency.

I thought Susan would be a perfect mother, a willing hostess, an efficient homemaker, but she turned out to be a human being, an individual, a woman who would not simply fit into the roles I had imagined for her. Obviously if she were only what I had to make her out to be, we would have remained married. We would not have been two human beings, mutually respecting and loving each other, but we would have been content. As it was, she resisted the work required to entertain and run a home, she continued to cry out ME TOO!

Having been an "ideal" student, on my way to being a professor, I knew the importance of filling out one more role, that of being the model husband. Those who watched and judged demanded it. I demanded it of myself because I didn't want to repeat my parents' mistakes, more immediately because, ironically, I sensed the model was a bad one (and I was certainly made to feel it was a bad one by Susan), and I wanted to do something about it. Though at one level I would have liked Susan to be a glorified maid, I knew that it was deadly to expect that of anyone and in my guilt I did much more than my colleagues to lighten the load at home. So our household appeared all the more serene.

In the process of being a model husband I was a model father too, spending time with the children, working with them in the yard, teaching them to play tennis, dragging them to cultural events. With them there were moments of tenderness and delight such as I could not find with Susan and that made it easier to maintain the facade, even to ignore the fact that it was a facade we were maintaining. There were precious few moments of tenderness and delight with Susan for the simple reason that I was not in competition with my children and was, though I did not know it at the time, in competition with her.

As had been the case from my earliest years, competition precluded intimacy. While getting A's, making teams, winning prizes, I kept my distance from my schoolmates and they kept theirs from me. While becoming what my parents and what I thought society wanted me to be, I deprived myself or was deprived of intimate relationships with boys and girls, men and women. I looked on marriage as a refuge from the competitive world I had known. In choosing a mate I tried to avoid competitiveness, tried to be best from the start so that finally, in marriage, I could find intimacy.

Such was the meager legacy of my earlier years. Nothing in it would help me recognize the real competition I had entered nor build on what intimacy existed in spite of that legacy. Rather than avoid competition, I ran into more than I could handle, or, what is sadder, given all the waste, I didn't really know that Susan and I were in competition. We never fought but we continually struggled: who would do the shopping? who the cleaning? who would sleep late? who would nap? who would take care of the children? Always, who would take care of the children? The facade was maintained but the struggle went on. If Susan was victorious—got a nap, say—I would begrudge her her success. If I succeeded—particularly out there, in the "real world"—Susan would be resentful. To overturn the old terms of endearment, we couldn't do enough for each other. And all the while we could not admit to our real needs, to our deep needs for pleasure and love, nor, of course, could we meet those needs in each other, not even with a counselor's help. We could not even see, we were not mature enough to realize, the predicament we were in. As the struggle wore on I wore out and began to look for intimacy elsewhere. Eventually the competition ended. This time everybody lost.

SISSYHOOD IS POWERFUL

DAN WAKEFIELD

Many of us males should be rooting for the acceptance of women in sports for—just as you suspected—our own per-

---

Dan Wakefield's most recent novel is *Home Free*, published by Delacorte Press/ Seymour Lawrence in 1978. He is the author of other nonfiction books *(Island in the City)* and novels *(Going All the Way and Starting Over)*, and his television writing includes the series *James at Fifteen*.

sonal chauvinistic selfish concerns, as well as the genuine desire to see females have the opportunity to participate in any sport they wish, from basketball to boxing.

James Baldwin pointed out in The Fire Next Time *that in any situation of social inequality it is both sides that suffer, it is both sides that are dehumanized, and this is as true of sexism as it is of racism. The case of athletics is a particular telling example, I think. There is no way of making a whole lot of little girls miserable by segregating sports according to sex without also making a whole lot of little boys miserable. The hurt is simply inflicted in a different way.*

Just as the girl who is good at sports is labeled "unfeminine," so the boy who has no ability at athletics is labeled "unmasculine." From childhood, the boy who can't make a tackle or hit a ball is soon likely to be called a "sissy," and made the butt of ridicule by the other kids on the block or at school. A boy who strikes out in a sandlot softball game is likely to be accused with the most embarrassing judgment his jeering little mates can think up: "Ah, ya swing like a girl!" It's the kids' interpretation of the parental charge, "You're not masculine," or, as it is more terrifyingly expressed, "You're not a man!" This is followed, in high school, and at camps, by the grim, grown-up coach or counselor telling the skinny, uncoordinated kid, "Johnson, I'll make a man out of you!" And little Johnson knows he's in for a great deal of mental and physical punishment.

As you might have guessed, I was and am lousy at sports. I was one of those pudgy little kids who tried like hell, but who just didn't have it as even an average athlete. I once wrote about my experience as a high school freshman trying to grab onto some little rag of athletic achievement by practicing the mile run, which I assumed could be conquered by sheer determination. I even bought a stopwatch. After my rigorous training, I ran the mile at dusk on a nearby high school track and found that my time was

7:02. Most grandmothers could have done it in less. I trained longer and harder, and when I next dropped across the finish line I found that my time was seven minutes flat. I had not been able to break the seven-minute mile. The seven-minute mile is roughly comparable to the five-foot broad jump.

It took me years to admit to that humiliation, but when I finally wrote about it I received a number of letters from sympathetic men, other "closet-milers," among them the writer Kurt Vonnegut, who said he was glad to know he was not the only man in modern American history who had failed to break the seven-minute mile.

In the physical training courses required for high school graduation, I learned to remain as unobtrusive as possible. I made a genuine high school friendship with another such boy when we realized we were doing the same thing. In phys. ed. softball games we always volunteered for the outfield, and we played so far back that we were nearly hidden among a grove of trees behind the diamond.

"What are you doing back here?" I asked him one day as I edged carefully farther into the foliage, and he said, "Same thing you are—trying to avoid the ball." In high school, that was a hard thing for a boy to admit. I admired his honesty, which I came to learn was a human quality not inferior to catching a fly ball. We became friends.

In college at Columbia I found to my vast relief that I could satisfy part of my physical education requirement by taking a course in bowling. It was held at a bowling alley in the basement of the Riverside Church, and there I was at ease among my fellow non-athletes.

I came to appreciate the fact that some of the finest men were not necessarily athletic. I will never forget the time when, having finished a Columbia phys. ed. class in basketball, one of the few sports I enjoyed since I was a fairly good shot (due to millions of hours of practice at my backyard net in Indianapolis), I was told that in the next period a famous upper-classman of the college would appear. I had heard about this fellow's brilliance, his popularity, his great future in the arts as predicted by the giants of the faculty, and I was anxious to see who he was. The class he was in came out onto the floor, dressed identically in blue trunks and white T-shirts, and formed a line to go in and take layups under the basket.

"Which one is he?" I asked a companion.

"That's him, coming in for a layup right now."

I looked, but could not believe my eyes. The famous fellow came stomping up to the basket, his feet wide in a duckstyle walk, his eyes alarmed behind thick, jiggling glasses, and, when the ball was fed to him he leaped upward, arms and legs moving like a threshing machine gone berserk. The ball careened off his cheek, and he fell to the floor in a jumble of confused limbs.

"I can't believe that's him," I said.

"Why not?" my companion asked. "Einstein probably couldn't make a layup either."

It seems a simple observation, and yet it is not one that comes easily in a society that brainwashes males with the notion that "manhood" is equivalent to athletic prowess. Getting rid of that concept is inextricably connected with getting rid of the notion that women who enjoy and excel at sport and who want to make a pastime or even a profession of it are not somehow deficient in "femininity" or aberrant in their behavior.

I sincerely look forward to the time when Dick and Jane can run and jump and sew and read and paint pictures according to their inclinations and talents rather than to the arbitrary rules of their respective sexual roles as dictated by society. See Dick bake a cake! See Jane knock a homer! Hurray for Dick and Jane!

RUNNING AS A PROVING GROUND FOR HUMANISTIC VALUES

DAVID BROAD

Running is rapidly becoming the most participated-in sport in America. In 1978 there were over sixteen million regular runners in the United States.[1] *The image of the runner has changed from that of a physical fitness nut to embrace people of every conceivable description. If it continues, the phenomenon of running, as a social event as well as a personal experience, will have wide-ranging effects on the definition of sport, sex roles, and even class relations.*

The meaning of running, like the meaning of all human activity, ultimately resides in its social context. What we say, hear, and think about what we do is inextricable from the doing. There is a symbolic connection, a dialectical process in human experience that makes it unique.

In one phase of this process, experience generates symbols. Images, sounds, feelings, are perceived and catalogued in light of already patterned and interpreted perceptions and concepts. In the reciprocal phase the symbols we have catalogued become expectations, goals, dreams, that reach out and frame new experiences. Thus we learn by first creating symbols and then applying them.

The contemporary American experience with running is part of the dialectical process we have described. It has a history and a symbolic heritage that structures much of our consciousness of it, and it has an existence which brings new life to that consciousness and challenges related beliefs and values.

David Broad, a marathoner, is a lecturer in sociology and coach of cross country at the State University College at Buffalo.

The symbolic context of the current running boom is partly defined by our concept of sport. Thorstein Veblan traces the origin of sport to the stage of human development he calls predatory barbarism. Many central social institutions have roots in this historical period, and their development thus reflects the predatory temperament. In the era of predatory barbarism, men where valued for their prowess as hunters and warriors. Among the earliest symbols of success were women seized from enemies in battle and displayed as trophies.

> This practice [of seizing enemy women] . . . gave rise to a form of ownership-marriage, resulting in a household with a male head. This was followed by an extension of slavery to other captives and inferiors, besides women, and by and extension of ownership-marriage to other women than those seized from the enemy.[2]

The desire to display evidence of exploits not only provided a motive for coercive marriages but established the custom of ownership of people. The concept of people as property was then extended to include the products people made and various means of production, including land.[3]

Veblen saw sport as a modern survival of barbaric displays and demonstrations of prowess. Hunting and warfare provide the models for many sports, sporting language, and the athletic subculture in general. Key sports concepts such as targets and territoriality, offense and defense, winning and losing, to name just a few, all derive from predatory and barbaric occupations.

The desire to display prowess culminates, for Veblen, in the development of the leisure class. This class consists of subscribers to a code of living that measures a person's standing by his or her ability to devote time and energy to *nonproductive activities, activities designed to demonstrate the worthiness of prior exploits. The sporting gentleman typifies this modern expression of predatory posturing for the upper class, and the profile of values he represents is emulated by other classes in leisure pursuits and in participation in athletics.* Conspicuous consumption *is the chief form taken by the middle and lower classes' attempts to associate themselves with leisure-class canons. The effort to attain status through wasteful displays finds some expression in the running culture, through the buying and wearing of designer warm-ups and togs and gimmicky accessories.*

Underneath the predatory aspects of human character is the more basic need to be productive. To be human is to be dependent upon social commerce, and some of our products must have enough durability and utility to give them commercial value. Veblen describes our awareness of this need to produce useful things as an instinct of workmanship. Our desire to emulate our predatory forebearers through sports, the instinct of sportsmanship, is to Veblen a perversion of these productive impulses. It is unsatisfying because it does not contribute to the real socioeconomic base of the community, only to the repute of the sportsman. It is invidious because it diverts us from pursuing a peaceable life and progress through human industry.[4]

In an increasingly technological and bureaucratic world, we are largely denied the opportunity to fully experience our own productivity. We are cut off from essential phases of production by unrepresentative ownership and management, overspecialization, and a nondemocratic system of distribution and therefore we are alienated. Viewed in this dominant social context, running can be an invaluable clue to our basic productive character. Running is easily accessible to virtually everyone. It requires no ponies like polo, no courts like tennis, no pool like swimming. There can be no monopoly of the means of running by any class, social group, or gender. At world-class levels of performance, specialization is required, but most runners set whatever pace they choose, from a white-hot sprint to a blissful ramble on a country road.

These then are two aspects of running: It is a way of emulating our barbaric ancestors and a gilt-edged opportunity for lessening our alienation from our own world. There is no doubt that competitive running requires some sacrifice, but as a display of prowess it is a tie to our barbaric roots:

> The competitor is concerned with winning—rank, records, fame, awards—all types of recognition for accomplishment within the competitive social system. By focusing on athletic success, the competitive athlete must subordinate other areas of his life such as study, work, family and social responsibilities in order to fulfill his dominant goal.[5]

It is competition, however, that has been chiefly responsible for the symbolically important fulfillment of human potential in many cultures, providing models of excellence for all.

On its humanistic side, running is an opportunity to participate in a productive process free of the restrictions and expectations we encounter in most of our productive relations. Its easy accessibility, the directness and intensity of the shared experience of a run, produce an empathy that is new and exciting to generations of people who have been led to be skeptical of their own sensibilities and schooled to rely on expert judgments in most matters.

The two sides of running—competition and satisfaction—complement one another. The understanding of oneself and others produced by the experience of running free the competitor from some of the isolation of competition. The technical knowledge of physiology, nutrition, etc. gained from competition and competitive training help the humanistic runner attain the strength, agility, and stamina (s)he needs to enjoy a run more fully. This convergence enriches the meaning of the sport for participants entering from either mode.

Running is a bridge between existence and consciousness, an example of the connectedness of being and knowing. The potential for de-alienation through running reaches its zenith in the marathon—the archetypical test of human endurance.

The place of the marathon in western history and thought, and the contemporary usage of the word, exemplify the impact of the running experience on our culture. The literate and enlightened classical period of Greece began in 490 B.C., when the threat of Persian conquest was decisively ended at the battle of Marathon. As H. G. Wells writes in his Outline of History.

> This remarkable culmination of the long-gathering creative power of the Greek mind, which for three and twenty centuries has been to men of intelligence a guiding and inspiring beacon out of the past, flared up after the battle of Marathon . . . had made Athens free and fearless, and without any great excesses of power, predominant in her world.[6]

This landmark event in the history of western civilization is tied to the long run that bears its name by the legend of Pheidippides, which is known to nearly every marathoner. Pheidippides, an Athenian soldier, was a trained and heralded runner. He ran the twenty-four miles from the battlefield at Marathon to Athens to report to the *anxious throng the outcome of the battle. He arrived at Athens, gasped "Victory is ours on the plain of Marathon," and fell dead.*[7] *When contemporary marathoners speak of "dying" on the now standardized 26.2-mile courses they are usually referring to a profound state of exhaustion, but they do know that they have been to the threshold of some other world. As Dostoyevsky found, "suffering is the sole origin of consciousness."*[8]

The marathon is a standard of the physical dimension of culture, a testimony to the potential of body and soul. It has stretched our conception of human limitations, making running a touchstone of human indomitability. As a symbol of endurance the word marathon has many usages. There are dance marathons, kiss marathons, and marathon bargaining sessions, to cite but a few popular expressions.

The running experience, crowned by the marathon, tells us not only about the potential of human beings in the abstract, but about the capabilities of people and groups in particular. Stereotypes of age and sex are shattered by performances that were unheard of yesterday and will be routine tomorrow. As an outgrowth of its roots in the predatory past, participation in distance running was long restricted by myths concerning both age and the "natural" frailty of women. Today, sixty-year-old men are running marathons in what were world-class times in their youth, and women are bettering the winning time of the 1948 London Olympic marathon.[9]

From a social standpoint, nothing about running is more dramatic than its effect on sexual stereotypes. Conventional male supremicist wisdom about what women can and can't do is rapidly being reduced to folly by what women do. The majority of male runners, whose self-images are tied to traditional models, find their athletic prowess eclipsed by a growing number of women. Some attempt to rationalize this apparent anomaly by calling their female betters unfeminine, but the weight of evidence demonstrates that women runners have feminine identities at least as strong as those of nonrunners.

Running is existentially well-suited, and the running phenomenon is historically well-timed, to provide American society with a proving ground for emerging humanistic values. It is a path to health and emotional attunement. Runners universally attest to its benefits in this regard. Since runners are generally more aware of air quality and the interdependence of people and nature, running is also an individual and societal spur to ecological concern. Running also furnishes us with a model of nonalienated production, since runners themselves enjoy the valuable results of their labor. Finally, running provides a test of the wisdom of traditional patriarchal norms compared to sexual egalitarianism. Runners are coming to realize that, as in other areas of society, men and women on the track or the open road are very much more alike than not.

FOOTNOTES

1. *The Toronto Star* (February 9, 1979).
2. Thorstein Veblen, *The Theory of the Leisure Class* (New York: Viking Press, 1931), p. 23.
3. Ibid., p. 270
4. Ibid.
5. Howard Mickel, "Going Beyond Competition," in Runners World Magazine, eds., *The Complete Runner* (New York: Avon Books, 1974), p. 5.
6. H.G. Wells, *The Outline of History* (Garden City, N. Y.: Garden City Publishing Company, 1920), p. 290.
7. David E. Martin, Herbert W. Benario, and Roger W. H. Gynn, "Development of the Marathon from Pheidippides to the Present," in Paul Milvy, ed., *The Long Distance Runner* (New York: Urizen Books, 1978), pp. 1–32.
8. Quoted in Garrett Tomczak, "Is the Pain Necessary?" in

Runners World Magazine, eds., *The Complete Runner*, p. 14.

9. Nina Kuscsik, "The History of Women's Participation in the Marathon," in Milvy, ed., *The Long Distance Runner*, pp. 32–46.

GETTING BEYOND EXERCISE AS WORK

DONALD F. SABO, JR.

Exercise is intrinsic to the jock culture. Work and sports have been central proving grounds of masculinity, and both serve as arenas for competition and combative camaraderie. They determine a male's sense of self-mastery or failure and engender feelings of superiority to women. The work and sports ethics are also underpinned by a similar social mythology of success, potency, and prestige. The self-made-man formula for fame is a theme shared both by the Horatio Alger hero and tales of successful jocks from John L. Sullivan to former president Gerald Ford. Moreover, work and sports similarly shape the male personality and generate such traits as independence, ambitiousness, dominance, objective detachment, and competitiveness. Like certain jobs, many sports are traditionally considered "masculine" by definition and endow males with an ascetic sense of self-denial, an aura of toughness and ruthlessness deemed necessary to achieve success. This constellation of personality traits implies an active and instrumental attitude that is related to the ways a male sees himself and others, which requires conquest, competitive skills, and a preoccupation with the end results of activity.

Considerable overlap, then, has existed between the work ethos and the male approach to exercise. To put it simply, men have defined and experienced exercise as work. The term "workout" used to describe an afternoon at the gym or a calisthenic session, amply reflects this identification. Exercise is usually approached with ascetic rigor or purpose. Varying degrees of physical pain and sweaty exhaustion are accepted as natural derivatives of the process. Competition is an integral part of the activity. The individual competes directly against others or more subtly against himself. In addition, the end products of exercise are uppermost in the exerciser's consciousness—a better physique, health, muscular development, or sexual vitality. The mind regards the body as an object to be moved, manipulated, and developed in order to achieve desired results. The body is experienced as a machine to be set in motion or an obstacle to be surmounted rather than an amicably organic entity. The notion that exercise is or can be a pleasurably sensuous activity in itself is alien to the jock ethos.

Getting Beyond Exercise As Work: A Non-Jock Approach

Due to its immersion in the work ethos, exercise fosters the development of traditional masculine personality traits that, in turn, help to maintain sexist attitudes and social relations. A small step might be taken toward women's and men's liberation by redefining exercise in a nonsexist way. Such a non-jock approach to exercise would be predicated upon the pleasure principle and not on the glorification of strenuous physical toil. Sensual enjoyment would replace ascetic self-denial. The body would be perceived organically and not mechanically. Consciousness would focus upon the moment and upon immediate physical sensations, not on visions of future rewards. The exerciser would passively participate in the bodily process rather than attempting to control it.

Body-Awareness Exercises:
Tuning in to Body

The following exercises are designed to induce new states of body awareness and to restructure consciousness away from a traditional masculine motif. Each exercise can be explored alone or in a group. Above all, try not to approach the exercises as a crusade for self-improvement. Crusades end up being work, and the passively oriented participant is more likely to experience a sense of self-improvement.

BODY FANTASIES

Masculine identity is a social product. The individual male has learned to perceive and interpret bodily sensations from within a masculine self-concept. The first two exercises encourage mild transformations in our everyday consciousness through which changes in body awareness can be experienced. The mind beckons and the body follows. Restructuring our fantasies allows sensory input to be perceived in new ways. The old culturally conditioned perceptions, the ways we have learned to interpret.physical sensations in the past, can be gently displaced by an organismic sensitivity.

Each fantasy exercise should be carried out in a relaxed position. Sit comfortably or lie down on the floor or a couch. Keep your eyes closed.

1. "THE IDEAL BODY FANTASY." Think of your mind as an empty movie theatre. You are seated in the front row. Before you is a large movie screen. Visualize a male body on the screen that you would like for your own. If you could live inside another body, the body on the screen would be your ideal choice. Picture the body walking, swimming, or moving freely about a room.

292

Imagine how it would feel to be inside such a body. Focus on your immediate physical sensations. Think about them. Let yourself feel.

Now slowly visualize the screen going black. You are alone again in a totally dark theatre and back in your own body. Become aware of your breathing. Feel the positioning of your neck, head, and arms. Now take your hands and explore the contours of your face. Touch your cheeks, chest, and stomach. Stroke your legs and grip your knees. Be thankful for your body. Regard it as a gift. Contemplate its wonders. When you are ready, slowly open your eyes.

2. *"THE HOLDING IN YOUR BELLY FANTASY. Once again, you are in a darkened movie theatre. This time, however, visualize yourself upon the screen. Picture yourself in a situation in which you are scantily clad and self-conscious about your body. Perhaps you are at a beach or undressing before a lover. Think about your self-consciousness. How concerned are you about other people's eyes? How do you cover up your embarrassment? How does it feel? Try to determine the bodily tensions you are experiencing. Are you holding your belly in? Is your chest out? Are you tensely conscious of your posture?*

Again, let the screen go black. You are alone in your body. Focus on your breathing. Locate any stiffness or tension you feel. Try to specify the region of your body where the tension is. Is it your neck? Your lower back or abdomen? Now direct each exhalation of your breath to the locus of the tension. Imagine that, with each exhalation, the tension is gradually dissipating. Be conscious of any signs of increased relaxation. When you feel relaxed, open your eyes.

STRETCHING EXERCISES.

Most bodies are stiff. Our bodies are too frequently the reluctant vehicles of consciousness. While one suffers from disuse, the fluidity of another is impeded by an overdeveloped musculature. The body is perceived as a constraint, an alien object to be overcome and pushed forward. Thus the jock phrase "pushing yourself" means ordering the body about against its will.

The instrumental orientation of the male character is exemplified in the jock approach to stretching exercises. They are a preparatory endeavor. They are done to get ready for a physical challenge or to avoid a torn muscle. They are a preparatory endeavor. The body-machine must function well and respond to commands. When a jock stretches, he is punching a timeclock to begin work.

The non-jock approach to stretching exercises stresses the unity of mind and body. Cooperation is a key word. Relaxation is the mind-set. Here, the body beckons and the mind follows. Only two stretching exercises are described below, but you can easily use the ideas presented there to invent others.

1. *"THE SUN-REACH." Stand comfortably with your hands at your side. Become conscious of your breathing. Focusing upon physical sensations, slowly raise both arms above your head. Think about the experience while it is happening. What is occuring in your body? Next stretch your hands skyward as far as possible. Don't strain. Feel your spine stretch upward. What is the impact on your sense of balance? Now lower your arms to their original position. Look for a sense of relaxation. Repeat the exercise several times.*

2. *"THE LEG-BACK STRETCH." Stand with your legs far apart. Focus on your breathing. Slowly bend forward*

and stretch your hands toward the floor at a point midway between your feet. What and where are you feeling? Listen to your body making adjustments to maintain balance. Get into that balance. Let yourself relax. Let your arms hang. Slowly stand upright again. Look for a sense of relaxation. Repeat this exercise as often as desired or whenever you feel fatigued or stiff.

SLOW-MOTION CALISTHENICS.

Calisthenics are seldom done for pleasure. Fitness is the usual aim. Fear of unfitness is often the motive. Calisthenics are performed mechanically and dutifully. Each repetition is counted, and the tally denotes the degree of achievement.

Non-jock calisthenics wed awareness with physical motion. Fitness is a byproduct, not the aim. Mind and body dance. Counting repetitions is needless. The focus is upon bodily cues and processes. The idea is to explore the body, not to discipline it. The types of non-jock calisthenics are innumerable, so feel free to try others as well as the two described below.

1. "ROLLING THE ARMS." With your eyes closed, stand comfortably with your arms extended sideways. Be aware of your breathing. Think of a reason you are glad to be alive. Slowly begin moving both arms in small circles. Focus upon your arm muscles and the movements of your shoulder joints. What are you feeling? Progressively increase the size of the circles. Let your mind follow the body's movements. Slowly decrease the size of the circles until your arms return to their original position. The exercise may be repeated and speeded up but not to the extent that your sense of unity with the body's motion is disturbed.

2. *"PUSHING."* Lie face down in the pushup position. Breath as comfortably as possible and relax. Allow your body to go limp. Think of yourself as a child asleep on its belly. Next, very slowly, begin to push yourself upward. Feel your arm muscles tense. Feel the weight of your body. How is your breathing? Your arms should eventually be straightened. How is your mind translating the event? Do you feel light or heavy, strong or weak? Begin lowering your body toward the floor. Embrace the motion. Rest when you are finished. Repeat the exercise as often as you wish, but avoid strain. Don't expect too much of yourself. Be yourself. Let your body define its strengths and limitations to your consciousness.

The Non-Jock Approach to Exercise and Women's and Men's Liberation

The jock approach to exercise, so inundated by the work ethic, encourages the formation and preservation of traditional masculine personality traits. Moreover, athletic activities reinforce the relation between a male's consciousness and his body. This relation may be described as alienated, instrumental, and objectified. The average male perceives his body as a thing to be stoically ignored or controlled rather than an organismic grounding of his self. Research indicates that males are less aware of their bodies than females (Fisher, 1974). Men are less unified with their bodies than women and less sensitive to bodily cues. As culture conditions consciousness, the body becomes the vesicle of identity which, in turn, shapes the self-concept. The body contains the history of its social origins. Mind, body, and society ceaselessly interact. The biosocial wheel turns onward. Hence, traditional masculinity and sexism are organically as well as socially perpetuated.

The non-jock approach to exercise attempts to help men move from beneath the wheel by discovering and deriving pleasure from bodily sensations and to restructure consciousness away from traditional masculinity. Wilhelm Reich's character analytic framework illustrates the potential of the non-jock approach to exercise to provide sensual enjoyment and changes in personality. Reich conceives of the body as the structural embodiment of character. Thus the posture and facial expressions of a paranoid, for example, may appear guarded and rigidly defensive. An individual's social and emotional history is processually embedded in his or her musculature and nervous system. Reich defines the mannerisms, patterns of speech, postural attitudes, and bodily motions by which an individual manages inner tensions and wards off threats from the outside world as her or his character armour. Reich's therapeutic technique to repeatedly call attention to an undesirable character trait and compel the patient to experience the mannerism associated with it. The patient's heightened awareness of the trait leads to its eventual dissolution and thus to improved psychic health (Reich, 1972; Boadella, 1974).

The body-fantasy exercises described above are consistent with Reich's orientation in that they persuade the participant to explore bodily sensations in various imagined psychosocial contexts. In this way he learns to make conscious connections between certain bodily states and corresponding masculine images and roles. One moment a man visualizes and experiences his body in a social role. The next moment, he is his body. The stretching exercises and slow-motion calisthenics are also intended to enhance male body awareness and induce mind-body unity, thus supplanting the traditional body-as-object relation. To some degree, such experiences promote better understanding of what it means and how it feels to live within a culturally conditioned male body—a body generally severed from its residing consciousness and treated as an implement in the world of work.

The traditional male mind-body relation has been characterized as both alienated and objectified. This mode of psychical-biological organization is evident in many social behaviors. Feminists have been outraged by the proneness of males to regard women as sexual objects rather than persons. Heterosexual and homosexual rape are male crimes, whereas cases of sexual assault by women are virtually unknown (Kanowitz, 1969, 18). Males are also vastly more prone to commit crimes of violence than females (Simon, 1975). Boxers and football players are trained to deny their own pain, yet they are expected to hurt or cripple their opponents. The great daredevils who risk life and limb for fame have been largely male. Warfare, almost always a male preserve, entails the risk of one's own physical being as well as the denial of the enemy's right to life. Genocide has been almost exclusively a male activity. Dehumanizing institutions such as slavery and the early factory system were initiated and justified by men of power.

To imply that these social behaviors and institutions are outgrowths of an inherently male mind-body relation would be reductionistic. Nevertheless, the available evidence indicates that a restructuring of male consciousness and the male mind-body relation is a prerequisite to the evolution of full sexual equality.

REFERENCES

Boadella, David. *Wilhelm Reich: The Evolution of His Work.* Chicago: Henry Regnery Company, 1974.

Fisher, Seymour. *Body Consciousness.* New York: Jason Aronson, 1974.

Kanowitz, Leo. *Women and the Law.* Albuquerque: University of New Mexico Press, 1969.

Reich, Wilhelm. *Character Analysis*. New York: Farrar, Straus and Giroux, 1972.

Simon, Rita James. *Women and Crime*. Lexington, Mass. Lexington Books, 1975.

THE FUTURE
OF WOMEN'S SPORT:
ISSUES, INSIGHTS,
AND STRUGGLES

BONNIE A. BECK

PERHAPS,
Before there were Gods there were Goddesses;
Before there was Man there was Woman;
Before there was Sport there was Play;
Before the Roboticized-Automatons there were
Life-Living/Loving-Free-Spirited/Joyful
Humans-Be-ing, and PERHAPS, there will be again.

Through this article I will attempt to turn away from the Death-March of NowSport/ManSport, to create the possibility of the existence of EuSport/Woman-Identified NewSport born of collective gynergy.* This is a Journey upon which we must all embark if we are to reunite ourSelves with other-Selves in the playful abandon/reunion of com-testing (Oglesby, 1978, p. 197), that is, playing with others in the quest for Self-Knowing, Self-Be-ing, Self-Creation, univer-

---

**Author's note: The inspiration for this article is directly attributable to Mary Daly's new work *Gyn/Ecology: The Metaethics of Radical Feminism* (Boston: Beacon Press, 1978).

Dr. Bonnie A. Beck is an assistant professor on the Faculty of Physical Education at the State University of New York College at Brockport.

sal Spiraling, Spinning, Connecting on the playing fields of JoySport.

ManSport is a creature of the Patriarchy and as such reflects the dominant values of both patriarchy and capitalism. As such, ManSport is male-dominated and for-profit. WomanSport (there used to be such a thing, that is, play days, sports days, telegraph com-tests) was of WomanBorn and reflected a union of players, a striving for joy in the com-test well played, an activity for everyWoman and everyWoman in an activity. The question to be asked then is, "Does NowSport reflect the best of both ManSport and WomanSport?" The answer is no! I will show in this article how WomanSport has been co-opted by the Patriarchy and what the consequences of this are for Sister-Players.

Many writers have used the words "humanism" or "androgyny" to suggest an evolution and an integration of humans-being in sport. The intent was to blend two opposites, two halves, the "masculine" and the "feminine," or ManSport and WomanSport. However, as Mary Daly (1978) suggests, this only creates pseudo-integrity or pseudo-wholeness, since masculinity and femininity are but social constructs born of an androcratic world. She writes:

> Feminist theorists have gone through frustrating attempts to describe our integrity by such terms as androgyny. Experience proved that this word, which we now recognize as expressing pseudo-wholeness in its combination of distorted gender descriptions, failed and betrayed our thought. . . . When we heard the word echoed back by those who misinterpreted our thought we realized that combining the "halves" offered to consciousness by patriarchal language usually results in portraying something more like a hole than a whole. . . . androgyny is a vacuous term which not only fails to represent a richness of be-

ing, it also functions as a vacuum that sucks its spellbound victims into itself. Such pseudwholeness, which characterizes all false universalisms, (. . . humanism, people's liberation) is the deep hole—the chasm—which Spinsters must leap over, which we must span. (pp. 387–88)

Daly (1978) urges those who would "connect two things" or "span" differences to be wary of "bridging over" two undesirable or inimical things. We are urged to explore different meanings of "span" that would include "an encompassing of" and "a setting of limits" on what is presented as the structure/idea/or direction of any patriarchal institution (including ManSport). With this in mind, throughout this article "woman-identified" will connote neither sex-separateness nor union with "man-identified," but rather a spiraling, spinning, swooping evolutionary process that focuses on seeing clearly what is in NowSport/ManSport, measuring precisely whose energy is tapped to perpetuate NowSport/ManSport, and holding at arm's length in a firm grip the phallocratic (Daly, 1978) myths that support ExistingSport while moving to set in motion movement toward ecstatic, Whole Humans-Be-ing moving.

An exposing of the myths born of gynocide is but one way to start on the Journey to ideas about EuSport/NewSport/OurSport. In the fratricidal/soroticidal world of NowSport/ManSport, keen sight, acute hearing, and delicate antennae are basic essentials for those who would stop/shift/redirect the patriarchal institutions of sexism, racism, ageism, and classism. NowSport/ManSport oppresses all, even those to whom it gave birth. With life-risking conviction we must demand new life-energizing com-tests, play days, sport days, JoySport, activities for AllSelves and AllSelves in every activity.

NowSport con-tests are male-defined/derived to show

males parading in front of each other in all their glory. Within the NowSport/ManSport social subculture males have both power and privilege solely by virtue of their sex. It is also in the male interest to maintain that power and privilege. Within this social subculture males oppress women in personal relationships, in groups, and on the sporting terrain, for there is status in the ability to oppress another regardless of the oppression males themselves may suffer.

Women, also, may participate in the oppression of their sisters. As women move into greater involvement in the androcratically defined NowSport/ManSport world of con-testing, either as con-testers or as organizers of con-testers, they risk being manipulated/mutilated by male dogma designed to co-opt them. Moreover, there is a risk of a too-eager need for acceptance by the NowSport/Man-Sport world which may make women "docile tokens mouthing male texts, employing male technology for male ends, and accepting male fabrications as the true texture of reality." (Daly, 1978, p. 5) Women who believe in and argue for an ideology of social reform which postulates that what men have is good and that women want half of it, that is, women who perceive the existing social institutions (including NowSport/ManSport) to be of value and want to move into the mainstream along with and beside men, might well ponder this feminist's admonition:

> Amazon expeditions into the male-controlled "fields" are necessary in order to leave the father's cave and live in the sun. A crucial problem for us has been to learn how to repossess righteously while avoiding being caught too long in the caves. In the universities, and in all of the professions, the omnipresent poisonous gases gradually stifle women's minds and spirits. Those who

carry out the necessary expeditions run the risk of shrinking into the mold of the mystified Athena, the twice-born, who forgets and denies her Mother and Sisters because she has forgotten her original Self. "Reborn" from Zeus she becomes Daddy's Girl, the mutant who serves the master's purpose. The token woman, who in reality is enchained, possesses, "knows" that she is free. She is a useful tool of the patriarchs, particularly against her sister Artemis, who knows better, respects her Self, bonds with her Sisters, and refuses to sell her freedom, her original birthright, for a mess of respectability. (Daly, 1978, p. 8)

Androcentric/patriarchal values permeate the structure and function of NowSport/ManSport, and by virtue of sex-role definitions men are "able to manipulate women's behavior by ignoring, misrepresenting, devaluing, and discrediting women or their accomplishments, especially when women deviate from the traditional roles." (Freeman, 1979, p. 595) In addition to defining where, when, how, with whom, and in what women shall con-test, men also maintain an unequal balance in the sporting options extended to females and males. Women who do attempt to break out of "Daddy's Cave" often find themselves labeled social deviants or their progress blocked by male control of the economic institutions necessary for the development and progress of WomanSport. A prime example of this economic boycott is the NCAA-supported lobbying effort to block Title IX guidelines calling for equal per-capita expenditures for women's and men's sports in colleges and universities. Within a few weeks the patriarchy of Now-Sport/ManSport raised over $1 million from institutions of higher education (one-half of whose population is female) to be used to block legislation that would have given

women economic support and a base for program development in NowSport/ManSport. Title IX guidelines proportion-
ally equalizing funds for women's and men's sports, which
were to have been published in April 1979, continue to be
buried by massive lobbying efforts by the phallocracy.

Not only have males used their normative, institutional, and economic powers to control women's choices in
sport, they have also become quite adroit at doling out differential rewards for "appropriate" and "inappropriate"
behavior on the part of women. Their intention to continue
doing so is reflected in a statement by the president of the
University of Georgia regarding HEW's enforcement of Title
IX guidelines that would have required equal per-capita
expenditures for women's and men's sports:

> The University, with President Fred C. Davison at
> the helm, has responded to HEW requests by
> stepping into the lead in the fight against imple-
> mentation of current Title IX guidelines. [Italics
> mine.] "The whole thing is ridiculous. It has noth-
> ing to do with what the public wants," Davison
> said. (Red and Black, 1978)

A few months later, in the same student newspaper,
the University of Georgia Red and the Black the following
ad appeared:

> BE A GEORGIA GIRL
> The University of Georgia Athletic
> Department needs attractive young
> ladies (currently enrolled in school)
> to assist with their recruiting program
> for the fall quarter.

Help us make the University of
Georgia's Football program Number 1
in the Nation!
Call . . .

(Red and Black, 1979)

The double message to women is loud and clear. "Appropriate" behavior (helping recruit young men to football) receives positive recognition or is rewarded; "inappropriate" behavior (forcing the equitable funding of women's and men's teams) is negatively reinforced or dismissed as "of no value to the public."

Assuming that the normative, institutional, and differential rewards/uses of power are not sufficient to keep women in their place, males can always resort to "the power of expertise." Women moving into NowSport/ManSport must often rely on men for advice concerning "the game." It is highly likely that much of the advice freely given serves the interests of male supremacy or male values rather than the interests of womenSporters.

When all other tactics fail to keep women down, out, and quiet, then males can and often do turn to psychological power; they assert that, solely by virtue of being born male, they alone belong naturally in the NowSport/ManSport world of con-testing. Anyone other than a Male entering that world is unnatural. If even this fails to keep women out, then Brute Force is exercised. Witness the physical and verbal abuse heaped on the heads of women who dare to be jockeys, football players, wrestlers, baseball umpires, and sports reporters. Marauding males quickly show trespassers what happens to women who dare to invade male sanctuaries.

Daddy's message to daughters-of-all-time was to dismiss, harshly and seriously, the value of sport/play for women. The effect was to keep women out of the mainstream of NowSport/ManSport. The women's movement and the resurgence of feminism in the 1960s and 1970s changed the message, but not the result. Women contesters or organizers of contests, co-opted by the patriarchal NowSport/ManSport world that is hellbent on a Death-March at the end of which lies roboticized existence and nonSelves, screech, "Equal Opportunity," "Separate but Equal Teams," "You have it and we want it," "We'll take one-half of what you've got!" In reality they are calling for judgment/participation/involvement to continue to rest on sex. As a class, women athletes are being made subject to exclusion from all or any games they would choose to enter. By embracing the phallocratic model of Now-Sport/ManSport women have joined hands with men on the Death-March, and the gynocide begun under the Patriarchy continues under the new-Mothers, the Association of Intercollegiate Athletics for Women, the National Association for Girls and Women's Sports, and all other women's organizations that screech "separate but equal."

As early as 1923, Foresisters and Great Grandmamas, both com-testers and teachers, advisors, officials, and managers of the com-test, developed guidelines (alternatives to the androcratic con-test) that permeated Woman-Sport until the later 1950s and early 1960s. These woman-identified guidelines for com-tests included a covering ideology and specific aims, which are summarized below:

> The Woman's Division believes in the spirit of play for its own sake and works for the promotion of physical activity for the largest possible proportion of persons in any given group, in forms suitable to individual needs and capacities, under leadership and environmental conditions that foster health, physical efficiency, and the development of good citizenship. (Gerber, 1974, p. 72)

Foresisters and Great Grandmamas attempted to create a structure for WomanSport that promoted broad-based participation for all girls and women, not merely a select few. One motto that persisted for years was "a sport for every girl, a girl in every sport." Additionally, Foresisters and Great Grandmamas encouraged com-testing for its own sake, play for the enjoyment of playing, with winning and extrinsic rewards being only incidental to the experience of playing hard, sweating profusely, scoring a goal, bonding with other women in the exaltation of a com-test well played. Foresisters and Great-Grandmamas tried to protect the com-test from spectators and exploitation, to discourage sensational publicity, to make well-trained and well-qualified women the managers of com-tests, to make certain all girl and women players had adequate medical checkups, to insist on an environment conducive to healthy com-testing, to eliminate gate receipts, and to "eliminate types and systems of competition which put the emphasis upon individual accomplishments and winning rather than stressing the enjoyment of sport and the development of sportsmanship." (Gerber, 1974, pp. 72–73)

This woman-identified concept of participation in physical activity, WomanSport, persisted in the United States until the middle of the twentieth century. However, the years from 1957 to 1979, almost one-quarter of a century, saw WomanSport move in the direction of Now-Sport/ManSport, away from the com-test and toward the male-established, male-defined, male-developed, and male-governed world of the sports con-test. Many of the Woman-identified concepts of the com-test were gradually dis-placed/replaced/dis-re-membered by contemporary Sister Con-testers/organizers who had been tamed/mutilated/manipulated by the androcratic Sport-Death-March.

Con-testing experiences for women and men today

contribute strongly and effectively to the gradual but persistent demise of Life-Living/Loving, Free-Spirited, Joyful, Creatively energized Humans Be-ing. Gynergy has been sapped/tapped by Male Necrophiliacs who themselves were drained/chained by the Killer/Entrapper/NowSport/ManSport. Necrophiliacs, vampires in need of transfusions (students, money, status, or image) encouraged the emerging She/moths with promises of excellence/glory/rewards/visibility/power. Encouraged, applauded, and permitted limited participation of Fe-Males in the NowSport/ManSport Death-March to NoWhere. Women were encouraged to come along on Male-terms, to play Male-games; to Look, Act, Dress, and be Like-Males, for then their presence would be tolerated, not so disturbing. For in NowSport/ManSport Males Dominate/Regulate/Perpetuate. Females and their accomplishments in the NowSport world will always be ignored, misrepresented, devalued, and discredited. Women athletes in the NowSport/ManSport world become either men or exaggerated Barbi Dolls. Neither is palatable, genuine, nor representative of feminist intentions.

The Association of Intercollegiate Athletics for Women (AIAW) and the National Association for Girls and Women's Sports (NAGWS), once hopes for NewSport/EuSport/OurSport, whisper for sex-separatist con-testing structures. They wish to build their con-testing pyramids alongside/identical to the models of their male peers and thus offer to girls/women Death of the Spirit/Death of Artemis once again, only more insidiously this time, for it comes through the image/appearance/form/mouths/bodies of Women.

Women's organizations that stand for "separate-but-equal" opportunities for Unborn-Daughters/Living-Sisters in the con-testing world offer false hopes/shams/swords clothed in satin and camera lights. Scholarships glisten *along the eerie Death-March and recruitment packages hide the sinister timebombs. Look around us, LADIES, at the GENTLEMEN created by the Wide-wide World of Sport! Look and Listen, Sisters, Aunts, Grandmamas, Mothers, to the sounds of dying on prime Sports/time. Look around you, once-strong, nobel, dreamers-of-being-Artemis, what do you really want? In what Woman/Shadow do you stand? Listen Mothers, Daughters, Aunts, Grandmamas to the screams. screeches, and howls of the fans: BLOOD! MORE BLOOD! GUTS! SPILL YOUR GUTS (you blue-chip young-men and now youngwomen)! Harken to the call of a nation committed to a Death-March (with NowSport leading the way). See clearly the strobe-lit path of glory of Now-Sport/ManSport as BloodAlley, lined with Necrophiliacs burping out false promises, lies, doubletalk, reversed truths, newspeak, male/female-accepted quilts covering the truth. The life promised in NowSport/ManSport is Death of the Self.*

Superficial/casual superlatives mask the horrors of NowSport/ManSport. Youngmen (then), now young-women, too, are drawn to the floodlights like ants to honey; and the hungry, watchful AdultColony gathers around awaiting the feast. Gynergy is sapped once more to feed the hordes. Breasts that once could suckle only the young are now bared to feed us all. Oh yes, we'll drink from her creative SportEnergy and be renewed; and when her breasts lie flat, muscles no longer supple, firm, young, we'll toss her, too, on the dung heap with her brother, having already eaten most of him alive.

Observing society from a radical feminist perspective I find that equal opportunity in sport/EuSport/NewSport/Our-Sport can be realized only through the total integration of females and males in all areas of society without regard for sex/gender identity. All games/activities/dances/forms of movement, must welcome both women and men, girls and boys, *My approach to this is absolute. Any organization, regardless of the sex of its membership, that argues for co-equal structures of WomanSport and ManSport, with each sex being relegated to its appropriate court/field/activity/or space may be for women's rights; but it is definitely not for women's liberation. Human liberation must come from social structures and institutions that are based on the concept of* Integration with Equality. *Only then will true liberation/equality exist. When social structures (including EuSport/NewSport/OurSport) encourage and reward all humans be-ing regardless of their sex, race, age, sexual preference, class, or handicap, then human liberation begins.*

Kathie Amatniek (1979) of the New York Radical Women writes:

> *Forming separate women's groups on issues other than women's rights and liberation is reactionary. It falls right within male supremacist designs for keeping women segregated, excluded, and "in their place." Only if the* stated *purpose of a woman's group is to fight* against *the relegation of women to a separate position, and status in the world, to fight for women's liberation, only then does a separate women's group acquire a revolutionary rather than a reactionary character. Then separation becomes a basis for power rather than a symbol of powerlessness.* (Feminist Revolution, 1979, p. 154)

To date, it does not appear that women-staffed governing bodies for WomanSport have begun to build visible power bases from which to demand integration with equality in EuSport/NewSport/OurSport. Too little has been said about women's liberation, and too often what is said about women's rights is whispered in familiar closets. Strong women's organizations governing con-testing for women must begin to voice their opposition to the rising-floodwater values of the phallocracy. We/they must begin/continue shouting Women's Liberation from any sex-defined place/space. Women con-testers and organizers of con-tests must relook/re-member/re-unite in Sisterhood to re-live the com-test. We must begin/continue to bond with other women to share com-testing experiences, and we must form sisterhoods/motherhoods/grandmamahoods to begin/continue to understand our Journey which began before we lived and will continue long after we are gone. Women must refuse to participate in the male-designed/male-connected procession of NowSport/ManSport and begin to create EuSport/NewSport/OurSport.

How then do we stop this procession toward NonSelf? Where do we begin our own Journey of Ecstacy, our own March of Joy/Integration/Reunification? We start first with ourSelves: Self-change, redefinitions, ripping off the masks handed us by the Patriarchy and looking at ourSelves clearly, accurately; rejoicing in the Beauty reflected in NewMirrors cast from gynergy. We begin to create new patterns of movement/forms of moving/ways of moving that emphasize Wholeness/Integration/Connectedness. We begin boldly, surefootedly, lithe of body, to trust our vision for NewSport born of gynergy. We begin to move in natural ways, spinning, spiraling, darting, dipping and swooping in ever-widening circles until our creative energy, released in movement, attracts other self/energized humans be-ing; and then we soar to quiet places with rapidly beating hearts, sweating bodies, full lungs, and pulsating auras that cry "One. I am One. We are One."

Along with self-change comes change in our relationships with others. We begin reaching out to the writings of the Grandmamas, our Foresisters, our ForeAunts who had visions of WomanSport. We learn our GynoSportStory and build bridges from their vision. We read each other's ideas and connect with one another through conversations, letters, and conventions. We reach out to the SportSisterhood and examine clearly and critically the processes, structures, and activities designed, developed, for WomanSport and always ask the questions "Whose energy is being sapped to sustain the activity?" "Is creative energy being generated through the activity?" We look at the accomplishments of womenMoving and use experience as our first source of accurate information. We trust our experience over androcratic texts, research, records, and computerized data bases. We begin/continue to develop Sister/Support/Systems in Sport, and through these we share experience and build bases from which to spin newThreads in EuSport/NewSport/OurSport.

Collectively, we begin to erode the MalePowerBase in all our social institutions and specifically in the institution of NowSport/ManSport. As one feminist indicated, we do this through Legal Action, Direct Action, Moral Pressure, and Building Skills (Freeman, 1979, p. 601). Felshin (1974) argued that once women worked through the "apologetic" in sports participation they would resort to the forensic or legal arena to wrest from the Patriarchy rights due them under the Constitution. This has, in fact, happened. Numerous lawsuits involving defendants as diverse as Little League and universities have been filed on behalf of girls and women who have been discriminated against solely on the basis of sex. A majority of the cases have been decided in favor of the women who brought the suits. Often they have received back pay, permission to play on a team previously considered "for men or boys only," or reinstatement in a workspace. Such legal actions on the part of our Sisters must be supported by each of us, both morally and financially. Sisters-in-Sport who allow themselves to be scrutinized by the cruel eyes of the Patriarchal court bear witness to the continuation of gynocide.

The direct actions that can be taken by women include sit-ins, economic boycotts, and other actions necessary to draw attention to illegal and unjust institutional practices (Freeman, 1979). Any sporting activity or organization whose sexist practices continue at the expense of women must be held accountable through public sit-ins, letters to the editor, letters/to or conferences with college presidents, peaceable marches with posters dramatizing the situation, speaking up whenever and wherever discrimination is encountered. We must always look critically with a feminist eye, hear acutely with a feminist ear, and speak boldly with a feminist tongue. We must rip off the masks of the Patriarchy and acknowledge the beauty of free/liberated women/men in motion. Humans spinning yarns to form newThreads; whirling rapidly in many directions, facing about; humans turning quickly on eager heels toward EuSport/NewSport/OurSport; darting sideward, forward, backward, daintily and strongly, creating new patterns of humans be-ing in motion. Whirling dervishes, women and men, black and white, old and young, homosexual and heterosexual, rich and poor, maimed and well, blending in motion of creative/energy/born. Integrated motion/spiraling connectedness of living/loving humans be-ing together in motion, splendid/suspended/upended in flight toward never/ending, no/pretending, body/blending EuSport/NewSport/OurSport.

Our Journey has begun. EuSport/NewSport/OurSport, integrated with equality, connected, free form, with all who wish to move in new ways/free ways/open ways joining in the glory and excitement of the com-test, in the exhilaration of meeting other humans be-ing playful/YEA/ful to Life.

REFERENCES

Daly, M. *Gyn/Ecology: The Metaethics of Radical Feminism.* Boston: Beacon Press, 1978.

Felshin, J. The Triple option . . . for women in sport. *Quest,* 21, 36, 1974.

Freeman, J., *WOMEN: A Feminist Perspective.* 2nd ed., Pala Alto: Mayfield, 1979.

Gerber, E., et al. *The American Woman in Sport.* Reading, Mass.: Addison-Wesley, 1974.

Johnson, T., ed. *The Complete Poems of Emily Dickinson.* Boston: Little, Brown, 1980.

Morgan, R. *Going Too Far: The Personal Chronicle of a Feminist.* New York: Vintage Books, 1978.

Oglesby, C., ed. *Women and Sport: From Myth to Reality.* Philadelphia: Lea and Febiger, 1978.

Sarachild, K., ed. *Feminist Revolution.* New York: Random House, 1979.

Ulrich, C. The woman in your life: witches, bitches, and shrews. Amy Morris Homans Lecture, Milwaukee, 1973.

CREATING NEW SPORTS FOR MEN AND WOMEN: AN INTERVIEW

WARREN FARRELL

EDITORS' INTRODUCTION: *For several years, Warren Farrell has applied his imagination to the problem of formulating practical alternatives to sexist social practices and values. One of his goals has been to develop new forms of*

Warren Farrell, Ph.D., is the author of *The Liberated Man* (New York: Random House, Bantam, 1975) and currently teaches at the California School of Professional Psychology in San Diego.

athletics that do not reinforce traditional sex-role stereotypes and differences in power between men and women. He is not alone in this endeavor. Under the collective banner of the "new games movement" or the "cooperative games movement," many people are restructuring games and athletics in cooperative, nonviolent, and nonsexist, ways that build self-esteem. We wanted to tap Warren's current ideas along these lines. What follows is an edited transcript of a telephone interview that took place on July 8, 1979.

EDITORS: *What do you see as the functions of sport?*

FARRELL: *Ideally, to rejuvenate, to reduce stress, and to contribute to an integrated personality and a well-rounded body.*

EDITORS: *What is it about contemporary sport that you find socially destructive to individual physical and emotional well-being?*

FARRELL: *I see it as doing more to create a specialized personality, a specialized body, alienation, and the development of a "winner's circle" that leaves, ultimately, seventy million spectators behind a TV while twenty-two "players" win the victories through which the rest of us live vicariously, while unconsciously becoming insecure about our physical inadequacies relative to these "supermen."*

EDITORS: *Would you repeat that? How does this all begin?*

FARRELL: *It starts, I think, with defining athletics as a predominantly male activity. This defines us as more of a man if we succeed in sports. Although this definition has at least legally begun to change, there are still enormous differences between recruitment practices for boys and girls (in Little League, for example), in the amount of money spent on men's and women's athletic programs, and in parental channeling of boys as opposed to girls. An everyday event during the grammar school and high school years is "choosing sides"—basically a culturally approved male-pecking-order system. A group of boys informally choose two captains—usually the best players—who, in turn, choose sides. The remaining boys are picked one by one, until finally the last boy is assigned the lowest ranking within the group. In effect, most boys receive a type of "report card" of their masculinity every lunch hour, five days a week, sometimes after school, and often twice a day on weekends. Perhaps for ten years. Eventually we pick up message number one: If we're not among the best in one sport, then switch to another. I would like to see message number one be "it's OK to excel in a sport; but also find a sport you're not good at, and use that sport to develop the more deficient parts of your coordination." The second message is, if we're not good at sports at all, drop out. By the time we get into high school, 90 per cent of the boys have dropped out and are winning out their victories vicariously through the 10 per cent who are varsity players. It's stage one in the creation of vicarious maleness.*

For those who make the varsity, the basic message is to concentrate on developing that part of your body which is most proficient; that is, we learn that the purpose of sport is not to round out our body but to specialize in order to enhance our ability to compete with other males and, consequently, to gain status as a man by gaining the respect of men and the support of women.

EDITORS: *What do you see as the implications of this female "support" system?*

FARRELL: *The successful male athlete is able to secure the attention of a whole cadre of allegedly "supportive" women. We call them cheerleaders. I saw my first cheerleaders in grammar school. It was my first introduction to the most attractive women in school, thrusting their bare legs in front of me with dresses so short that I actually thought I was seeing their underwear! It was the strongest motivation I had to play basketball or football, rather than being "just a track star." It was my introduction to the sexuality part of heterosexuality. I thought of these cheerleaders as supporters. I didn't understand their real role as "pressures." Pressure to make me choose a particular playing field (football or basketball), in preparation for my future role to choose a particular type of job (doctor, lawyer). And once I had chosen that playing field, pressure to be the best performer on it—as long as I expected those bare legs to be shaking for me. I didn't see the connection between the sex object and the success object then. Nor did I understand that I was being teased by that sexual promise to be successful; that if I wasn't successful, it could be withdrawn and given to another man; that this sexual promise was their power over me. Nor did I understand that for the females this was their only form of power, their only form of participation, which was vicarious. For the females, this was their preparation to play the housewife role, supporting or pressuring me to perform in the breadwinning role. To perform not only enough to support me, but to support her, my wife and my wife's aspirations, my children and my children's aspirations, and all their expectations of me. A whole audience of expectations. Mostly, though, I didn't understand in grammar school that when I wasn't playing on the team, I, like the women, was beginning to live my life vicariously as well. If I did this in too many sports I'd be, in fact, just like the women. But as a male, I wouldn't be a cheerleader. I'd be a sissy!*

EDITORS: *Do you think not understanding these complexities allowed you to enjoy sports more than if you had understood them?*

FARRELL: *When I was able to put my finger on the pressure (both to succeed and be attractive to the attractive women), I was able to enjoy sports for different reasons: for the process rather than the victory or the tension about po-*

tential victory. But I had to recognize that pressure creates motivation. But it is anxiety-stimulated motivation. I had to substitute self-motivation, which is a different type of enjoyment.

EDITORS: *With all this pressure and motivation, why do so many men drop out of sports?*

FARRELL: *Because the larger pressure is to succeed. And when a boy learns he cannot make it in sports, he tries to succeed elsewhere. But, in the gut, he's still needing to prove himself in sports. So he does it vicariously, because doing it directly no longer offers the chance of proving himself. So just as all but an elite of women learned to live through men, all but an elite of men learned to live through sports.*

Editors: *You mentioned before "stage one" of vicarious maleness. What's stage two?*

FARRELL: *I guess I'd call stage two understanding how proving one's masculinity through the victories of "our team" is linked to proving one's masculinity vicariously through the victories of "our country." It's not coincidental that we pledge allegiance or sing the national anthem at major sports events. In the article in Part One of this anthology [*"The Super-Bowl Phenomenon"*], I clarified this link. Since writing this article, I've constructed what I believe might be called "The Unconscious Pledge of Allegiance":*

I pledge allegiance
to vicarious identity
in the United States of America;
one team, under God
to win victories making me feel
better about myself.

EDITORS: *How does this "vicarious identity" operate on an everyday level?*

FARRELL: *Three examples come to mind right away: (1) through a man's predictions of which team will win or lose, (2) through his personal identification with superstars or the "best" team, and (3) through armchair quarterbacking or retrospective analyses of why teams fail or succeed. None of these vehicles for men to integrate sports into their own lives requires any direct participation or enjoyment of athletics which would allow men to develop their physicality or humanity.*

The real significance of this, though, is that it serves as a communications crutch for us men. We think we are communicating with each other. In fact, we're avoiding each other. We're focusing on sports—not our feelings toward each other, our hurts, our joys, or even our relationships. Vicarious participation in sports is a distancing mechanism while giving the appearance of being a bonding mechanism. That is, a woman might see a group of men "bonded together" at a bar (or the office) and feel excluded because we're discussing the latest game. It may appear to her that we have close camaraderie. She is unaware that any man with the same knowledge can participate—that we're basically interchangeable parts because we don't know each other. That's why we can return to a college reunion, see our "best buddies" and, after five minutes, have nothing in common because the sport we had in common is gone.

Vicarious identity in sports, then, not only avoids direct participation in our physicality, it also avoids direct participation in our emotionality, our ability to develop friendships, to really know others, and, ultimately, to know ourselves.

EDITORS: *Do you feel sports contributes to a less hierarchical society insofar as it provides opportunities for minorities?*

FARRELL: *Overall, I think it presently contributes to an ex-*

clusive society, in which elites and celebrities enjoy higher status and greater opportunities than the masses. For minorities it creates an illusion of upward mobility. While minorities, blacks in particular, represent about three-quarters of the 250 or so National Basketball Association players and are also overrepresented in baseball and football, millions spend their early lives trying to become part of the athletic elite. Many minorities focus much of their childhood and adolescent efforts upon athletics rather than channeling energies into more job-productive and career-productive activities than sports, only to be tricked in the end by not getting any real rewards.

EDITORS: *In light of these problems, how would you go about redesigning a high school athletic program?*

FARRELL: *By way of introduction, I would not like to see us move in the direction of simply replacing all competitive sports with cooperative types of athletic endeavors. I would like to see us develop maybe six or seven basic types of sports that give children the early message that there are many ways to approach athletics, ranging from competitive and nonviolent on the one hand to a form of relaxation and "centeredness" on the other. In addition, sports should be restructured in ways that allow for mutual participation by boys and girls, men and women.*

One category of sport might be one that integrates cooperation with competition. We might take a traditional sport like baseball and redesign the rules so that, at the end of each inning, each player would rotate from one position to another, similar to volleyball. By the end of nine innings, each of the nine players would have experienced each of the nine positions on the team. Teams can still win or lose by observing these rules, so interteam competition has not been eliminated. Some progress is made, however, toward eradicating the message to young people that one of the central functions of sport is specialization.

A second category of sport might emphasize cooperation in order to enhance self and partner's individual improvement. Frisbee is a good example. Participants simply enjoy throwing the frisbee back and forth, running, jumping, and performing tricks. Each individual improves tes* own skills and helps others improve theirs. Tennis volleying similarly encourages experimentation rather than specializing in the mastered area to win a victory.

A third area of innovation would be cooperative athletics with a group challenge. In a modified version of volleyball, for example, both teams could focus on getting the ball over the net to each other in such a way that would facilitate the other team's returning of the ball again. This cooperation dimension might be reinforced by a group-challenge dimension; challenging both teams, for example, to get the ball over the net as often as possible, assisted by as many participants as possible, within as short a time period as possible.

A fourth genre of sport I call competitive and nonviolent. An example might be a modified form of football. Touch football can preserve the potential for brilliant strategizing without the violence. Football is the closest physical game we have to chess and requires the execution of beautifully syncopated maneuvers of mind and body. Increasing the excitement level can be done by rule changes such as widening the field (without tackling, more running space is needed) or decreasing the number of team members (allowing for more direct participation per participant).

A fifth category would revolve solely around individual improvement in relation to a personal challenge. Yoga

---

*"tes" = his or her. It is part of the "human vocabulary" introduced in *The Liberated Man*. "Te" = he or she; "tir" = him or her.

or jogging without timing as the main goal are the most familiar examples here. A sixth category, individual improvement with an outside challenge, such as in jogging against a self-imposed improvement timetable, swimming, or gymnastics, is already familiar. Finally, a seventh category, usually not considered a sport, might be called "relaxation." Examples would be floating on our back in a pool, or body surfing in the ocean's smallest waves until our body is inches off the sand, just allowing the surf to carry our body with it. It's a great sport for learning to "go with the flow."

EDITORS: *What benefits would accrue for female and male participants within this modified sports structure?*

FARRELL: One of the fundamental changes in sports described above is that athletics become fully integrated across sex lines. For men integration means that sports are not, by definition, a sign of masculinity. It also means sending early childhood messages to boys that teach us that (1) we can enjoy the process of the sport as the end rather than the victory as the end, hence preparing men to value the process of their work rather than its economic outcome; (2) we can be well-rounded rather than specialists (preparing for career change rather than being prostitutes to one function and position our entire life); (3) we can remain on the playing field as primarily a method of participation rather than primarily a method of performance in response to cheerleaders and peers; (4) we can improve via experimenting rather than repeatedly performing the same tasks; (5) our father's attention might be procured not by performing like television athletes, but because of ourselves and our unique characteristics. The sex role benefits for women include those mentioned for men, plus (1) learning to take risks; (2) learning not to live vicariously through men's lives and achievements, as is the case with the cheerleader and housewife roles; and (3) learning to compete, cooperate, and experience the joy of developing their physical skills and potentials.

When combined, men and women learning to share participation in sports prepares them for sharing participation in the breadwinning and homemaking roles. At present we give men and women "divorce training"—teaching them to be attracted to each other the more unlike each other they are. Secondly, when both sexes learn to share sports roles, and therefore breadwinning roles, it prepares both sexes to be free to question the institutions that employ them, or to try something creative that could increase the chances of failure. The training of the sports specialist means only a few make it, and those who do get the rewards of performing but few rewards of life diversification. They are quickly has-beens. And they are never sure whether women are attracted to them for who they are or what they've achieved. They lose if they win, and lose if they lose!

EDITORS: *What would be the role of coaches in this newly devised athletic program?*

FARRELL: *One of the big challenges for the future of sport is the changing role of coaches. For creative coaches, it is an opportunity for "job creation"; that is, creating jobs that do not exist, rather than competing for a notch in a bureaucracy that does exist. The coach might start by simply selling tes* school and the schools in the geographical area, for example, on implementing "rotating baseball," described above. The schools might still compete, maintaining the excitement that can accompany competition; but the message about specialization would differ. As this step becomes accepted, sports with interteam cooperation might be sold.*

---

*his or her

The "selling points" of this approach include every-thing mentioned above, which, it might also be argued, are more compatible with communication in family life than are solely competitive, victory-oriented athletics. It also facilitates wider athletic participation among a given student body. From a cost-benefit perspective, all but a few athletic programs are a drain on fiscal resources and, at the same time, serve the athletic needs of a small number of individuals rather than a majority of a school's populace. High schools, with rare exceptions, do not make money from their varsity sports programs. In short, therefore, we would be creating a structural base for a larger number of participants with probably a smaller amount of cash outlay and a series of messages far more compatible with a true education.

EDITORS: *Do you think it is possible to restructure sport without first restructuring American society at large?*

FARRELL: *There is no such thing as restructuring American society at large without first beginning to restructure every bit and portion of it. This is the essential socialist fallacy. There will never be a socialist revolution in a country in which its traditions lead to a debate between Ronald Reagan, Jimmy Carter, and Gerald Ford. There will only be an evolutionary type of change in this country, unless something extraordinary occurs. Waiting for a comprehensive socialist revolution is like a religious zealot waiting for God to come knocking at the door; no one can say it definitely won't happen, but you better not wait around for it. And if it did happen without preparation, we'd have a socialist structure superimposed on a capitalist mentality. The only way out of that is back to capitalism or a socialist dictatorship. The first is no real change, and the second is unacceptable. A more practical recipe for change is to begin both individual reassessments and political action at every level of society, to encourage each person or group to effect change in a relatively immediate area of influence. One of my central messages to "revolutionaries" is to figure out, first, what we enjoy doing; second, what makes a social contribution; third, what is not already being done; fourth, how to make a living doing it; fifth, how to recognize when we're beinning to no longer grow doing it, and then to prepare to start the five steps over again. That gives us full-time social change agents, rather than people working for the system during the day and against it at night.*

REFERENCES

For reading materials that discuss cooperative athletics or games nobody loses, see Jim Deacover, *Cooperative Games: for Indoors and Out* (write to Family Pastimes, RR #4, Perth, Ontario, Canada K7H3C6); Terry Orlick, *The Cooperative Sports & Games Book* (New York: Pantheon Books, 1978); Andrew Fluegelman, ed., *The New Games Book* (write to the New Games Foundation, P.O. Box 7901, San Francisco, CA 94120); T. Schneider, *Everybody's a Winner: A Kids' Guide to New Sports and Fitness* (Boston: Little, Brown, 1976).

CONCLUSION

MEN'S LIBERATION AND SPORTS

This book has aimed at a critical analysis of sports in American society from the perspective of men's liberation. We have examined the impact of sports upon male identity, the reinforcing connections between the athletic ethos and dominant cultural conceptions of masculinity, and various interrelationships between sport and other social institutions such as the military, big business, and the media. For male liberationists and social scientists, sport is a crucial area to explore because it is perhaps the most important institution socializing boys into traditional male roles. Since sport is so pervasive an institution, we believe an understanding of its social dynamics can be an effective vehicle for generating and testing theoretical constructs concerning the male sex role in American society. For men outside academia and unidentified or unfamiliar with men's liberation, we feel a greater awareness of the influence of sport upon men's lives may enhance their understanding of themselves at a time when definitions of masculinity are undergoing a metamorphosis.

Men's Liberation:
Its Origins and Ethos

The men's liberation movement emerged in the early seventies, largely in response to feminism. It is composed of predominantly white, middle-class, college-based males interested in confronting the issue of sexual inequality and redefining their relationships with women and other men. While there is much diversity of opinion in the movement, its general objectives are summarized in this statement prepared by the Berkeley Men's Center in February 1973:

329

We, as men, want to take back our full human-
ity. . . . We no longer want to feel the need to per-
form sexually, socially, or in any way to live up to
an imposed male role. . . . We want to relate to
both women and men in more human ways—
with warmth, sensitivity, emotion, and hon-
esty. . . . We want to be equal with women and to
end destructive competitive relationships with
men. We are oppressed by conditioning which
. . . serves to create a mutual dependence of
male (abstract, aggressive, strong, unemotional)
and female (nurturing, passive, weak, emotional)
roles. We believe that this half-humanization will
only change when our competitive, male-domi-
nated, individualistic society becomes coopera-
tive, based on [the] sharing of resources and
skills. We want to use our creative energy to serve
our common needs and not to make profits for our
employers. [1]

It is difficult to describe the present stature and character of the men's liberation movement. Perhaps the best historical parallel is to compare the incipient men's movement
with the early consciousness-raising efforts of feminists in
the 1960s. Although Betty Friedan spearheaded an effort to
centralize and bureaucratize feminist activities by founding
the National Organization for Women (NOW) in 1966, the
women's movement at large displayed essentially anar-
chistic social and political origins, with small feminist
groups springing up throughout the country independent of
one another but in tune with the overall ethos of feminism.
During this early phase, the majority of women attracted to
the new feminism responded primarily to its developing
ethos more than to a sense of affiliation with a firmly en-
trenched social and political movement. Men's liberation

began as an ethos; but unlike feminism, it has remained so, not developing into a bona fide social-political movement.

As a cultural ethos, that is, a set of predominant ideas, values, and ideals that possess a distinctive character, men's liberation has attracted large numbers of sympathizers who support and identify with its overall objectives and perceive it as a viable means of bringing about personal and social change. A social basis of a men's liberation movement, however, has developed through a growing network of small, autonomous men's consciousness-raising or support groups formed in the United States and Canada. Just as women, moved by the emotional call and issues of women's liberation, came together in small consciousness-raising and study groups, so men have begun to meet with one another to explore their lives and feelings within a sexist society.

The purposes of these groups are many and range from providing a space for individuals who may feel lost and confounded by rapidly changing values and lifestyles to securing a supportive atmosphere for men to grow together. The types and concerns of groups vary. Divorced males may gather to discuss their loneliness, alimony, recollections of a broken marriage, or the children they may or may not see on weekends. Experienced and new fathers share insights concerning child-rearing or problems with authoritarianism. Friendships or love relationships may be the theme of another meeting's ruminations. Gay men share and shape new consciousnesses and help one another take the difficult steps from closet to community. Using literature, films, or the works of Marx and Lawrence, study groups explore the terrain of masculine identity, sexuality, life within and alternatives to a sexist society. Political thinkers and activists peel back the layers of the traditional male role and plan strategies for personal and social change.

While the idea of men's groups is still fairly new, their experiential ethos and aims can be generally summarized. An interpersonal atmosphere of supportive acceptance and emotional openness is developed. The traditionally combative and competitive motif of male interaction is consciously avoided. Striving for dominance is out and sharing is in. Excessive intellectualizing is looked upon with suspicion because, for men, intellectualism has too long been a guise for stoicism and egocentricity, which are key components in maintaining social and emotional distance among males and from women. An unthreatening atmosphere in which genuine expressions of anger, affection, confusion, or playfulness are possible is sought. Participants attempt to feel and think through the varied and complex ways in which sex role stereotypes and social institutions limit their ability to understand and relate more authentically to men and women. The effect of a men's group, if the commitment of the participants is sustained over several meetings, is likely to be both powerful and profound, particularly on men's struggles against sexism and their efforts to forge new identities and lifestyles in a changing institutional milieu.

There is no way to estimate the numbers of men's groups in America or the scope and influence of the movement itself. The activities and ideologies of members and sympathizers equally defy handy categorization. Though annual national conferences on men's liberation have been held since 1975, no national leadership or organizational structure has evolved through which more programmatic policies and political actions could be formulated.

A majority of male liberationists seem particularly concerned with understanding and liberating themselves from the psychological oppression resulting from socialization into destructive sex roles that limit their opportunities for emotional expression and interpersonal fulfillment. Others, more political in thinking and activities, locate the sources of sex-based oppression in institutions external to the individual and strive to develop insights and strategies designed to make the social structure itself more humane. Many men identified with the liberation movement focus upon specific issues such as how men relate to one another, how men deal with careers and work, or gay liberation. Many others have defined their politics as ancillary to feminism and actively support feminist efforts to establish day-care facilities, secure rights for welfare mothers, obtain passage of the Equal Rights Amendment, expose and eliminate violence against women in the media, or achieve humane abortion policies. Some men have joined feminist-inspired and controlled groups such as NOW or the National Women's Political Caucus. Since 1972, various spokespersons for the movement have created a growing public awareness of men's liberation, as well as developing an analysis of sexism from a male perspective.

Social scientists have also begun to apply their energies to the analysis of men's roles. Partly in response to women's changing social, economic, and political roles in the twentieth century, the growth of the feminist movement and women's studies, and the resulting articulation of a feminist analytic paradigm in social science, contemporary sociologists and psychologists are scrutinizing the role of patriarchal values and sex stratification in men's as well as women's lives. Theoretical debate is flourishing, and the area of men's studies is rapidly expanding.[2]

Whether the ethos of men's liberation will continue to grow remains to be seen. It is certain, however, that men's lives will change unremittingly in the future, and understanding the links between sports and male identity will help men to make the difficult transition from their traditional embattlement with women and one another to a new era of empathy and cooperation. As Margaret Mead counsels, "For the future, our one sustaining strength will be a sense of our common humanity."[3]

SPORTS AND MALE IDENTITY

What have we learned from our study of sports and male identity? First, we feel the analysis of the relationship between sports and masculinity adds impetus to the argument that male identity and behavior *is learned* and not instinctive. Unlike nineteenth-century thinkers, contemporary social scientists generally agree that social and cultural influences, and not biological impulses or sex-based physiological factors, account for differences in male and female identity. The social-role explanation of sex role differences has displaced the nineteenth-century dictum "anatomy is destiny."[4] To put it simply, the belief today is that the male sex role is defined by a culture and learned by individuals. Once learned, the constellation of expectations, beliefs, and values that are culturally regarded as masculine do much to shape the attitudes and behavior of boys and men. Through their identification with and participation in sports, many males learn to feel superior to and exploit women, to suppress their emotions, to act aggressively and affect an air of bravado, to seek and exercise power over others, and to enhance or maintain their position in the social hierarchy.

The competitive structure and teleology of sport as it is presently defined by American society encourages the development of the kind of behavior and values associated with striving for dominance. One individual is pitted against another; boxers beat their opponents into submission, while high jumpers and hammer and javelin throwers contest the forces of gravity and inertia. There is nothing inherently evil or socially destructive in the essential character of the athlete's struggle against others and the limits imposed upon physical accomplishment by nature. However, to the extent that the ethos of athletic competition and excellence is associated with the ideology of male supremacy, sexual potency, and a desire for power, sports legitimize a social hierarchy in which men enjoy greater status than their female counterparts. In a way sadly consistent with the Hobbesian legacy, sports encourage men to forever compete with one another, never trusting and never feeling, and to regard women as frail underlings who are far removed from the panoply of patriarchal pugnacity and privilege. Evidence mounts that competition has lost its functional effectiveness in both personal and social life. The interpersonal anomie of modern culture and pressing economic, political, and ecological problems beckon the birth of a new ethos of cooperation. One seldom succeeds in muscling one's way through loneliness or a shattering relationship, and it is doubtful that we can pole vault over the coming energy crisis.

A predilection and respect for violence is yet another result of male socialization in sports. Aggression was long thought to be an outgrowth of physiological drives abundant in men and relatively absent in women. Hence the rough-and-tumble antics of boys, barroom brawls, or occasional incidents of wife beating were often regarded as "natural" derivations of masculinity—*the acting out of innate biological urges. Today, however, most social scientists believe aggression is learned.*[5] Studies of hockey players, for example, show that assaultive behavior on the ice is a function of peer influences.[6] In many sports, violence is considered normal and is not limited to the players. There has been an alarming rise in the incidence and severity of spectator violence at sporting events:

> *At a National Football League game at Foxboro, Mass., between the New York Jets and New England Patriots, rowdy fans continually ran out on the field, stopping play a dozen times. By the time the game ended, two fans had died of heart at-*

> *tacks, 30 were taken to a hospital with cuts and bruises, 49 were arrested, a policeman's jaw was broken and a spectator had been stabbed. In the parking lot a policeman was giving mouth-to-mouth resuscitation to a heart attack victim when a drunken fan urinated on the officer's back.*[7]

For social scientists interested in explaining the rising tide of violence in American society, our advice is to tune in *Monday Night Football* or the Stanley Cup finals for reflective fodder.

A good case can be made that the sports subculture furthers the adoption of violence-generating premises by susceptible individuals. Moreover, because they are vehicles of the machismo syndrome, sports do much to equate demonstrations of violence with manhood. This dynamic juxtaposition of violence and masculinity, described in Wolfgang and Ferracuti's Subculture of Violence,[8] is also found in other predominantly male groups such as the military and the police. Just as football players are taught to hate their opponents, American soldiers were conditioned to despise the Japanese in World War II and the Vietnamese in the 1960s. Soldiers and athletes have always been twin pinnacles of manhood, and more recently, thanks to television, the police have come to share the symbolic limelight. (Kojak may be bald, but "he has balls.") In a case study of changing law-enforcement practices in Buffalo from 1830 to 1970, Elwin H. Powell sees a trend away from community-based policing toward a developing paramilitary bureaucracy, and he documents the traditional proneness of policemen to violence.[9] Considering the growing prevalence of allegations regarding police brutality and indifference to violent crimes against women, such as rape and wifebeating, we would do well to explore the associations between violence and masculinity in the law-enforcement subculture.

As we have pointed out before, as an institutional network for stereotypical male socialization and the dissemination of a patriarchal ideology, sports function to preserve the existing power structure and a system of stratification by sex. Hopefully, this book has shed some light upon the political economy and sexist role of sport in the American social order.

Summary

This collection of articles was intended to deepen and enliven the discourse on men's liberation and to take us a step closer to understanding both the psychological and the institutional nature of sexual inequality. Sports in our culture play a major role in perpetuating traditional sex-role stereotyping furnishing an ideological firmament that promotes and rationalizes an unequal distribution of power and status between men and women. Because sport is such a widespread institutional fountainhead of traditional masculine values and comprises a fertile ground for stereotypical male socialization, it provides an excellent analytic medium for exploring the myriad ways men are oppressed by sexual inequality, as well as the role played by men in the oppression of women. Perhaps the most essential problem of men's liberation is getting men to understand themselves *individually* as victims of sexual inequality without losing sight of why they are the *collective* oppressors of women. Such a recognition of the awkward and perplexing position in which men find themselves in their efforts to comprehend and combat sexism would facilitate further analysis, research, and political action. As Nona Glazer observes,

> *there has been a singular neglect by men of any analysis of men's power over women. Hence, the men's liberation movement has largely neglected*

> *to investigate such questions as how men con-*
> *tinue to victimize women, how men themselves*
> *resist sharing male privileges with women, how*
> *men manage to resist changing their relation-*
> *ships with women toward sexual equality.*[10]

We feel the contributors to this edition have made some headway toward correcting the analytic deficiencies Glazer outlines. Their writings indicate that, if full sexual equality is ever to be gleaned from the social and historical process, the structure and attendant ideology of contemporary sport must be radically altered. This is a formidable undertaking that will require both a restructuring of male consciousness at the individual level and a continuing struggle for humane change at the institutional level. If the ethos of men's liberation is to survive, the legacy of the locker room must be abandoned and new modes of sporting activities must be created. If true sexual equality is to be achieved, men must discover new ways to play together that do not prohibit emotional expression, encourage violence and dominance striving, glorify ruthless competition, and maintain traditional notions of male supremacy.

FOOTNOTES

1. For a copy of the entire statement, see Joseph H. Pleck and Jack Sawyer, eds., *Men and Masculinity* (Englewood Cliffs, N. J.: Prentice-Hall, 1974), pp. 173–74.
2. For a review of the literature on men's studies see James B. Harrison, "Men's Roles and Men's Lives," in *Signs: Journal of Women in Culture and Society* 4, no. 2 (1978): 324–336. Also, a *Men's Studies Bibliography* may be obtained by writing to The Humanities Library, Massachusetts Institute of Technology, Cambridge, MA 02139.
3. Margaret Mead and Ken Heyman, *World Enough:*

Rethinking the Future (Boston: Little, Brown, 1976), p. 216.

4. Laurel Richardson Walum, *The Dynamics of Sex and Gender: A Sociological Perspective* (Chicago: Rand McNally, 1977), pp. 1–66.

5. Richard Sipes, "War, Sports and Aggression: An Empirical Test of Two Rival Theories," *American Anthropologist* (February 1973), pp. 64–86. See also Albert Bandura, *Aggression: A Social Learning Analysis* (Englewood Cliffs, N. J.: Prentice-Hall, 1973), and Erich Fromm, *The Anatomy of Human Destructiveness* (New York: Holt, Rinehart & Winston, 1973).

6. Michael D. Smith, "Significant Others: Influence on the Assaultive Behavior of Young Hockey Players," *International Review of Sport Sociology* (March 1974), pp. 126–31.

7. Joe Falls and Bill Surface, "War in the Grandstand: Sports Fans Grow Violent—Why?" *Parade Magazine* (Dec. 26, 1976), pp. 7–9.

8. Marvin Wolfgang and Franco Ferracuti, *The Subculture of Violence: Toward an Integrated Theory in Criminology* (London: Tavistock, 1967). See also Hans Toch, *Violent Men: An Inquiry into the Psychology of Violence* (Chicago: Aldine, 1969), pp. 187–97.

9. Elwin H. Powell, *The Design of Discord: Studies of Anomie* (New York: Oxford University Press, 1970), chap. 8.

10. Nona Glazer and Helen Youngelson Waehrer, eds., *Woman in a Man-Made World* (Chicago: Rand McNally, 1977), p. 391.

SUPPLEMENTAL READINGS

Amdur, Neil. *The Fifth Down Democracy and the Football Revolution.* New York: Delta, 1972.

Angell, Roger. "The Sporting Sense—The Long Green," *The New Yorker* (April 25, 1971), pp. 103–29.

Ashe, Arthur. "An Open Letter to Black Parents: Send Your Children to the Libraries," *New York Times* (February 6, 1977), sec. 5, p. 2.

Axtheim, Peter. *The City Game.* New York: Harper's Magazine Press, 1920.

Ball, Donald W. "Failure in Sport," *American Sociological Review* 41 (August 1976): 726–39.

Ball, Donald W., and John W. Loy, eds. *Sport and Social Order: Contributions to the Sociology of Sport.* Reading, Mass.: Addison-Wesley, 1975.

Berger, Richard A., and Donald H. Littlefield. "Comparison Between Football Athletes and Nonathletes on Personality." *Research Quarterly* 40 (December 1969): 663–65.

Bergman, John. "From the Cradle to the Playing Field: America's Emphasis on Highly Organized Competitive Sports for Preadolescent Boys." *Journal of Sport History* 21 (1975): 112–31.

Berkowitz, L. "Sports, Competition and Agression," in *Proceedings:* 4th Canadian Psycho-Motor Learning and Sport Symposium (Ottowa, 1972).

"The Boom in Leisure: Where Americans Spend 100 Billions." *U.S. News and World Report* (May 23, 1977), pp. 62–63.

Bouton, James. *Ball Four: My Life and Hard Times Throwing the Knuckleball in the Big Leagues.* New York: World, 1970.

Boyle, Robert H. *Sport—Mirror or American Life.* Boston: Little, Brown, 1963.

Brenton, Myron. *The American Male.* New York: Coward McCann, 1966.

Brower, Jonathen G., ed. "Children in Sport." *Arena Review* 1 (Winter 1978): entire issue.

Buchanan, Hugh Troy, Joe Blankenbaker, and Doyice

Cotten. "Academic and Athletic Ability as Popularity Factors in Elementary School Children." *Research Quarterly* 47 (October 1976): 320–25.

Caldwell, F. "Adults Play Big Role in Children's Games." *The Physician and Sports Medicine* 5 (1977): 103–08.

Chandler, Jean M. "TV and Sports." *Psychology Today* 10 (April 1977): 64–76.

Coakley, Jay J. *Sport in Society: Issues and Controversies.* St. Louis: Mosby, 1978.

"Comes the Revolution: Joining the Game at Last, Women are Transforming American Athletics." *Time* (June 26, 1978), pp. 54–60.

Cooke, Chris, ed. *The Men's Survival Resource Book: On Being a Man in Today's World.* Minneapolis, Minn.: M.S.R.B. Press, 1978.

Creamer, Robert. "Women's Worth," *Sports Illustrated* (January 17, 1977), p. 6.

Deford, Frank. "Religion in Sport." *Sports Illustrated* (April 19, April 26, and May 3, 1976).

Dickey, Glenn. *The Jock Empire.* Radnor, Penn.: Chilton, 1974.

Dowell, Lewis J. "Environmental Factors of Childhood Competitive Athletics." *The Physical Educator* 28 (March 1971): 17–21.

Durso, Joseph. *The All-American Dollar: The Big Business of Sports.* Boston: Houghton Mifflin, 1971.

Edwards, Harry. "Change and Crisis in Modern Sport." *Black Scholar* 8 (1976): 60–65.

———. "The Myth of the Racially Superior Athlete." *Intellectual Digest* 2 (March 1972): 58–60.

———. *The Revolt of the Black Athlete.* New York: Macmillan, 1969.

———. *Sociology of Sport.* Homewood, Ill. Dorsey, 1973.

Edwards, Harry, and Van Rackages. "The Dynamics of Violence in American Sport: Some Promising Structural and Social Considerations." *Journal of Sport and Social Issues* 1 (Summer/Fall 1977): 3–31.

Elias, Norbert, and Eric Dunning. "Dynamics of Group Sports with Special Reference to Football." *British Journal of Sociology* 17 (1966): 388–401.

Eitzen, D. Stanley. "Athletics in the Status System of Male Adolescents: A Replication of Colemen's 'The Adolescent Society'". *Adolescence* 10 (Summer 1975): 267–76.

———. "Sport and Social Status in American Public Secondary Education." *Review of Sport and Leisure* (Fall 1976): 139–55.

———. ed. *Sport in Contemporary Society: An Anthology*. New York: St. Martin's Press, 1979.

Eitzen, D. Stanley, and George H. Sage. *Sociology of American Sport*. Dubuque, Iowa: Brown, 1978.

Elias, Norbert, and Eric Duaney. "The Quest for Excitement in Unexciting Societies." *The Cross-Culture Analysis of Sport and Games*, edited by Gunther Luschen. Champaign, Ill.: Stipl, 1970, pp. 31–51.

The Embattled Human Male." Special issue of *Impact of Science on Society* 21, no. 1 (1971).

Engle, Kathleen. "The Greening of Girls' Sports. *The Nation's Schools* (September 1973): 27–34.

Fasteau, Brenda Feigen. "Giving Women a Sporting Chance." *Ms.* 2 (July 1973): 56–58, 103.

Felshin, Jan. "The Triple Option . . . for Women in Sport." *Quest* 21 (January 1974): 36–40.

Feltz, Deborah L. "Athletics in the Status System of Female Adolescents." *Review of Sport and Leisure* 3 (Fall 1978): 8–108.

Figes, Ev' . *Patriarchal Attitudes*. New York: Stein and Day, 197'

Fireston , Ross. *A Book for Men: Visions of the Male Experience*. New York: Stonehill, 1975.

Fisher, A. Craig. "Sports as an Agent of Masculine Orientation." *Physical Education* (Oct. 1972): 120–22.

Fixx, James F. *The Complete Book of Running.* New York: Random House, 1977.

Flood, Curt. *The Way It Is.* New York: Trident Press, 1970.

Frayne, Trent. "Parents, Pressure, and the Puck." *Quest Magazine* (November 1972), pp. 41–43.

Gallico, Paul. *Farewell to Sport.* New York: Knopf, 1938.

"Games Big People Play." *Mother Jones* (September/ October 1976).

Gent, Peter. *North Dallas Forty.* New York: Morrow, 1973.

Gerson R. "Redesigning Athletic Competition for Children." *Motor Skills: Theory Into Practice* 2 (1977): 3–14.

Gilbert, Bil, and Nancy Williamson. "Women in Sport." *Sports Illustrated* (May 28, June 4, and June 11, 1973; July 29, 1973).

Goldstein, Jeffrey H., and Robert L. Arms. "Effects of Observing Athletic Contests on Hostility." *Sociometry* 34 (March 1971): 83–90.

Goodman, Cary. "Degoaling Sports," *Sport Sociology Bulletin* 5 (Fall 1976): 11–13.

Greendorfer, Susan. "Role of Socializing Agents in Female Sport Involvement." *Research Quarterly* 48, no. 2: 304–10.

Harding, Carol, ed. "Women in Sport." Special issue of *Arena Newsletter* (April/June 1977).

Harris, Donald S., and D. Stanley Eitzen. "The Consequences of Failure in Sport." *Urban Life* 7 (July 1978): 177–88.

Harris, Dorothy V., ed. *Women and Sport: A National Research Conference.* Penn State HPER Series no. 2, the Pennsylvania State University, 1972.

Hart, M. Marie, ed. *Sport in the Socio-Cultural Process.* Dubuque, Iowa: Brown, 1972.

Hein, Fred V. "Competitive Athletics for Children," In *Contemporary Philosophies of Physical Education and Athletics,* edited by Robert A. Cobb and Paul M. Lepley. Columbus, Ohio: Merrill, 1973.

Hellison, Donald R. *Beyond Balls and Bats*. Washington, D. C.: AAHPER, 1978.

——— . *Humanistic Physical Education*. Englewood Cliffs, N. J.: Prentice-Hall, 1973.

Herron, R., and Brian Sutton-Smith. *Child's Play*. New York: Wiley, 1971.

Heywood, Lloyd A., and Rodney B. Warnick. "Campus Recreation: The Intramural Revolution." *Journal of Physical Education and Recreation* 47 (October 1976): 52–54.

Hoberman, John. "Sport and Political Ideology." *Journal of Sport and Social Issues* 1 (Summer/Fall 1977): 80–114.

Hoffman, Abigail. "Super-Jock in Decline: Liberating Sport from Sexist Stereotypes." *Canadian Dimension* (August 1971), pp. 41–49.

Hogan, Candace Lyle. "Fair Shake or Shakedown?" *WomenSports* 3 (September 1976): 50–54.

Horn, Jack. "Parent Egos Take the Fun Out of Little League." *Psychology Today* (September 1977), pp. 18, 22.

Hotchkiss, Sandy. "Parents and Kids' Sports." *Human Behavior* 7 (March 1978): 35.

Huckle, Patricia. "Back to the Starting Line." *American Behavioral Scientist* 21 (January/February 1978): 379–92.

Huizinga, Johann. *Homo Ludens: A Study of the Play Element in Culture*. Boston: Beacon, 1950.

Isenberg, Jerry. *How Many Miles to Camelot?* New York: Pocket Books, 1971.

Issacs, Neil D. *Jock Culture U.S.A.* New York: Norton, 1978.

Jackson, C. O. "Just Boys, Not Little Adults." *The Physical Educator* 18 (May 1961): 42.

Jackson, Myles. "College Football Has Become a Losing Business." *Fortune* (December 1962), pp. 119–21.

Johnson, Arthur T., ed. "Political Economy of Sport."

American Behavior Scientist 21 (January/February 1978): entire issue.

Kahn, Roger. *The Boys of Summer.* New York: Signet Books, 1973.

Kay, R. S. et al. "Sports Interests and Abilities as Contributors to Self-Concept in Junior High School Boys." *Research Quarterly* 43 (1972): 208–15.

Kennedy, Roy, and Nancy Williamson. "Money: The Monster Threatening Sports." *Sports Illustrated* (July 17, July 24, and July 31, 1978).

Klofs, C. E., and M. J. Lyon. *The Female Athlete.* St. Louis: Mosby, 1978.

Kokopeli, Bruce, and George Lakey. "More Power than We Want: Masculine Sexuality and Violence." *Win Magazine* 29 (July 1976): 4–8.

Koppett, Leonard. *The Essence of the Game Is Deception.* Boston: Little, Brown, 1973.

Kramer, Jerry, ed. *Instant Replay.* New York: World, 1968.

——— . *Lombardi: Winning Is the Only Thing.* New York: World, 1970.

Lahr, John. "The Theatre of Sports." *Evergreen Review,* 13 (November 1969): 39–76.

Landers, Daniel M., ed. *Social Problems in Athletics: Essays in the Sociology of Sport.* Urbana: University of Illinois Press, 1976.

Larson, David, Elmer Spreitzer, and Eldon E. Snyder. "Youth Hockey Programs: A Sociological Perspective." *Sports Sociology Bulletin* 4 (Fall 1975): 55–63.

Lawson, R. A. "Physical Education and Sport: Alternatives for the Future." *Quest* 21 (January 1974): 19–29.

Leah, Vince. "The Case for Abolishing Hockey Leagues for Youngsters." *McLeans Magazine* (April 1964), 62–65.

Leonard, George B. *The Ultimate Athlete: Re-visioning Sports, Physical Education and the Body.* New York: Viking Press, 1975.

———. "Overemphasis on Winning Makes us a Nation of Losers." *The National Observer* (April 12, 1975), 16.

Leonard, John. "No Sweat: The Coming Leisure." *New Times* 8 (January 7, 1977), 64–68.

Lever, Janet. "Sex Differences in the Games Children Play." *Social Problems* 23 (1976), 479–87.

———. "Sex Differences in the Complexity of Children's Play and Games." *American Sociological Review* 43 (August 1978), 471–83.

Ley, Katherine. "Women in Sports: Where Do We Go from Here Boys?" *Phi Delta Kappan* 56 (October 1974): 129–31.

Lipsky, Richard. "Toward a Political Theory of American Sports Symbolism." *American Behavioral Scientist* 21 (January/February 1978): 345–60.

Lipsyte, Robert. *Sportsworld: An American Dreamland.* New York: Quadrangle/New York Times, 1975.

Lowe, Benjamin, and Mark H. Payne. "To Be a Red-Blooded American Boy." *Journal of Popular Culture* (Fall 1974): 383–91.

Loy, John W., and Alan Ingham. "Play, Games, and Sport in the Psychosociological Development of Children and Youth," In *Physical Activity: Human Growth and Development,* edited by G. L. Rarick. New York: Academic Press, 1973.

Loy, John W., and George S. Kenyon, eds. *Sport, Culture and Society.* New York: Macmillan, 1967.

Loy, John W., Barry D. McPherson, and Gerald Kenyon. *Sport and Social Systems: A Guide to the Analysis, Problems and Literature.* Reading, Mass.: Addison-Wesley, 1978.

McMurtry, William R. *Investigation and Inquiry into Violence in Amateur Hockey.* Report to the Ontario Minister of Community and Social Services, Toronto, 1974.

Magill, R., et al. *Children and Youth in Sport: A Contemporary Anthology.* Urbana, Ill.: Human Kinetics, 1978.

Malmisur, Michael C. "Social Adjustment Differences Between Student Athletes and Student Non-Athletes as Measured by Ego Development." *Sport Sociology Bulletin* 4 (1975): 2–12.

———. "Title IX Dilemma: Meritocratic and Egalitarian Tension." *Journal of Sport Behavior* 1 (August 1978): 130–38.

Marine, Gene. *A Male Guide to Women's Liberation.* New York: Avon Books, 1974.

Martens, Rainer. "Kid Sports: A Den of Inequity or Land of Promise?" Proceedings of the National College Physical Education Association for Men. Chicago: University of Illinois at Chicago Circle, 1976.

———, ed. *Joy and Sadness in Children's Sports.* Champaign, Ill.: Human Kinetics, 1978.

Martin, Thomas W., and Kenneth J. Berry. "Competitive Sport in Post Industrial Society: The Case of the Motocross Racer." *Journal of Popular Culture* 8 (Summer 1974), 107–20.

Meggyesy, Dave. *Out of Their League.* Berkeley, Calif.: Ramparts Press, 1971.

Mehl, Jack, and William W. Davis. "Youth Sports for Fun—and Whose Benefit?" *Joper* 49 (March 1978): 48–49.

Michener, James. *Sports in America.* New York: Random House, 1976.

Miller, Arthur. *Death of a Salesman.* New York: Viking Press, 1958.

Miller, Stuart. "New Directions in Sport." *Intellectual Digest* 4 (September 1973): 48–50.

Mitzel, John. "Sports and the Macho Male," *A Manifest Destiny* pamphlet (July 1973).

Morgan, Thomas B. "The American War Game." *Esquire* 64 (October 1965): 68–72, 141–48.

Nelson, Linden L., and Spencer Kagan. "Competition, the Star-Spangled Scramble." *Psychology Today* 6 (September 1978): 53–56, 90–91.

Nichols, Jack. *Men's Liberation: A New Definition of Masculinity.* New York: Penguin Books, 1975.

Ogilvie, Bruce C., and Thomas A. Tutko. "Sport: If You Want to Build Character, Try Something Else." *Psychology Today* (1971), pp. 61–63.

Oliver, Chip. *High for the Game.* New York: Morrow, 1971.

Olsen, Jack. *The Black Athlete: A Shameful Story of Integration in American Sport.* New York: Time-Life Books, 1968.

Opie, Jona and Peter. *Children's Games in Street and Playground.* London: Oxford University Press, 1964.

Orlick, Terry, and Cal Botteril. *Every Kid Can Win.* Chicago: Nelson-Hall, 1975.

Parrish, Bernie. *They Call It a Game.* New York: Dial, 1971.

Phillips, John C., and Walter E. Schafer. "Consequences of Participation in Interscholastic Sports. A Review and Prospectus." *Pacific Sociological Review* 14 (July 1971): 320–38.

Pleck, Joseph, and Robert Brannon, eds. "Male Roles and the Male Experience." *Journal of Social Issues* 34, no. 1 (1978).

Ralbovsky, M. *Destiny's Darlings.* New York: Hawthorn Books, 1974.

―――. *Lords of the Locker Room.* New York: Wyden, 1974.

Real, M. "Superbowl: Mythic Spectacle." *Journal of Communication* 25 (Winter 1975): 31–43.

Rehberg, Richard A., and Michael Cohen. "Athletes and Scholars: An Analysis of the Compositional Characteristics and Damage of These Two Youth Culture Categories." *International Review of Sport Sociology* 10 (1975): 91–107.

Rentzel, Lance. *When All the Laughter Died in Sorrow.* New York: Bantom Books, 1972.

Riesman, David, and Reuel Denney. "Football in America: A Study of Cultural Diffusion." *American Quarterly* 3 (Winter 1951): 109–319.

Roberts, Michael. *Fans! How We Go Crazy Over Sports.* Washington, D. C.: New Republic, 1976.

Rozark, Anne C. "Court Rejects NCAA Challenge to Ban in Sex Bias in Sports." *The Chronicle of Higher Education* (January 16, 1978), p. 1.

Rudin, A. James. "America's New Religion." *The Christian Century* 89 (April 9, 1979): 384.

Russell, Bill. "Success Is a Journey." *Sports Illustrated* (July 8, 1970), pp. 81–93.

Sack, A. L. "Big Time College Football: Whose Free Ride?" *Quest* 27 (Winter 1977): 87–97.

Sadler, W. A. "Competition Out of Bounds: Sport in American Life." *Quest* 17 (January 1973): 124–32.

Sage, George H., ed. *Sport and American Society: Selected Readings.* Reading, Mass.: Addison-Wesley, 1974.

Schafer, Walter E. "Participation in Interscholastic Athletics and Delinquency: A Preliminary Study." *Social Problems* 17 (Summer 1969): 40–47.

———. "Sport and Male Sex-Role Socialization." *Sport Sociology Bulletin* 4 (Fall 1975): 47–54.

Scott, Jack. *The Athletic Revolution.* New York: Macmillan, 1971.

———. *Athletics for Athletes.* Berkeley, Calif.: Otherways, 1969.

———. "Making Athletics a Masculinity Rite." *Ramparts* 10 (January 1973): 64.

Seefeldt, Vern, and John Haubenstricker. "Competitive Athletics for Children–The Michigan Study." *Joper* 49 (March 1978): 44–47.

Shaw, David. "The Roots of Rooting." *Psychology Today* (February 1978), pp. 48–51.

Shaw, Gary. *Meat on the Hoof: The Hidden World of Texas Football.* New York: St. Martins, 1972.

Shecter, Leonard. *The Jocks.* Indianapolis: Bobbs-Merrill, 1969.

Sillitoe, Alan. *The Loneliness of the Long Distance Runner.* New York: New American Library, 1959.

Simpson, George. "College Football's B.M.O.C. Crisis: Battered and Maimed on Campus," *Sport* 63 (November 1976): 26.

Sipes, Richard. "War, Sports and Aggression: An Empirical Test of Two Rival Theories" *American Anthropologist* 75 (February 1973): 64–86.

Slusher, Howard. *Man, Sport and Existence: A Critical Analysis.* Philadelphia: Lea and Febiger, 1967.

Smith, Michael D. "Hostile Outbursts in Sport." *Sport Sociology Bulletin* 2 (Spring 1973): 6–10.

———. "Significant Others' Influence on the Assaultive Behavior of Young Hockey Players." *International Review of Sport Sociology* 9 (1974): 45–56.

Smoll, Frank L., Ronald E. Smith, and Bill Curtis. "Behavioral Guidelines for Youth Sport Coaches." *Joper* 49 (March 1978): 44–47.

Smoll, Frank L., and Ronald E. Smith, eds. *Psychological Perspectives in Youth Sport.* Washington, D. C.: Hemisphere, 1978.

Snyder, Eldon E. "Aspects of Social and Political Values of High School Coaches." *International Review of Sport Sociology* 8 (1973): 73–87.

Snyder, Eldon E., and Joseph E. Kivlen. "Perceptions of the Sex Role Among Female Athletes and Nonathletes." *Adolescence* 12 (Spring 1977): 23–29.

Snyder, Eldon E., and Elmer Spreitzer. "Correlates of Sport Participation Among Adolescent Girls." *Research Quarterly* 47 (December 1976): 804–09.

———. *Social Aspects of Sport.* Englewood Cliffs, N. J.: Prentice-Hall, 1978.

———. "Sociology of Sport: An Overview." *Sociological Quarterly* 15 (Fall 1974): 467–87.

Spady, W. G. "Lament for the Letterman: Effect of Peer Status and Extracurricular Activities on Goals and Achievements." *American Journal of Sociology* 75 (January 1970): 680–702.

Spring, Joel. "Athletics and the Modern Industrial State." *Phi Delta Kappan* 56, no. 1 (1973): 114–15.

Stevenson, Christopher. "Socialization Effects of Participation in Sport: A Critical Review of the Research." *Research Quarterly* 46 (October 1975): 287–301.

Stone, Gregory P. "The Play of Little Children." *Quest* 4 (Spring 1965): 23–31.

Strenk, Andrew. "Sport as an International Political and Diplomatic Tool." *Arena Newsletter* 1 (August 1977): 3–9.

Sutton-Smith, Brian. "Child's Play: Very Serious Business." *Psychology Today* (December 1971), pp. 66–69, 87.

Talamini, John T., and Charles H. Page, eds. *Sport and Society: An Anthrology.* Boston: Little, Brown, 1973.

Thomas, Jerry R. "Is Winning Essential to the Success of Youth Sports Contests?" *Joper* 49 (March 1978): 42–43.

Tolson, Andrew. *The Limits of Masculinity.* London: Tavistock, 1977.

Tunis, John R. *Sports: Heroics and Hysterics.* New York: John Day, 1928.

Tutko, Thomas, and William Bruns. *Winning Is Everything and Other American Myths.* New York: Macmillan, 1976.

Underwood, John. "Taking the Fun Out of the Game." *Sports Illustrated* (November 17, 1975), pp. 86–98.

Veblen, Thorstein. *The Theory of the Leisure Class.* New York: Mentor Books, 1953.

Voigt, David. *A Little League Journal.* Bowling Green, Ohio: Bowling Green University Popular Press, 1974.

Watson, G. G. "Family Organization and Little League Baseball." *International Review of Sport Sociology* 9 (1974): 5–31.

———. "Games, Socialization and Parental Values: Social Class Differences in Parental Evaluation of Little League Baseball." *International Review of Sport Sociology* 12 (1977): 17–47.

Weiss, Paul. *Sport: A Philosophic Inquiry.* Carbondale: Southern Illinois University Press, 1969.

Wenkert, Simon. "The Meaning of Sports for Contemporary Man." *Journal of Existential Psychiatry* (Spring 1963): 397–404.

Wilmore, Jack H. "Inferiority of the Female Athlete: Myth of Reality." *Sports Medicine Bulletin* 10 (1975).

Wolf, Dave. *Foul! Connie Hawkins, Schoolyard Star, Exile NBA Superstar.* New York: Holt, Rinehart and Winston, 1972.

Wolf, Gary K. *Killerbowl.* Garden City, N. Y.: Doubleday, 1975.

Yiannakis, Andrew et al., eds. *Sport Sociology: Contemporary Themes.* Dubuque, Iowa: Kendall/Hart, 1979.

INDEX

353